D0207096

The Artificial River

Carol Sheriff

THE ARTIFICIAL RIVER

The Erie Canal and the Paradox of Progress
1817–1862

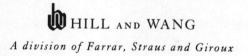

HILL AND WANG

A division of Farrar, Straus and Giroux

Hill and Wang
A division of Farrar, Straus and Giroux
19 Union Square West, New York 10003

Copyright © 1996 by Carol Sheriff
All rights reserved
Published in Canada by HarperCollinsCanadaLtd
Printed in the United States of America
Designed by Fritz Metsch
First published in 1996 by Hill and Wang
First paperback edition, 1997

Fifth printing, 2000

THE LIBRARY OF CONGRESS HAS CATALOGUED THE HARDCOVER EDITION AS FOLLOWS:

Sheriff, Carol.
   The artificial river : the Erie Canal and the paradox of progress,
1817–1862 / Carol Sheriff.
      p.   cm.
   Includes bibliographical references (p.) and index.
   ISBN 0-8090-2753-4
   1. Erie Canal (N.Y.)—History.   I. Title.
F127.E5S54   1996
974.7—dc20   *96-2219*

For my parents

ACKNOWLEDGMENTS

I began this book as a dissertation while a graduate student at Yale University and completed it while an assistant professor at the College of William and Mary. Along the way, many institutions and people offered a great deal of assistance, and it is a pleasure to acknowledge their contributions.

Several organizations provided generous financial support. The American Antiquarian Society, Yale University (through its John F. Enders Research Assistance Award), the Yale History Department, and the New York State Library all funded extensive research in distant archives and libraries. A fellowship from the Mrs. Giles Whiting Foundation enabled me to spend a full year writing my dissertation without distractions. The College of William and Mary provided two summer research grants to turn the dissertation into a book.

Many institutions opened their rich historical collections to me. I am deeply indebted to the staffs at the American Antiquarian Society, the Buffalo and Erie County Historical Society, the Buffalo Public Library, Cornell University Library, the Erie Canal Museum (Syracuse), the Erie Canal Village (Rome), the New York State Archives, the New York State Historical Association, the New York State Library, the Oneida County Historical Society, the Onondaga Historical Association, the Rochester Historical Society, the Rochester Museum and Science Center, the Rochester Public Library, the University of Rochester (Rush Rhees Library), the Smith College Library, the Library of the State University of New York at Buffalo, Syracuse University

(George Arents Library), the Tonawanda-Kenmore Historical Society, the Valentown Museum, and the Yale University libraries. While many, many people helped me at these institutions, a few stand out for special thanks: Joanne Chaison of the American Antiquarian Society; Judy Haven of the Onondaga Historical Association; Karl Kabelac of the University of Rochester; and Don Wilson, formerly of the Erie Canal Museum. The reference staffs at Yale's Sterling Memorial Library (especially Paul Constantine, Ann Ferguson, and Paul Musto) and at the New York State Library cheerfully assisted with what were often rather obscure inquiries.

As a graduate student, I benefited greatly from the insight and enthusiasm of a dissertation committee made up of four outstanding scholars and teachers. William Cronon, who directed this project from its inception, has unfailingly lived up to his own high standards as a teacher, critic, and mentor. Like Bill, Howard Lamar and John Demos guided my intellectual endeavors throughout my days as a graduate student; acknowledging their help on the thesis only begins to describe my indebtedness to them. Ann Fabian joined my dissertation committee in the final stretch and managed in a short time to provide years' worth of thoughtful advice. I cannot adequately express my sense of appreciation to an ideal dissertation committee.

My colleagues in the Department of History at William and Mary have provided a supportive and caring environment in which to complete this manuscript, while setting high standards for scholarship and teaching. My students, too, have contributed to this book by encouraging me to clarify my explanations of antebellum history and, in particular, to reconsider the importance of party politics in explaining social change.

The Artificial River has benefited directly from the generous contributions of a number of scholars who graciously took time away from their own work to improve mine. Edward Balleisen, Chandos Brown, and Jonathan Cedarbaum commented abundantly on multiple versions of the manuscript, contributing significantly to both its substance and its prose; each engaged with me in countless conversations about antebellum history, and each has influenced my thinking in ways too numerous to list. Although I have never met Paul Johnson or Ronald Shaw, I have long admired their scholarship and feel privileged to have received detailed comments from each of them on an earlier draft of the manuscript; they forced me to reconsider many issues, and the book is far better as a result. Robert Gross's extensive comments on the dissertation clarified my interpretation of the impact of the Erie Canal and helped me to reshape the manuscript in crucial ways. Craig Williams, of the New York State Museum and the Canal Society of New York State, had a profound influence on this work: he alerted me to the existence of the Canal Board Papers; read the entire manuscript at least three times, saving me from numerous mistakes; and provided unending research assistance. Glenn Wallach's years of support culminated in a long and perceptive critique of the manuscript. Richard Buel, Jr., who instructed me when I was an undergraduate history major at Wesleyan University, read the dissertation and offered important suggestions for revising it, many of which, I'm afraid, will have to wait for another project. Aari Ludvigsen accompanied me on my first frigid adventure to explore the Erie Canal and then, fittingly, was the work's final reader, offering marvelous suggestions on both content and style. Elaine Chubb, at Hill and Wang, provided patient and insightful copy editing.

While I did not subject everyone to the entire manuscript, many others read significant portions or contributed in other substantial ways. Melvin Ely, Cindy Hahamovitch, Leisa Meyer, Scott Nelson, and James Wooten each offered valuable comments on parts of the book. Mia Bay, Deborah Elkin, and Beth Wenger read almost the entire dissertation in draft form, while Elizabeth Abrams, Martha Boonin-Vail, David Godshalk, Xiaohong Shen, and Anne Standley commented on sections of it. Liz Skoler responded to an extended abstract of the dissertation and—along with Joanna Skoler—helped me settle on a title for the book. Daniel Linke not only tracked down references to the Erie Canal but forced me to keep a sense of humor about what often seemed like a daunting task. Scott Nelson rescued me from several computer-related disasters.

I have also benefited from discussions with Parley Agner, Jeffrey Auerbach, Elise Broach, Cathy Corman, Clyde Haulman, Ludwell Johnson, Susan Johnson, F. Daniel Larkin, David Montgomery, Stephen Nissenbaum, Karen Sawislak, and Billy Smith. Bruce Boling, Catherine Brekus, Dona Brown, Steve Bullock, Reeve Huston, and Kirby Miller—along with other people mentioned earlier—supplied me with important sources about the Erie Canal; their particular contributions are acknowledged in endnotes. Bernard Cedarbaum, Miriam Goldman Cedarbaum, Kirsten Gruesz, Bill Moses, Liz Skoler, and Amy White exhibited endless patience for hearing about antebellum society and debating appropriate word choices; Kirsten also took my author's photo.

Because my research took me away from home for long periods of time, I often found myself relying on the generosity of others—not just for food and lodging, but for the less material comforts of home. I owe much to David Cedarbaum and Barbara Mitchell; Marion Goldstein; Robert and Marcia Moss; Ruth and Russell Peck; Dan Linke and Sarah Ritchie; Craig Williams and Helen McLallen; and Barbara and Bob Willner.

I'd also like to express deep appreciation to my family, especially my parents, Selene and Seymour Sheriff. In addition to their constant support, they each read the dissertation twice and pointed out logical flaws as well as editing mistakes; they also graciously helped correct the book's page proofs in record time. My brother, Steven, commented on the dissertation, offering useful suggestions for making the book more enjoyable for non-historians. My sisters, Ellen and Susan, supplied bountiful encouragement, as did Michele Alperin, Tim Kempka, and Jim Rogers. Jacob, Alison, Aliza, and Emmy never fail to remind their aunt that there is indeed life beyond the Erie Canal.

It has been a tremendous privilege to work with such a talented and good-humored editor as Arthur Wang. Since no one has awaited the final word more eagerly, it seems only proper that it should be for him: Thanks!

CONTENTS

ILLUSTRATIONS

BRIEF CHRONOLOGY

of state and national events linked to

THE ERIE CANAL

1792: Western Inland Lock Navigation Company incorporated to open navigation from the Hudson River to Ontario and Seneca lakes; during remainder of decade, constructs dams, locks, and canals of no more than two miles.

1807–8: Jesse Hawley's essays outline feasibility of a canal between the Hudson and Lake Erie.

1808: New York State Legislature authorizes a survey of possible canal routes.

1810: Appointment of first New York State canal commissioners.

1811: Commissioners ask for aid from federal government and neighboring states.

1812–14: War of 1812; industrial development booms in Northeast.

1817: President James Madison vetoes federal funding for a New York canal; DeWitt Clinton elected governor of New York; state-funded construction begins on the Erie Canal, and then on the Champlain Canal; famine in Ireland encourages emigration.

1819: Completion of ninety-eight-mile portion of the Erie Canal along the middle section; Missouri applies for statehood with a constitution allowing slavery; nation gripped by economic crisis after end of post–War of 1812 boom.

1820: Navigation opens on Erie's middle section; major portion of western section completed; work begins on the eastern section; Missouri Compromise temporarily removes issue of slavery from national politics.

1823: First boats pass from the Erie Canal and the Champlain Canal into the Hudson River.

1825: Completion of the entire Erie Canal between Buffalo and Albany marked by "Grand Celebration" and "Wedding of the Waters"; "Great Canal Act" authorizes the surveying of seventeen other canal routes; Charles Finney first preaches in New York.

1826: Canal Board established.

1828: American Seamen's Friend Society founded; Clinton dies; Andrew Jackson elected President.

1831: Completion of first New York railroad, connecting Albany and Schenectady; evangelical revivals peak in New York's "Burned-Over District."

1833: Whig Party founded in opposition to Jacksonian Democrats.

1836: Work begins on the Erie Canal Enlargement; American Bethel Society expands effort to reach out to canal workers.

1837: Financial panic sweeps the nation; U.S. Supreme Court hands down ruling in *Charles River Bridge* case.

1838: William Seward elected governor of New York as a Whig.

1839–42: Major economic depression.

1842: "Stop and Tax" law halts most canal construction.

1845: Mass Irish immigration to the United States begins.

1847: Work resumes on the Erie Canal Enlargement.

1851: State exempts railroads from canal tolls.

1853: Consolidation of New York Central Railroad.

1854: Republican Party founded.

1858: Seward—U.S. senator since 1849—delivers "Irrepressible Conflict" speech in Rochester.

1860: Abraham Lincoln elected President; South Carolina secedes from the Union.

1861: Creation of Confederate States of America; Seward begins serving as U.S. Secretary of State; Civil War begins with firing on Fort Sumter.

1862: New York State legislative act declares completion of Erie Canal Enlargement; Lincoln issues initial Emancipation Proclamation.

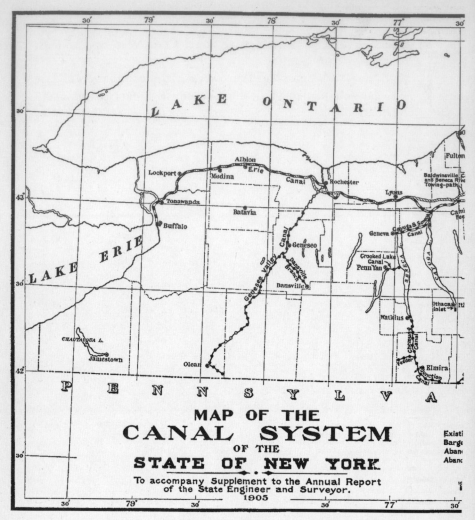

(Noble E. Whitford, *History of the Canal System of the State of New York* . . . ,
Canal Society of New York State)

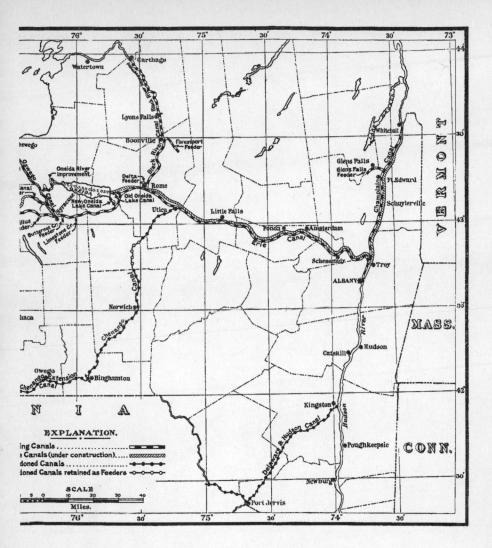

The Artificial River

INTRODUCTION

Fresh Oysters and
Sour Deals

"OYSTERS! Oysters! beautiful Oysters," trumpeted a headline in a Batavia, New York, newspaper in 1824. "While we partake of the fresh and delicious [Long Island oysters]," the paper's editor continued, "let us remember that Providence is the author of the ocean, and DeWitt Clinton the Projector of the Erie Canal."[1]

In the years after the Erie Canal linked the Great Lakes to the Atlantic Coast, many settlers in the western hinterlands of New York marveled at the availability of fresh oysters so far inland. Unlike the more common pickled and stewed varieties, fresh oysters spoiled easily and could be consumed only within a few days' travel from the coast. In 1817, the year construction began on the Erie Canal, freight could take several weeks to reach a town like Batavia from the port city of New York, having traversed hundreds of miles over water and land before reaching its destination. The difficulty and expense of the land portion of the journey meant that many goods did not travel between these two points at all. DeWitt Clinton, the future governor of New York and soon to be the most vocal proponent of the Canal, had remarked in 1810 that the road leading to Batavia "is bad; it runs through swampy ground, and is sand with bogs." After the completion of the Erie in 1825, cargo moved along the same route with greater ease, in much less time, and at a small fraction of the expense. That one could now savor fresh oysters so far from the sea symbolized the single greatest triumph of the Erie Canal:

it compressed distance and time in ways that had previously seemed impossible.[2]

Yet many New Yorkers who applauded the waterway's accomplishments also mourned the loss of what they perceived as a simpler, more moral way of life that disappeared with the arrival of the Canal. Dr. Alexander Coventry, an otherwise ardent supporter of the Erie Canal, complained in 1825 about "the sharp tricks of the day." The doctor had intended to sell one of his animals at an auction of canal horses in January of that year. Before the auction began, "a very genteelly dressed young man" offered to buy Coventry's horse and promised to return later with the money. Assuming that he had contracted to sell his horse to a credible buyer, Coventry did not put the animal up for sale at the auction. But the well-dressed man never returned. The young stranger, it seems, turned out to be merely posing as a prospective buyer so that his partner, who wanted to sell inferior horses at the auction, would not have to compete with the "best" livestock, as Coventry considered his own. Thus when the doctor remarked that "[c]analling is hard business for horses," he was not expressing sympathy for the animals who towed canal boats. He was lamenting instead what he saw as impersonal market conditions that made business transactions difficult for an honest horse seller like himself. While "sharp" dealing obviously long predated the new waterway, it was the Canal that brought such practices into the everyday lives of men such as Alexander Coventry.[3]

Fresh oysters and sour deals were among the daily reminders of the ways in which the Erie Canal was reshaping the lives of ordinary Americans. Part of the larger transportation revolution, the Erie Canal played a major role in the transformation of the young Republic's geography and economy and helped to set off the industrial and marketing revolutions that swept across the northern United States early in the nineteenth century. Because the Canal also brought changes to the intimate details of people's lives—from the food they ate to the way they transacted business—residents of upstate New York regularly grappled with the new waterway's impact on their habits and values.[4]

The story of the Erie Canal thus offers a rich perspective on the tumultuous era between the War of 1812 and the Civil War. This period in American history saw dramatic changes in the ways people perceived and organized their lives. *The Artificial River* uses the Erie Canal region as a microcosm in which to explore the relationships between some of the antebellum era's important transformations: widespread geographic mobility; rapid environmental change; government intervention in economic development; market expansion; the reorganization of work; and moral reform. Among the middle classes, these changes would be grouped together as signs of "progress" or "improvement." For them progress meant, in large part, that men and women were taking an active role in realizing a divinely sanctioned movement toward the perfectibility of the natural and human worlds.[5]

This understanding of progress would play a central role in defining Northern sectional identity in the decades leading up to the Civil War. The revolutions in transportation, marketing, and industry, along with rapid urbanization, created the infrastructure for the North and Midwest's growing regional distinctiveness. These changes, which were as much social as structural, led Northerners and Midwesterners to perceive themselves as different from the South, a region of the country which to them seemed hopelessly attached to a semifeudal economic and social system. Southerners seceded from the Union to preserve their way of life based on slavery, but we cannot forget that Northerners refused to let them leave. Their unwillingness to do so stemmed in part from a refusal to compromise their vision of an America based on the culture of progress. *The Artificial River* explores many components of that culture.[6]

The geographic region through which the newly born Erie Canal flowed presents a compelling, if far from universal, pattern for the antebellum North. The North was hardly a monolithic

region, and neither was upstate New York. Like the rest of the
North, the Canal corridor—the area that fell within a day's
wagon ride (approximately twenty miles) of either side of the
waterway—was predominantly agricultural on the eve of the
Civil War. But, also like the rest of the North, it was undergoing
rapid economic and social change. It had pockets of land that
had not yet been settled by Euro-Americans, but it was also
home to several of the most rapidly growing cities in the country.
It provided fertile lands to yeoman farmers (primarily native-
born white Americans), but it also fostered a large population of
ethnically diverse wage laborers. And earlier in the nineteenth
century, the upstate region played an important role in igniting
the Second Great Awakening, a fiery evangelical movement that
eventually made its way across the country and that fed a rise in
abolitionist sentiment in much of the North. As more of the
North and Midwest embraced the culture of progress during the
antebellum period, the Canal corridor became increasingly less
exceptional.[7]

By focusing on the entire Canal region, rather than a particular
town, this book more fully captures the intricacies of the era's
ever-growing web of commercial and social networks. The cost
of expanding the book's bounds beyond a single community is,
of course, that it cannot pursue in depth questions about the
Canal's impact on individual lives; it cannot systematically explore how the Canal influenced people's production, income, mobility, and affiliations. Yet the regional overview compensates for
this sacrifice of detail by enhancing our ability to answer a whole
other set of questions: questions about how people of diverse
circumstances and ambitions perceived the swift and profound
transformations brought about by the revolution in transportation.

The Artificial River recounts, then, a chapter in American perceptions and aspirations. It does not seek to retell the familiar
history of the Canal's impact on westward expansion and northeastern industrialization; rather, it looks at the men and women
who visited the Canal's locks, lived along its banks, and steered

its boats. Aware that they were caught up in a time of dramatic change, many residents and travelers alike recorded their thoughts about the new waterway, either in letters for distant relations or in diaries for posterity. Not content simply to let the Canal alter their lives, New Yorkers also tried to guide the Canal's reshaping of upstate life. They petitioned the state government for changes in Canal policy, mailed their complaints to newspapers, and participated in reform movements—and left a paper trail behind them. I have been fortunate enough to have access to collections of documents that have only recently become conveniently available to historians, particularly the extensive Canal Board Papers. New Yorkers addressed the Canal Board, a group of state officials, about issues like property damage, toll rates, employee transgressions, route alterations, boating disputes, construction contracts, and technological innovations. While the attitudes expressed in these documents can rarely be taken at face value, they offer an unusual glimpse at people's ideas toward the Canal and the progress it symbolized.[8]

Like all works of history, this book seeks not just to explain the complexities of people's lives and dispositions; it strives also to explore change over time. Unsurprisingly, perhaps, New Yorkers' ideas about progress underwent notable transformations during the antebellum period. Their ideas about the environment, community, political economy, market relations, and work all evolved—and became increasingly at odds with those of other New Yorkers. I trace the ways in which the Erie Canal contributed to a more fluid society of competing impulses, interests, and classes—a society no longer compatible with the political culture that sponsored and built the Canal in the first place. Out of those competing interests would emerge a new political culture, one that was no less committed to progress but that adapted the meanings of progress to fit changing ideals and circumstances.

The Artificial River follows the story of the Erie Canal from its ground-breaking in 1817 to the 1862 official completion of a quarter-century-long project to widen, deepen, and reroute the waterway. As boats began carrying freight from Buffalo to Albany in the 1820s, virtually all New Yorkers could celebrate the Canal as a wonder of human progress, an accomplishment representing the seemingly unlimited potential of a nation founded on republican principles. The new canal would not only expand agricultural and commercial opportunities; it would, they hoped, keep the new nation bound together, an especially pressing concern for Americans as the country once again confronted the slavery issue with Missouri's 1819 application for statehood.[9]

By the 1860s, residents of the Canal corridor took the Canal —and progress—for granted. They argued with one another about just what progress meant, and often they shared Alexander Coventry's disapproval of certain aspects of progress itself. Yet despite their disagreements and ambivalence, upstate New Yorkers generally shared a commitment to the notion that humans could improve and perfect the world around them. When many of those New Yorkers joined other Northerners in taking up arms to preserve the Union, they carried that commitment with them. The young soldiers who boarded canal boats to begin their journeys to the front lines could not remember the days when there had been no artificial river connecting the Great West to the East Coast. The waterway seemed as natural to them as their Northern way of life. Yet neither would have been even imaginable to their grandparents, the generation that had ratified the Constitution. *The Artificial River* traces the ways in which the citizens of New York took one of the extraordinary achievements of the young Republic and rendered it—along with the culture it helped create—ordinary.

I

Visions of Progress

ON JULY 4, 1817, at daybreak, cannons boomed as a crowd assembled near Rome, New York, to watch the digging of the first spadeful of Erie Canal dirt. The honor fell to Judge John Richardson, who had been awarded the first contract to build a section of the waterway. Richardson addressed the gathering, proclaiming, "By this great highway unborn millions will easily transport their surplus productions to the shores of the Atlantic, procure their supplies, and hold a useful and profitable intercourse with all the marine nations of the world." He then drove his spade into the ground, and—according to the *Utica Gazette* —"was followed by the citizens, and his own laborers, each vieing with the other in this demonstration of joy of which all partook on that interesting occasion."* Amid an enthusiastic and popular celebration of the nation's Revolutionary heritage, the state of New York had begun construction on what was to be one of the longest artificial waterways in the world.[1]

Events leading up to that sunrise ceremony began hundreds of millions of years earlier, with a series of continental collisions giving rise to the Adirondack and Appalachian mountains. By

* While some quotations have been abbreviated for clarity, otherwise the original punctuation, spelling, grammar, capitalization, underlining, and italics have been maintained. These variations reflect the educational levels and emotional tones of their authors, helping to convey the medley of nineteenth-century voices that remarked on the Erie Canal and the paradoxes of progress.

producing intimidating obstacles to human migration, those natural barriers—together covering an area between what are today
southern Canada and northern Alabama—checked the westward
expansion of the vast majority of Euro-American settlers in the
original colonies, and in the newly formed states, of North America. Those who did venture beyond the Atlantic basin took advantage of several gaps left by the prehistoric collisions. In the
northern colonies, the only such break was the one through
which the Mohawk River flowed easterly from central New York
to the Hudson River, which in turn ran southward into the
Atlantic Ocean. While Dutch and British colonists took up
farming along the Mohawk and other natural rivers and lakes of
central New York, they, too, found their westward migration
restrained once they reached Lake Oneida, near the head of the
Mohawk. From that point, more than 150 miles east of Lake
Erie, no major waterway permitted easy access through the western interior. Until shortly before Judge Richardson broke ground
on the canal that would extend 363 miles between Lake Erie
and the Hudson, residents of the region had no reason to believe
that such a waterway would ever exist in their lifetimes.[2]

But some western New Yorkers dreamed it might. The desire
for a canal running the width of upstate New York emerged in
the early eighteenth century and reveals something about the
aspirations and values of settlers in the region. If eighteenth-
century inhabitants generally dismissed such an artificial waterway as mere fantasy, an undertaking beyond the realm of human
accomplishment, they did project more realistic, shorter channels. For them, the topography of upstate New York was evidence not of the shifting crust of the earth but of the Hand of
Providence. God, they reasoned, would not have created breaks
in mountain chains or riverbeds unless Man (to use the contemporary term) was destined to finish the work. Yet canals of any
length required great investments of labor and capital, and the
Dutch and the English governments had not seriously considered
devoting such resources to develop their New York colonies,
even though they had both undertaken extensive transportation

projects in their own countries. Still, local interest in canals suggests that at least some settlers on the New York frontier shared an interest in commercial exchange and modernization. As early as the seventeenth century, Iroquois and Dutch traders had made use of the region's natural waterways to exchange furs and guns. In more recent times, European settlers had been attracted to the region's river valleys precisely because of the connection to markets they provided.[3]

Of course, as many historians would be quick to point out, trade alone does not make for a commercial society organized around the ideal of progress. They would agree that farmers sought ways to unload agricultural "surpluses," but the very term "surplus," these scholars argue, suggests that the average farmer did not intentionally produce for trade, and certainly not for a market beyond the local community. And when farmers did exchange goods and services with neighbors, these transactions rarely involved cash—not because cash was in short supply, but rather because they saw no use for assigning monetary values. Instead, they calculated value in terms of social worth, and simply kept accounts of what they owed and were owed. A farmer, for example, might work for two days in his neighbor's cornfield in exchange for five chickens, since that was what it would take to feed his family during the time he spent away from his own farm duties. Or he might simply hold the neighbor accountable for two days' labor at some later time. These farmers sought, not to accumulate wealth, but to secure a "competency" that would allow their families to live a comfortable and independent existence in a community limited in geographic reach. Historians have found ample evidence suggesting that such a moral economy endured in some parts of the country into the nineteenth century. Whether New Yorkers of the colonial period tended to see themselves as peasants seeking a competence, businessmen pursuing profits, or consumers yearning for luxuries, their interest in canals suggests that at least some had aspirations to engage in broader market exchange.[4]

Certainly by the turn of the nineteenth century, families em-

igrating to New York—whether from New England or from the
Old World—saw access to markets as a prerequisite for settlement. To meet this demand, private land developers, such as the
Dutch-owned Holland Land Company, invested heavily in roads
connecting interior lands to commercial entrepôts. Access to
markets made the land much more valuable, and by the time
work began on the Erie Canal, upstate New York had a system
of turnpikes and roads linking remote farming areas to natural
waterways, over which settlers sent their produce to distant markets. Beginning in 1792, the Western Inland Lock Navigation
Company and the Northern Inland Lock Navigation Company
tried to turn a profit by improving some of the waterways themselves. Drawing on the financial resources of stockholders, many
of whom would become the strongest advocates of the Erie Canal,
the Western Company built canals, dams, and locks along the
Mohawk River. These efforts aimed to establish more reliable
commercial links among inland New York and the entrepôt of
Albany on the Hudson, from which goods could go on to the
Atlantic port of New York City. Although the company failed
to make a profit because of the scheme's technological limitations
and financial miscalculations, its goal nonetheless suggests that,
as early as the 1790s, investors believed that farmers wanted an
improved means of transporting their goods to an international
port.[5]

Settlers in upstate New York already took part in a system of
economic relationships that revolved around the long-distance
trade of goods and services for specie or credit. Some farmers
hoped to use these market relationships to gain no more than
economic independence and physical comfort—to sell the fruits
of their labor in exchange for things they did not make or grow
themselves. Mary Ann Archbald, who emigrated from Scotland
in 1807 with her husband and children, held such aspirations.
Three years after arriving in the United States, the Archbalds
sold their initial tract of land and bought a farm directly along
the banks of the Mohawk River to gain easier access to the New
York market. The Archbalds had considered moving to Ohio,

but worried that the new territory was "at a great distance from markets . . ." If the Archbalds hoped only to trade goods and services within a local community, the distance to "markets" would not have been an issue; instead they might have worried about isolation from neighbors. The Archbalds sold their cloth and wheat in New York City while also growing rye, corn, barley, peas, oats, and potatoes. Mary Ann Archbald manufactured the cloth herself from the wool shorn from the family's seventy sheep. The size of the flock alone suggests that the Archbalds produced for the market and did not merely find themselves with an unplanned "surplus" of goods. Yet Mary Ann Archbald spoke of her quest for "independence"—that is, her dream of owning their farm outright, of being free from indebtedness, and thus free from the control and whims of a creditor. Indeed, in 1828 Archbald would be able to boast, "There was also a considerable debt on the farm which [her son Jamie] had been paying as he earned it & expect to have it all cleared off this fall . . . now, as being out of debt is, in my estimation, being rich I trust that I will in my nixt [letter] be able to tell you <u>positively</u> that I am <u>rich</u>." For Archbald, wealth came in the form of independence.[6]

Personal motivations, though, often defy generalization. Other settlers had more entrepreneurial goals; they concentrated on reducing their production costs while selling their goods as dearly as the market allowed. In 1808, Mary Ann Archbald tried to offer a sweeping picture of her new home to the acquaintances she left behind. "We are a nation of traders in spite of all Mr. Jefferson can say or do," Archbald wrote. "[M]oney money is every thing . . ." Coming in the midst of the Jeffersonian embargo on international goods, Archbald's comment makes clear that not only were upstate New Yorkers engaging in trade; they were engaging in long-distance trade. Moreover, many of these settlers aimed not just to secure independence but rather to earn money and to profit from their connections to a larger commercial world. By cutting off legal trade with European nations, the embargoes had the unintended effect of raising the prices of those American goods that nonetheless reached European ports. Those

New Yorkers who continued to trade abroad expected a large sum of "money" in return. While Jefferson hoped to keep the new country free from the entanglements of European war, some citizens apparently cared less about possible enmeshments and more about their personal profit.[7]

It is not clear what distinguished independence-minded settlers from their profit-oriented neighbors. In fact, Mary Ann Archbald did not even have to look beyond her own home to witness entrepreneurialism. Her two sons tried their luck at mercantile ventures, activities she criticized as "speculation." That the Archbald children and their mother held different ideas about economic gain suggests that settlers' generational or gender backgrounds played into their attitudes toward market exchange. Mary Ann immigrated to the United States with her husband to establish an independent livelihood. Her sons, though, grew up in a "nation of traders" and eagerly looked forward to earning a living through the buying and selling of other people's goods. They bought lumber and wheat from western farmers and tried to sell it at a profit to other merchants in the eastern cities of Albany and New York.[8]

Still, those sons did not exclusively concern themselves with their personal gain. Jamie, who helped build the section of the Erie Canal passing in front of his mother's farm, did not make money from the venture, contrary to his expectations. Obviously disappointed, he nonetheless appreciated how his efforts would help the "general utility." While engaging in individualistic, or liberal, pursuits of wealth, Jamie also retained belief in the founding principles of the Republic: that the goals of individuals should be subordinated to the common good, or the commonwealth. It was Jamie's mixture of liberal and republican impulses, not his mother's, that would represent the nation's future.[9]

American politicians began planning for that future before the ink had dried on the Constitution. Even as they debated the principles that should govern their unique political experiment, the new nation's leaders could not ignore the pressing problems that emerged in the years after the Revolution. The United States urgently needed to accommodate its swelling population, to pay its war debts, and to reduce its dependence on Europe. Under the first party system that emerged in the 1790s, the Founding Fathers divided into two main schools of thought about how to develop the country's economy. Federalists, with Alexander Hamilton at their helm, supported a strong central government that would help sponsor commercial expansion, industrial and urban development, and international trade. Democratic-Republicans, under the leadership of Thomas Jefferson and James Madison, favored placing power in the hands of the states and limiting any role the federal government might play in commercial development. Unlike the Hamiltonians, who wanted to promote manufacturing, the Jeffersonian Republicans foresaw the nation remaining predominantly agrarian. Limited manufacturing, in their view, would provide a domestic outlet for agricultural surpluses, but it should not be the mainstay of the developing economy. Whereas Hamiltonians wanted to expand over "time," Jeffersonians envisioned expansion taking place over "space"—in the language of the day.[10]

Whichever method of economic growth they preferred, the first generation of national leaders recognized the importance of internal improvements. A system of roads and canals would allow settlers, raw materials, and finished goods to move affordably between the nation's thinly populated interior and its increasingly crowded coastal basin. Because the colonial powers had invested so little in commercial transportation routes, in 1800 shipping a ton of goods thirty miles into the interior of the United States cost as much as shipping the same goods all the way to England. Clearly, the situation needed improvement if the nation was to prosper.[11]

The notion of "improving" the physical world did not originate with the American Revolution, but it took on new meanings in its aftermath. Americans often ranked the founding of the American Republic as an event secondary in importance only to the creation of the earth. While the physical world had been the work of God alone, the Revolution had been a divinely sanctioned endeavor to perfect the human world. However limited the visions of the Founding Fathers seem to us today, particularly in regard to human equality, in their day the Declaration of Independence and the Constitution offered adult white men unparalleled rights and responsibilities. Drawing on the fervor and ideology of their Revolution (and, in the North, borrowing from their Puritan heritage), Americans believed that they had been placed on earth to finish God's work in shaping the New World. Their destiny was to perfect the human and physical world. Where God left gaps in the Appalachian Mountains, in other words, He intended humans to create their own rivers.

Motivated by a combination of economic and ideological imperatives, politicians on both the national and state levels embraced initiatives to expand the young nation's transportation networks. The federal government concentrated on financing roads for pedestrians, stagecoaches, and livestock. Its greatest achievement came with the opening of the National Road in 1818, connecting points in Virginia and Maryland; ultimately, the road would extend to Illinois. More extensive national efforts to improve transportation routes suffered from the scruples and inclinations of some Republicans, who controlled the federal government from the so-called Revolution of 1800 (when Jefferson won the Presidency from the Federalist John Adams) until the evolution of the second party system in the 1820s (after Andrew Jackson defeated John Quincy Adams's bid for reelection). Jefferson and his successor, Madison, both subscribed to narrow constitutional interpretations of the scope of federal authority, which made them hesitate to approve any measures not specifically falling within the purview of the national government. Their critics argued that these first two presidents in the "Virginia Dynasty" became particularly scrupulous when it came to authorizing transportation improvements north of the Mason-Dixon Line. But in both the South and the North, most public works projects proceeded with the help of state rather than federal money.[12]

The states concentrated their efforts on constructing turnpikes, which helped to open the West to settlement but which also suffered from serious limitations. Difficult to maintain, these roads became clouded with suffocating dust in dry conditions and soaked with impenetrable mud in wet weather. Thickets of fallen trees blocked the passage of coaches and carts for days, or even weeks, at a time. Few governments, though, could afford to invest in the much more costly, but reliable, artificial waterways. While private companies like the Western Inland Lock Navigation Company undertook small canal projects, they often fell short of their investors' goals even with state subsidies, discouraging others from risking their capital in similar undertakings. Before work began on the Erie Canal, only three canals in the United States were more than two miles long. The longest extended a mere twenty-seven miles. Most Americans had no choice but to move their goods, and themselves, on unpredictable natural waterways and dependably bad roads.[13]

As a result, Long Island oysters, even the pickled variety, rarely reached a town like Batavia before the Erie Canal made possible the reliable and inexpensive transportation of goods between the Atlantic Coast and the Great Lakes. And Batavia was no isolated outpost. As home to the offices of the Holland Land Company, Batavia was a business center and transportation hub in the 1810s. But the bulk of trade into and out of Batavia followed natural waterways, which ran to the south and north. Had some merchants been determined, nonetheless, to move goods to Batavia from New York City, they would have sailed (or, increasingly after 1815, steamed) up the Hudson, loaded their freight on a wagon in Albany, and followed the turnpike westward. Unlike passage on waterways, turnpike travel was rugged even under the best of conditions. In 1816, a visitor to central New York complained that "the great part was a causeway formed of trunks of trees and so sparing had the inhabitants been of their soil, that we could by our feelings have counted every tree we jolted over . . ."[14]

Because of the difficulty in transporting goods, East Coast

merchants limited their trade with settlers in the hinterlands. Yet those settlers, even those who went west in search of their simple "independence," did not want to give up the comforts of home—heavy furniture and fragile housewares, recent news, and frequent visitors. Without dependable and inexpensive ways to transport such amenities, relatively few Euro-Americans made claims on the vast and fertile lands west of the Appalachians. Since those settlers who did venture west had limited choices for marketing their produce, much of New York's commerce flowed out of the state, indeed sometimes out of the country. Some settlers in the western part of the state shunned completely the difficulties of hauling freight along the west–east route to the Hudson, especially since the Mohawk River remained largely unnavigable despite the early efforts to improve it. Instead they used natural waterways to reach Pittsburgh to the south and Montreal to the north.[15]

Eager to channel commerce through their own state, a number of business-minded New Yorkers began after the Revolution to devise ways to carve artificial waterways between the Great Lakes and the Hudson. The most prominent of these men was Jesse Hawley, a flour merchant in the Finger Lakes region. Beginning in 1807, during a twenty-four-month confinement in debtors' prison, Hawley wrote fourteen essays outlining a system of waterways that, by tapping the vast resources of Lake Erie, would transform New York's landscape, settlement, and commerce. Like Mary Ann Archbald, he realized that people wanted connections to international markets. The question was not whether an artificial waterway was desirable but whether it was practicable.[16]

Hawley argued that an east–west canal through upstate New York was in fact viable, since it would follow a course laid out by "the Author of nature." While his essays suggested a quite specific route for the "artificial river," as some contemporaries would nickname the project, politicians around the state did not rush to accept his proposal. Rather, the New York State Legislature funded, in 1808, a survey to compare Hawley's "interior route" to the "lake route" that others preferred. The interior route would involve one long canal running from the Hudson to Lake Erie, while the "lake route" would run through Lake Ontario; from there, boats would travel west to the Niagara River, down which they would pass to Lake Erie after a substantial portage around Niagara Falls. Each route had its advantages and limitations. The lake route, while much shorter and thus less expensive, relied on Lake Ontario, which was insecurely positioned near British territory—an issue that seemed all the more important as hostilities between the two countries escalated in the aftermath of the Jeffersonian embargoes. The interior route would be harder to build but would fall well within the bounds of American soil.[17]

From the outset, the debate in New York over the potential canal routes revolved as much around politics as around engineering and international security. In 1810, a joint resolution of the New York State Legislature appointed the first group of seven commissioners to oversee the state's canal-building. These original commissioners—Gouverneur Morris, Stephen Van Rensselaer, DeWitt Clinton, Simeon DeWitt, William North, Thomas Eddy, and Peter B. Porter—were all prominent and wealthy New Yorkers. In an attempt to avert party bickering, the legislature had chosen the commissioners with an eye toward representing each of the era's main political factions, Federalists as well as Democratic-Republicans of all stripes. Yet this attempt to build a political consensus on the canal-building issue did not prevent upstate politicians from waging campaigns to have the survey run through their portions of the state. Meanwhile, politicians representing the eastern and southern sections of the state, and especially New York City, opposed the canal project altogether, worrying that their constituents would bear the financial burden of an artificial waterway without reaping any of its benefits. Throughout the canal period, politicians and private citizens often took stands on internal improvements based not on party affiliation but on local concerns about prosperity.[18]

Hawley's essays also left unresolved who would fund what

promised to be a very expensive undertaking. When New York
conducted its 1808 survey, many of its legislators believed that
the federal government would back the project financially. They
pointed to the report issued in that same year by Albert Gallatin,
Jefferson's Secretary of the Treasury, calling for appropriations
for a national system of roads and canals. That report, which laid
the groundwork for the funding of the National Road, also mentioned a canal between the Hudson and Lake Ontario. The ensuing debates in Congress centered on whether the proposed
canal would benefit the country as a whole or whether it would
favor a particular section, while Jefferson and like-minded men
also worried that the Constitution did not allow the federal government to finance such projects. Before these questions were
decided, the War of 1812 interrupted matters.

That conflict turned the nation's attention and resources elsewhere, while also highlighting for New Yorkers the advantages
of an inland waterway. Because fighting took place mostly along
the border between New York and Canada, the war accentuated
the precarious nature of the Montreal market. A canal would
provide access to a more stable market for the nation's western
farmers. Moreover, the war and the embargoes leading up to it
set off a boom in manufacturing in the northeastern states. Since
Americans could no longer legally trade with Great Britain for
manufactured goods, they had to spin and weave their own textiles and sew their own shoes. The loss of access to European
trade made an inexpensive route for western agricultural products
even more essential, as a means both to feed industrial workers
and their families and to provide raw materials for factories.

New Yorkers still hoped that the federal government would
pay for their proposed waterway once peace returned. In 1817,
three years after the Treaty of Ghent brought hostilities to an
official close, Congress passed an internal improvements bill that
included funding for the New York canal, but Madison vetoed
the act on his last day in office, citing qualms over its consti-
tutionality. Without an amendment specifically authorizing
Congress to fund transportation projects, he argued, the federal

government could not legally sponsor projects like the Erie Canal, as desirable as those projects might be. Some critics accused Madison of having sectional biases, of not wanting to boost New York, the arch economic rival of his native Virginia. Whatever his motivations, it became clear that any such future transportation projects would have to be undertaken by the states. This was to be an era of state, rather than national, power.[19]

DeWitt Clinton then took the lead in piecing together a bill in the state legislature that funded an interior canal from New York's coffers. His task was not easy, since the war had inflamed political divisions within the state. In 1812, Clinton had come forward as a peace candidate for President, competing against his fellow Republican James Madison and, in the process, splitting the New York Republicans into Clintonians and anti-Clintonians. Since Clinton's name would become the one most associated with the Canal project (which critics derided as "Clinton's big ditch"), strong anti-Clintonian sentiment impeded his efforts to negotiate compromises over funding. While most politicians voted, in the end, for what they perceived to be their local interests, those who still wavered often chose sides on the Canal Bill based on their more general sentiments about the controversial Clinton, rather than on the merits of the waterway.[20]

In 1817, the bill passed by a comfortable, if not overwhelming, majority. It established the Canal Fund, administered by elected officials, which was to fill its treasury from a variety of sources: a loan from the state, to be repaid from toll revenue; the sale of land donated to the state by land speculators who hoped to profit from soaring property values if the canal succeeded; a levy on items sold at auctions; lotteries whose proceeds were designated for the Canal Fund; and taxes. The taxes, in particular, were designed to ensure that those who benefited most from the Canal would contribute the greatest amount to the expense of building and maintaining it. The state levied taxes on salt (abundant in the Canal region); steamboat travel (which would increase along the Hudson with the opening of the Canal);

and land within twenty-five miles of the Canal (property whose values would certainly increase from easy access to the market). Finally, the bill authorized the beginning of construction on the "Western Canal," as the Erie was often called in the early years, as well as the "Northern Canal," running between Albany and Lake Champlain. Also known as the Champlain Canal, the sixty-six-mile northern waterway had been part of the compromise to win approval from that part of the state.[21]

The exact route of the Western Canal continued to be the subject of political wrangling even after 1817. The Canal Bill divided the Canal into three sections, but it provided for construction on the middle section only, the stretch of canal running between the Mohawk and Seneca rivers. The exact course of the other two sections would be left to later legislation, as would the funding for their construction. Since the middle section would improve navigation in the upstate region regardless of whether the other two sections ever came into being, politicians reasoned that it would serve as a good test of the state's ability to oversee such a mammoth public works project, much larger than any other in the modern world. The middle section also promised to be the easiest to build, so the Canal's promoters hoped to bolster public confidence in the larger project by showing early signs of success; future funding depended on that confidence. Decisions about building the other sections came gradually over the next few years. Meanwhile, communities distant from the original Canal petitioned for the building of lateral canals to feed into the main waterway. While the state ultimately constructed eight other canals, and scores of smaller tributary waterways, it undertook only two projects between 1817 and 1825: the Erie Canal and the much shorter Champlain Canal.[22]

The decision to begin the Erie Canal's construction on the Fourth of July was not, of course, mere coincidence. Then, as now, the Fourth was a day of national unity, when Americans put aside their differences and joined in celebrating all that was admirable and special about their country. But then, unlike now, the Republic was quite young, and people sensed that they were participating in an untried political system that might still fail. In 1817, veterans of the American Revolution and the constitutional debates still harvested apples in New York, planted wheat in Virginia, and visited merchant houses in Philadelphia. They were in the final years of life and had seen many of their contemporaries die before them; yet they remained national heroes and regaled their children and grandchildren with stories of the birth of the Republic and the idealism and courage that accompanied it. When work began on the Erie Canal, the nation had just emerged from another war with Britain, a conflict that had in a sense tested the nation's independence. While the treaty ending the war resolved few of the disputes between the two countries, it nonetheless had not weakened the United States, which remained subject to intense international scrutiny.

In the wake of the Treaty of Ghent, the younger generation of Americans—the children of the founders—hoped to prove to skeptical Europeans that their republic permitted unprecedented political freedoms and played a leading role in God's plan to improve the earthly world. This new generation of Americans was also determined to make its mark. Even with God's grace, though, the Erie Canal involved undeniable risks. At worst it would be a dismal failure, at best an expensive success. But if Americans could succeed in crafting *the* technological wonder of their day, they would demonstrate that the United States—and republicanism—was very special indeed.

The Fourth of July, a day of national unity, often brought together people who disagreed with one another the rest of the year. While Americans generally accepted that they were part of a political experiment, they often disagreed strongly about how that experiment should proceed. The debate over the ratification of the federal Constitution had divided them into Federalists and Anti-Federalists, and the disputes of the early national period had created Federalists and Republicans. But on that Independence Day in 1817, the nation as a whole was in the middle of its short-lived "Era of Good Feelings" under President James Monroe, an era when it seemed as though the United States might actually realize George Washington's dream of a nation devoid of political parties. The Federalists were, for all practical purposes, no longer influential in national politics. Most Americans had come to support economic and geographic expansion, even if they held different notions of how that growth should take place. Moreover, the slavery issue had not yet resurfaced to haunt the nation's leaders. For the moment the country's leadership seemed unified, divided perhaps by personal differences but not by overarching political visions. It would be another year or two before these divisive issues would reemerge and reveal a major political realignment.[23]

DeWitt Clinton, the person most associated with the Erie Canal, in many ways personally embodied the political culture that helped give birth in the 1820s to the second party system, characterized by the rivalry between the Jacksonian Democrats and the Whigs. Clinton's outlook, like that of many of his contemporaries, exhibited both republican and liberal tendencies. He genuinely believed that the public good (the foundation of a republic) and private gain (the basis of a commercial economy) need not be at odds with each other. Clinton subscribed to "practical republicanism," which was the precursor to the Whig ideology that solidified in the 1830s and that, in turn, would evolve into the Republican ideology of Abraham Lincoln's sectional party.

Adherents to practical republicanism believed that the nation's common good depended on prosperity, individual opportunity, and an equal emphasis on rural and urban growth. These Northerners differed from Jeffersonian Republicans by adopting a mix of republican and liberal ideas and, in the end, had more in common with Northern Federalists than with Southern Republicans. Practical republicans thought the government should guide economic development by adopting protective tariffs and investing in internal improvements; they also rejected Adam Smith's ideas about a laissez-faire economy. To ensure a just and

virtuous commonwealth, they desired a government run by individuals who had proved their mettle in a market economy,
achieved financial success, and demonstrated a commitment to
good works. These successful men believed they had a moral
obligation to help uplift those below them, and in turn they
expected deference from those they helped. To practical republicans, morality and wealth sprang from the same source of virtue. And by improving the physical world around them, by
building highways of "profitable intercourse," Americans could
realize their special destiny of universal moral and material
prosperity.[24]

DeWitt Clinton's political philosophy and New York's plans
to build the Erie Canal both represented a growing commitment
in the North to the culture of improvement. The very term
"improvement," however, is loaded with seeming contradictions.
According to the scholar Raymond Williams, the word "improve" originally meant (before the sixteenth century) to "invest," in the monetary sense. It later referred in particular to
readying untamed land for agricultural purposes. Not until the
eighteenth century did the term also take on the meanings we
give it today: to make something better, generally in a moral or
social sense. Like the related term "progress," though, improvement retained its dual meaning: it could refer at once to economic and material advancement and to a less tangible sense of
human accomplishment. The sponsors of the Erie Canal claimed
both meanings for their new internal improvement, and residents
of the Canal corridor would struggle to find ways to make compatible the various meanings of improvement and progress. Their
struggles would in the years to come promote a new political
culture, one that DeWitt Clinton would not have recognized had
he lived to see it.[25]

By invoking the memories of the American Revolution, the
waterway's sponsors celebrated both the past and the future.
They saw the Canal's ground-breaking ceremony as the consum-
mation of efforts made possible by the political values of the
Revolutionary era. Yet that dawn ceremony also marked, they

hoped, the beginning of a new era of progress that would improve upon the nation's economic and moral past. Throughout the canal era, New Yorkers would continue to link the past to the future, and those links would grow ever more paradoxical. They set out with an image of their Canal corridor as a "middle landscape" between nature (the past) and civilization (the future)—an image American politicians and intellectuals consciously cultivated. By linking the wilderness of the West to the port cities of the East, the Erie Canal could occupy a middle ground between savagery and urbanization. On that Independence Day in 1817, the Canal also represented the middle ground between the known values of the Revolutionary generation and the uncertainties about what sort of social order—or disorder—might accompany progress.[26]

Judge Richardson played the leading role in an event staged to focus Americans' attention on their nationalistic and republican past so as to quell fears about the uncertainty of the future. His supporting cast, the laborers who took over the digging, probably for that moment shared Richardson's excitement over taking part in an event of international significance. The *Utica Gazette* took special note of the way the ceremony unified employer and laborer in the "joy" it brought them. In doing so, though, the *Gazette* may have hoped to spark additional support for the still-controversial and risky project; newspapers during this period intended to shape opinions as well as report them. Like their contemporaries who had established textile mills in Lowell, Massachusetts, just a few years earlier, the Canal's supporters wanted to reassure the population at large that economic development need not result in the class divisions that plagued Europe. Judges, citizens, and laborers could all join in celebrating progress. The Canal's proponents believed that the social decay associated with rapid market growth (unemployment, poverty, crime, anonymity) could be avoided altogether in America's interior and reformed in its ports because—unlike Europe—the United States was destined to political, physical, and moral greatness. And as construction began on the artificial river, many residents of the Canal corridor held similarly optimistic views.[27]

2

The Triumph of Art
over Nature

OVER THE NEXT EIGHT YEARS, while skeptics worried that Clinton's expensive ditch would never turn into a canal, residents of upstate New York celebrated virtually every milestone in the Erie's completion. They took pride in the way that people had made a river where previously there had been none —in the words of one ceremonial ode, in the way that "proud ART o'er Nature has prevailed." To finish Nature's work of creating a water connection between the Hudson River and Lake Erie had called for technological achievements considered wonders of their era. Men as revered as Thomas Jefferson, himself a master of invention, had rejected the proposed Canal as "madness," impossible to accomplish given the state of scientific knowledge in the early nineteenth century. But New Yorkers had succeeded in making their artificial river, and they turned out in droves to celebrate the accomplishment.[1]

Usually sponsored by political and social elites, these celebrations represented well-staged, self-conscious expressions of unrestrained optimism about the Canal's expected impact on New York State and the nation. The biggest events marked the passing of the first boat along a portion of the middle section in 1819; the uniting in the east of the Erie Canal to the Hudson River in 1823; and, with the completion of the waterway's western end in 1825, the navigation of the entire length of the waterway. While echoing the Revolutionary symbolism of the ground-breaking ceremony, these later celebrations took on greater proportions and included combinations of speeches, prayers, songs, parades, theatrical performances, and artillery salutes. The general public attended the outdoor parades and artillery salutes, while the emerging commercial classes reserved for themselves the more exclusive indoor dinners and dances catering to "ladies and gentlemen." Politicians and other "gentlemen," for the most part, took responsibility for the oratory at these occasions, and offered speeches and toasts that lauded what they saw as the Canal's accomplishments. When men like Alexander Coventry spent their time and money organizing these events, they put aside whatever unease they felt about the canal era and took the lead in applauding what all agreed was a triumph of human ingenuity and exertion.[2]

Many residents of the upstate region had contributed their efforts to the Canal, and their excitement about the project arose, in part, from a sense that its accomplishments were theirs. Those politicians who had joined ranks with DeWitt Clinton to fight for the project's approval congratulated themselves on their tenacity and vision. Merchants and speculators contributed first by petitioning state officials to endorse the project and then by donating land through which the Canal could flow. Farmers ceded sections of their modest properties, and—along with artisans and merchants—became contractors in charge of constructing short portions of the Canal. Other artisans—blacksmiths, stonemasons, carpenters—built locks and aqueducts. Laborers shoveled and picked their way through New York's solid landscape, and braved malaria and snakes in its swamps. While their husbands, fathers, brothers, and sons constructed the Canal, New York women boarded some of the laborers who did not have families in the area. After writing to a relative about the twenty Irishmen she and her daughters had lodged and fed, Mary Ann Archbald anticipated the obvious inquiry: "What are we doing you will ask with so many men?" The answer was simple: "digging the Canal . . ." A variety of New Yorkers identified their personal efforts with the artificial river, while others—like the factory girls who threw flowers at the governor during an 1820 celebration—simply delighted in the success of what had seemed an impossible feat.[3]

The Erie Canal was not the first important technological advance in the young nation. In addition to Robert Fulton's steamboat, first launched on the Hudson River in 1807, several other innovations had already enhanced human capacities to perform human tasks. Eli Whitney's cotton gin revolutionized cotton production after 1793, making it possible for one slave to do the work that would have previously required fifty. Slaves had long removed sticky cotton seeds with their fingers; now they could do so by turning a machine. Beginning in 1815, New England power looms, copied from British models, wove cotton into cloth. Previously women had used hand looms to manufacture textiles at home; now their productivity multiplied with the assistance of water-driven looms in factories.[4]

Yet in 1817, when work began on the Canal, these technological advances had directly touched the lives of only a small number of Northerners. Even farmers like the Archbalds, who were actively engaged in market trade, continued to make coarsely woven clothing into the 1820s. If few farmers wore ready-made clothing, even fewer would have laid eyes on the power looms of Lowell. Most early manufacturing took place in homes rather than factories and did not rely on new technology. Women braided hats and sewed shoes, tasks they had long performed, but now they did so to the specifications of a merchant who paid them by the piece and sold their wares for profit. Early industrialization and manufacturing relied on reorganizing work routines far more than it did on mechanization. As a result, the most intricate mechanisms most Americans would have been familiar with in 1817 were clocks or the waterwheels of a local flour or grist mill.[5]

Oddly enough, in some ways the Erie Canal also looked quite unremarkable. A mere four feet deep and forty feet wide, the artificial river could indeed resemble a big ditch. For two stretches of more than sixty miles—the "long levels"—the Canal simply meandered along the route nature had molded: between Utica and Syracuse the Canal ran on a summit level alongside the Mohawk River, and between Rochester and Lockport it paralleled the southern shore of Lake Ontario. Yet overall, from Albany to Buffalo, the Erie Canal had to overcome a 573-foot difference in elevation. Since the topography did not rise steadily along that course, but rather occasionally dipped into a valley or climbed a hill, the waterway had to travel over a combined ascent and descent of about 680 feet. Eighty-three locks raised and lowered boats in increments of from just a few feet to more than fifteen, while eighteen aqueducts carried the entire waterway, and the boats it transported, over river valleys. In an era when engineers and builders relied mostly on wood, the Canal's stone and iron structures helped to usher in a new age in American technology while adding durable additions to the New York landscape. Wooden structures would rot away; these locks and aqueducts promised to be longer-lasting, thus allowing future generations to prosper from the foresight of the Canal's builders.[6]

The artificial river near Buffalo

(Basil Hall, *Travels in North America in the Years 1827 and 1828,* 1829, Canal Society of New York State)

A view of the Rochester aqueduct circa 1825, from a piece of wallpaper lining a trunk. Canal scenes frequently appeared as household decorations
(New York State Museum)

The waterway's unprecedented length and its multitude of locks and aqueducts made the creation of the Erie Canal an extraordinary feat. One farmer likened it to "building castles in the air . . ." While aqueducts had carried water since ancient times and locks had lifted boats for hundreds of years, the Erie presented a completely different magnitude. Imposing aqueducts of classical design carried boats over deep ravines for distances of more than a thousand yards at elevations of up to thirty feet. Meanwhile, the "combined" locks at Lockport—which consisted of two sets of five locks stacked one on top of another—raised and lowered boats a total of sixty feet over what had been a daunting rock formation. Invited to ride in the very first boat to pass up those world-famous locks, the merchant Ira Blossom described his experience as "somewat calculated to bewilder the senses . . . Unmoved as I usually am by surrounding objects, I am willing to confess that I was more astonished than I ever was by anything I had before witnessed." A visitor to the region a decade later would write of Lockport: "Here the great Erie Canal has defied nature, and used it like a toy . . ." Unlike cotton gins, waterwheels, or clocks, the Erie Canal displayed human ingenuity operating at nature's scale. What made the engineering works on the Erie Canal so remarkable was that they appeared to defy not just the whims but also the very laws of nature. They seemingly made water run uphill, and they lifted an entire waterway into the air. Humanity, in brief, had outwitted nature.[7]

To nineteenth-century Americans, nature was a powerful force. It provided the essentials of life: fertile land, sun and rain, trees and plants. But nature could also be deadly, rearing up unexpectedly in the form of floods, blizzards, tornadoes, hurricanes. Given nature's strength, the destruction of natural fixtures was as impressive as the construction of artificial ones. By far the most impressive example of flattening mountains was the three-mile "deep cut" at Lockport, a length of canal bed blasted out of a towering mountainside. Essentially an artificial gorge, the deep cut let boats pass thirty feet below the natural elevation at Lockport. A British traveler would later describe the manner in which human effort at Lockport had surmounted even the most stubborn impediments nature threw in the way. "It was here [at the deep cut] that the greatest obstacles of the whole 363 miles had to be encountered; and it certainly strikes the beholder with astonishment, to perceive what vast difficulties can be overcome by the pigmy arms of little mortal man, aided by science and directed by superior skill." If gunpowder helped little mortals blast the rocks, and if oxen helped cart the smashed stone, humanity nonetheless used a combination of brains and muscle to defeat the most daunting aspects of nature.[8]

But art's ultimate triumph was that it forced nature to do what nature had neglected to do on its own: create a river where one was needed. In his speech at the ceremony marking the completion of the Lockport locks in 1825, the Reverend F. H. Cuming elaborated on the feats of art and the ways in which they had created an artificial river: "The mountains have been levelled; the vallies have been filled; rivers and gulfs have been

Thousands of workers excavated the "deep cut" near Lockport
(Cadwallader D. Colden, *Memoir,* 1825, New York State Library)

The completed "deep cut"
(Cadwallader D. Colden, *Memoir,* 1825, New York State Library)

formed over them, by the exertions of art, a channel in which
the waters of the distant Hudson, the waters of the still more
distant Atlantic, will unite with the waters of the remote west,
and constitute a river . . ." Nature had been at once friend and
foe: by supplying its own waterways and a break in the mountains, nature offered humanity a tantalizing challenge to finish
nature's work. That New Yorkers had met that challenge represented, in the words of Samuel Woodworth, the "progress of
mind." By combining natural simplicity with human genius, the
Canal would fulfill the Republic's destiny to finish God's work,
which in turn would hasten the onset of the millennium.[9]

New Yorkers saw themselves at once as working with nature
and triumphing over it, a combination puzzling to modern sensibilities. Yet, as Raymond Williams has declared, "Nature is
perhaps the most complex word in the [English] language." In
nineteenth-century America, the same person could use the term
in seemingly contradictory ways. People commonly used it syn-
onymously with God. When they spoke of how Nature had left
a gap in the Appalachians, they meant that God had created that
break. Art historian Barbara Novak has noted that "by the time
Emerson wrote *Nature* in 1836, the terms 'God' and 'nature' were
often the same thing and could be used interchangeably." But
clearly this equivalence is not what New Yorkers had in mind
when they boasted that art had triumphed over nature. God was
to be revered, even feared, but certainly not vanquished.[10]

So when Americans talked about triumphing over nature, they
probably had in mind another meaning of the term, one that
represented the wilderness. Wilderness generally meant untamed
lands, where wild animals and Indians hunted and foraged. At
the celebration of the Canal's completion in 1825, the sponsors
launched an eastbound boat called "Noah's Ark" filled with
"birds, beasts, and 'creeping things' . . . —not forgetting two
Indian boys in the dress of their nation . . ." Representing the
subjugation of the wilderness, including the subduing of its human inhabitants, the "Ark" stood for the westward extension of
civilization that the Canal would make possible. The wilderness

was defined mainly in terms of what it was not: civilization. The triumph of art over nature represented civilization's spread over regions that had previously been home to "wild" beings, those incapable of understanding God's power. The triumph of art meant the physical and, particularly, the moral progress of society.[11]

Canal enthusiasts did not just celebrate the Erie Canal as a triumph of art. It was, in particular, a work of American art, a tribute to republicanism. At the celebration of the Lockport locks, great ceremony surrounded the laying of a capstone reading: "Erie Canal. Let posterity be excited to perpetuate our free institutions, and to make still greater efforts than our ancestors, to promote public prosperity, by the recollection that these works of internal improvement were achieved by the *spirit and perseverance* of REPUBLICAN FREE MEN." Here was a concise statement of the canal sponsors' attitude toward progress: by looking to their republican past, Americans could improve upon the efforts of the Founding Fathers. While the nation's founders had to concentrate their efforts on establishing free institutions, the next generation of leaders had the luxury—as well as the imperative—to concentrate on spreading prosperity. People like DeWitt Clinton, struggling to find their place in a society in which an earlier generation remained national heroes, saw their contributions as being in the commercial realm. By following God's plan to build a water highway to the West, these leaders would lure enterprising settlers to a region where before only beasts and "savages" roamed. By bringing with them not just their knowledge of God but also their commitment to "free institutions," these settlers would spread civilization westward. This notion would, in the 1840s, come to be called manifest destiny.[12]

The Canal's sponsors took every opportunity to laud the waterway as an American achievement. They pointed with pride to the American-born engineers who surveyed the Canal's winding route, designed its locks and aqueducts, contrived machines to remove tree stumps, and discovered a waterproof cement to ensure the permanence of the artificial river's structures. The most prominent of these engineers—James Geddes, John Jervis, Nathan Roberts, Canvass White, and Benjamin Wright—had received no professional training in engineering. Not until 1824 would the United States have a single school of civil engineering, when several of these men founded the Rensselaer Polytechnic Institute in Troy, near Albany. RPI would graduate most of the Canal's later engineers, but in 1817 the Erie's designers had been schooled in other professions. Roberts, who laid out the plans for the Lockport locks, had started out as a surveyor. He and the other men learned the science of making rivers as they went along—and thus served as exemplars of American ingenuity.[13]

For all their ingenuity, though, the success of these engineers' plans depended on the brute strength of the laborers who felled forests, shoveled and piled dirt, picked away at tree roots, blasted rock formations, heaved and hauled boulders, rechanneled streams, and molded the canal bed. In their eagerness to tout the project as an American enterprise, the canal commissioners bragged in 1819 that three-quarters of canal workers "were born among us." What they neglected to mention was that foreigners made up only a tiny percentage of the population in the Northeast generally as well as in New York in particular. Foreigners were thus very disproportionately represented among canal workers from the outset. In the years after 1819, the number of foreign workers on the waterway continued to swell, so that by 1825 the number of American workers on the Canal had dwindled even further; by the 1830s, the majority of canal diggers in North America would be Irish. The exact composition of the Erie's construction workforce of almost nine thousand remains in question. Contractors, rather than the government, hired most of the workers, and few of them kept any documentation on their employees. Our strongest image of canal workers comes from folklore, which portrays the typical construction worker as a young Irishman recently off the boat.[14]

People at the time also thought that immigrants did much of the work. Stephen and Elizabeth Watson, themselves immigrants from England, complained in 1823 that "there is thousands of Irish" in Albany. Laura Haviland remembered that the Irish came to Lockport in the 1820s "by hundreds," and Mary Ann Archbald reported seeing many "wild Irish working upon the Canal." Irish immigrants, however, may well have drawn attention beyond their numbers. While other foreigners in the region—those of English, Scottish, Welsh, and German origin —ordinarily arrived in family groups, the Irish tended to be single and male. Living together in large groups, the Irish attracted notice. As young men living away for the first time from paternalistic oversight, whether of their parents or of bosses, many Irish workers apparently showed a proclivity for heavy drinking and carousing, which drew the vocal scorn of other New Yorkers, Americans and foreigners alike.[15]

Whatever the actual numbers of foreign workers, other nineteenth-century New Yorkers would have disagreed that "republican free men" had alone constructed the Erie Canal. Much less important than the birthplace of the canal diggers was the nature of the work they performed. The concept of "republican free men" carried very specific connotations in the early Republic, ones that most of these canal workers, even those born in the United States, would not have satisfied. In order to participate as a citizen in this republic, a man was not supposed to be beholden to anyone. Someone who worked for wages, or even rented the land he tilled, left himself open to the economic, and hence political, control of another person. A boss or a landlord, in this era before the adoption of the secret ballot, could coerce his economic dependents into voting how he wished.

Only adult white men (for citizenship was limited to them) who produced for no one but themselves and their families could truly achieve the independence necessary to give reasoned thought to how they voted. Republican free men, in other words, should vote not from fear but on the basis of calm deliberation. For this reason, state constitutions in the early nineteenth century made property ownership a prerequisite for suffrage. Although shortly after 1825 New York would relax those property requirements, during the construction phase of the Erie Canal only property-owning white men qualified as citizens. By these standards, the vast majority of male laborers at the Lockport locks and elsewhere on the Canal did not qualify for political manhood regardless of their ethnic background.[16]

Many contemporaries recognized the baneful conditions faced by canal construction workers and worried about the political and social implications. While more and more Americans had accepted commercialization as necessary, if not desirable, after the War of 1812, many continued to fear the development of a permanent class of "laboring poor." They shared the views of the eighteenth-century Scottish economist Adam Smith, who believed that economic growth and social progress could develop hand in hand and that such development would require an increasing division of labor. Yet at the same time, Smith and his American followers worried that too much division of labor would dehumanize workers and make them "stupid and ignorant." For this reason, Americans had imagined that their early factories, like the textile mills in Lowell, would be run by a revolving workforce of unmarried women and children, people who would leave the mills after a short while to assume their duties as either mothers or citizens. Yet the colossal Canal project demanded a large workforce of unskilled male laborers, and it would be upon the backs of these workers that the market revolution of antebellum America would be built. Nothing was more deadening to human sensibilities than the repetitive and brutish labor of digging ditches day after day for someone else. Americans partially resolved this contradiction for themselves by justifying such labor as a temporary stage in the process of opening the West to settlement, a place where men's digging would be transformed into the more productive labor of tilling fields.[17]

The men who held the status of canal laborer could not by any stretch of the imagination be called republican free men. They were not like the part-time diggers that the canal commissioners liked to boast of: those American-born farmers who worked on the Canal during slow periods in the agricultural cycle. These noble farmers, rather than devoting a moment to idleness, threw themselves into a project that promoted the "general utility." Everyone recognized that without the grunt of labor, the Canal would never be built. But virtually no one wanted to imagine a class of men who permanently held the status of ditchdigger. If Americans realized that not everyone would become a farmer, they nonetheless hoped that citizens would produce *something*. In 1825, the same year New York debated adopting universal manhood suffrage, a state engineer wrote to the canal commissioners explaining why they should consider an alternative route for one of the lateral canals then under consideration: the proposed route would interfere with eel fishing. "It is said," the engineer conceded, "that this employment is not of the brilliant national use, which is attached to agriculture . . ." But he insisted that

> those employed in it are citizens and men, and fill a niche in the general estimate; deprive them of this resource, and they will not become husbandmen; they will remain what they were—fishermen, or become something worse. They have elected to rake the waters for their supplies, and their surplus, they barter with the farmer for their bread, who is glad to make the exchange, rather than break in upon his profession to catch fish.

Hardly a tribute to American republicanism, these fishermen at least raked up food. Ditchdiggers shoveled up only dirt and stones. Their occupation was "something worse" and could seem at times to compromise the workers' most basic status as "free men."[18]

To many residents of the corridor, Irish immigrants in particular appeared less than fully human in their desperate willingness to work for low wages and live in poverty. One English couple wrote home that "there is so many Irish keep coming every day, and they work so cheap, that it makes it bad for laboring people." The idea that Irish immigrants hurt the prospects of workers in general certainly contributed to the tensions between the Irish and other ethnic groups, which occasionally erupted into brawls and even riots. Although tensions existed among Irish workers themselves, who divided along ethnic and religious lines, Irishmen of all backgrounds became the targets of violence. Despite the Protestant affiliations of many early Irish immigrants, other New Yorkers tended to assume that all Irish were Catholic, a religion they feared because of its adherence to hierarchical and seemingly superstitious practices. Mary Ann Archbald, who freely admitted her past dislike of the Irish, reported that one of her son's Irish workers had been "attacked . . . by 16 freeborn Yankees as they are pleased to style themselves & nearly murdered in the most shocking manner." Archbald attributed the assault to "prejudice."[19]

Other factors also contributed to the sense that canal laborers were somehow not completely "free." Even though it was a relatively new occupation in the United States, canal digging had a history associated with unfree labor. Southern canal builders relied almost exclusively on slave labor, and, closer to home, in 1817 the state of New York authorized the use of convict labor to haul stones on the Erie Canal. Canal work, in nineteenth-century eyes, merited the use of the most degraded, unfree labor.[20]

Many, if not most, canal laborers probably felt that their occupation was beneath them. If Irish immigrants were not "freeborn," they shared with Yankees the hopes of escaping their degraded status as wage laborers and, perhaps, qualifying as citizens of the Republic. While the famines of 1817 and 1822 drove Irish immigrants from their homeland, the lure of opportunity also pulled them to the United States. If many of these immigrants had been common laborers in their own country, they had reason to believe that they could find work in the New World that would eventually allow them to return to the landed occupations of their ancestors. These men did not come to the United States because they wished to remain dependent. Articles and letters in Irish newspapers painted the United States as "the best poor man's country," a place where affordable farmland and work opportunities abounded.[21]

When immigrants made the final decision to leave their homelands, at least some of them set sail with optimistic expectations. Because so few of these laborers have left written records, it is impossible to generalize about their motivations. But the later reflections of a canal laborer who fulfilled his goals illustrate the vision that probably attracted other immigrants to the "best poor man's country." Pádraig Cúndún, an Irish farmer who first worked as an Erie Canal laborer, observed in 1834, "I have a fine farm of land now, which I own outright. No one can demand rent from me. My family and I can eat our fill of bread and meat, butter and milk any day we like throughout the year, so I think being here is better than staying in Ireland, landless and powerless, without food or clothing." The United States had promised freedom—not just from poverty but from the control of landlords. It was a country that promised "power" to men who earned their independence.[22]

Few canal laborers—not even Cúndún—found their expectations met during the years of the waterway's construction. Landing in New York or Quebec, many immigrants found their employment prospects at best grim. They arrived as the United States was suffering a major economic slump, the depression of the late 1810s. Many immigrants found themselves at their port of arrival without prospects of work, let alone property ownership. The Erie Canal answered their immediate needs. In August 1817, *The Exile*, an Irish newspaper in New York City, advised disappointed new arrivals about several specific employment opportunities, including jobs on the Canal. The editor promised that the Canal "will afford steady and permanent employment, as laborers will work winter as well as summer." The Irish were not alone in turning to canal digging out of necessity. "If it were not for the canal," wrote the Welsh laborer William Thomas in 1818, "many of the Welsh would be without work." Artisans also accepted canal-related work during the economic downswing that brought the post–War of 1812 boom to a stunning halt.

"The carpenter who is out of work, works on the canal," William Thomas reported. Americans as well as foreigners saw the Canal as a way to earn money in the midst of a financial crisis that made cash a very scarce commodity.[23]

Canal work generally offered competitive daily or monthly wages, though the seasonal nature of some canal jobs—despite *The Exile*'s promises to the contrary—still left many of its laborers in poverty. Workers' earnings did not follow a set pattern, since individual contractors hired and set the terms for their workers. Some contractors provided room, board, and often liquor as part of their wages; others paid higher wages but provided no amenities. Peter Way, in his study of North American canals, has seen the former arrangement as an attempt to create a paternalistic bond between employer and employee, which would allow employers to maintain a certain amount of control over their workers' habits. Yet it seems more likely, on the Erie Canal at least, that a shortage of cash, particularly after 1819, led many contractors to offer a portion of their payments in kind.[24]

The desire of many contractors to shelter their workers in shantytowns suggests they had no intention of adopting the paternal role of instilling good republican values in their workers. By all accounts, workers were housed in these shanties like animals in barns; their very living conditions were dehumanizing. And these shanties stood physically removed from the "civilizing" influences of nearby settled communities. Contractors did not plan to hire these workers on a permanent basis, so their long-term character and work habits were of little import to their bosses. What workers did on their own time did not matter to their employers as long as enough of them showed up ready to dig the next day. Even a certain amount of absenteeism probably did not matter, since most tasks were interchangeable. Moreover, some employers had no choice but to find shelter for their workers performing tasks deep in the New York wilderness. No other options existed.

The cash part of workers' wages fluctuated with the supply of laborers and the demand of contractors, and it varied in different locations on the Canal. A Welsh laborer near Utica reported in 1818 that "wages on the canal are one dollar a day and thirteen to fourteen dollars a month with food and washing and half a pint of whisky a day. Those who provide their own food, wet and dry, get twenty-two to twenty-three dollars." Three years later, one company advertised for fifty laborers to construct a feeder canal near Rochester for ten dollars a month, and the following year another company offered twelve dollars a month to a thousand laborers at Lockport—presumably with food and lodging. It undoubtedly took greater incentives to lure a thousand men to the wilderness outside Lockport than it did to find fifty willing workers in the booming town of Rochester. The more general dip in wages after 1819 and the increased reliance on payment in kind probably reflect the national glut of unemployed workers as well as the national shortage of cash. That shortage of cash strained all aspects of the economy, encouraging local farmers, merchants, and craftsmen to supplement their incomes by building sections of the Canal. Many would-be contractors tried to underbid one another by cutting their single greatest expense: labor. Even accounting for variations, though, wages for canal laborers appear to have been comparable to those offered other Northern wage earners. During the years of the Canal's construction, wages in Philadelphia ranged from seventy-five cents to one dollar a day.[25]

Although canal work paid comparatively well, laborers found to their disappointment that their earnings did not buy them a better way of life. William Thomas, like other Welsh immigrants he knew, took work on the Canal when he could not find other employment. Life in the United States did not meet his expectations, nor did it seem worth the initial expense of emigration. "I beg all my old neighbors," he wrote, "not to think of coming here as they would spend more coming here than they think. My advice to them is to love their district and stay there." Thomas reported that he and many others were thinking seriously about returning to Wales. In 1818, another Welsh immigrant complained that "this country is not what we had heard about it in any way." As their dreams for independence faded, immigrants' appreciation of their former homes grew sharper.[26]

For those laborers who had anticipated working at their chosen trades or on their own farms, canal work could only have led to disenchantment. Construction laborers worked long hours, in good weather and bad, and many worked seasonally only, unable to perform their tasks after the onset of the upstate region's deep frosts. Those whose jobs did continue in winter faced truly frigid conditions. Summertime weather, too, brought problems, mostly in the form of epidemics. In 1819, more than one thousand canal laborers fell disabled by an unidentified disease that apparently had its source in a thirty-mile stretch of swamp filled with the "rankest vegetable luxuriance." Most of these workers survived after a long recuperation, but a few died. The only consolation for poor working conditions was that they drove up wages. When another fatal illness struck along the Oswego Canal, one of the lateral waterways connecting with the Erie, several of the contractors appealed to state officials for extra compensation. When these entrepreneurs had placed their bids to build their sections of the canal, they had not anticipated that disease would force them to raise wages and to bear other expenses related to their workers' sickness. "In consequence of the sickness that prevailed in this section and its vicinity," one of them wrote, "we were under the necessity of raising wages from twelve to fourteen and some as high as seventeen dollars per month for common Labourers, and pay Physicians for atten[d]ing to the sick, purchase Coffins and grave clothes, and attend with Hands to bury the Dead." Sometimes nature still triumphed over art.[27]

Art also had its flaws. Gunpowder explosions—used to blast through the rock-solid landscape—blew up some workers as well, while rocks sent flying by those explosions struck others, killing or injuring them. Collapsing canal beds smothered yet others. Some workers fell to their deaths from those great technological wonders, locks and aqueducts. The same issue of the *Lockport Observatory* that reported how its citizens lavishly celebrated the Canal's completion also made note of the death of

Orrin Harrison, a worker on the famed combined locks. Harrison "was leaning against one of the balance beams, and from excessive fatigue fell asleep, and was precipitated into one of the locks, in about 8 feet of water." His legs became caught in the lock's gates, and he drowned before he could be rescued.[28]

In some ways, canal work did not differ so much from the tasks independent farmers performed when clearing unimproved land. Farmers, too, felled trees, dug ditches, diverted streams— all of which involved physical dangers. Their work, too, was hampered by upstate winters. Canal work, though, came with frustrations that farming did not share. Canal laborers had bosses and worked for wages. While some farmers also employed agricultural laborers for wages, those farm workers tended to live in a more genuinely paternalistic relationship with their employers. If that meant restrictions on their freedoms, they also usually came with better food and warmer beds than those hastily constructed shanties that sheltered dozens of canal diggers. While farm work was also seasonal, each year predictably brought a new season. Any particular job on the Canal endured for but a short period of time, sending workers from job to job, with the uncertainty of when and where they would next find work. In the long term, canal work was not "steady" in the same way as farming. Even if workers moved on to other public works projects, those jobs would also provide neither independence nor security.[29]

What, then, did the Canal's sponsors have in mind when they memorialized the Lockport locks as the work of republican free men? Very few of the thousands of men who worked on the deep cut or the combined locks would have qualified as republican citizens—in either their own or other minds. The authors of the inscription on the locks there did not have these laborers in mind at all. They referred instead to the "spirit and perseverance" of the politicians and engineers who had overseen the project. Just as "nature" took on several meanings in the nineteenth century, so did "art." Many New Yorkers celebrated the "proud triumphs of the arts over the work of nature," or saw their villages as "the favored seat of contest between Nature and Art—in which the latter is victorious." This widely shared sense of accomplishment was made possible by the flexibility of the word "art." "Art," according to historian Paul Johnson, possessed at least two distinct meanings in the early nineteenth century, depending on the social class of the user. To artisans, "art" was an "identity-defining skill." It included "the whole range of combined mental and manual performances through which trained men provided the wants and needs of their communities." The stonemasons and blacksmiths who fashioned the Lockport locks would have had this meaning in mind when they joined the merchant Ira Blossom in applauding the astonishing feat they had accomplished. Meanwhile, to the emerging business classes, "art referred to the works of technology and entrepreneurial vision that were transforming nature and the social order . . ." Men like Ira Blossom, in other words, paid tribute to the visionaries who brought to fruition the project that would usher in a new commercial age.[30]

Although people attending celebrations heard scores of toasts offered to politicians and canal commissioners, and a handful praising artisans, virtually none of the hundreds of speeches and toasts offered at the official gatherings honored the common laborers whose physical strength made the Canal possible. On the rare occasions when orators mentioned the efforts of labor, their meanings were ambiguous. In his speech at the Lockport ceremony, for example, the Reverend Cuming emphasized that "THE LONG LABOR IS OVER." After mentioning the leveling of mountains and the filling of valleys, Cuming said these accomplishments had been made possible "by the exertions of art." Cuming may have been alluding to the physical labor that went into constructing the Canal; his use of the passive voice, however, obscured any direct recognition of laborers' contributions to the "art" that brought the Canal into being. He could just as easily have been referring to the years of effort by politicians who first envisioned the Canal, promoted it, and overcame the competing demands of representatives from areas along proposed alternative paths of the artificial waterway.[31]

Common laborers remained strikingly absent from reports of the many official Canal celebrations. After Judge Richardson handed them his spade in 1817, they faded into obscurity. They did not sing public odes, march in parades, or offer toasts. Only one group of semiskilled workers played any role in the official festivities over the course of the next eight years; in 1825 the Albany cartmen—or drivers of freight wagons—led a parade in which the governor and canal commissioners also marched. But when the cartmen offered toasts that evening, they made no direct reference to the Canal project. Instead, they saluted themselves and their future prosperity.[32]

Artisans, by contrast, did take part in Canal-related festivities, though they had their own set of reasons for doing so. A song written for the Grand Celebration by a "mechanic of Buffalo" proclaimed, "Matter and space are triumphed o'er. Gigantic genius led the van." The mechanic, in other words, joined in the praising of politicians and engineers whose "genius" made the Erie Canal possible. But he gave credit to more than genius alone. The song continued, "While sturdy toil fulfilled the plan." Some New York artisans publicly commended the sponsors' art, the vision that shaped the Canal project, yet they also championed their own contributions and causes. At the 1825 Grand Celebration in New York City, printers distributed sheets with the lyrics to an "Ode to the Canal Celebration" written by one of their journeymen. Yet the other artisans, who turned out in great numbers for what would be one of the most elaborate public spectacles in nineteenth-century America, displayed banners and floats that celebrated their crafts but that rarely, if ever, mentioned the Canal. Few of the New York City paraders, in fact, had actually worked on the Canal. Like a group of mechanics and shoemakers who marched in Albany in 1823, they seized the celebrations as an opportunity to exhibit their occupational pride and their political presence.[33]

But unlike the cartmen and the craftsmen, the canal diggers did not belong to a well-organized, tradition-minded guild. Canal work was a relatively new occupation in the United States, and, moreover, most of them probably did not see canal work as an "identity-defining skill." Laborers took jobs on the Canal, as we have seen, only when their hopes for other employment had been dashed; nor did they willingly identify themselves with an occupation they shared with slaves and convicts. Their dependence on this unsteady occupation also meant that many, if not most, of them would have left town by the time of the official celebrations. While other New Yorkers marched and sang about the triumphs of art, the laborers began digging another ditch somewhere else.[34]

Those who remained may have lacked the desire to participate in official celebrations, whether for reasons of principle or otherwise. Some historians have found evidence that workers on other public works intentionally disrupted similar celebrations. Peter Way, for example, describes how Irish workers used rocks to pelt the elite participants at the ground-breaking ceremony for the Illinois and Michigan Canal in 1836; "rather than from any discontent with the patriotic celebration, [their actions] more likely resulted from mischievousness and a sense of pique at their exclusion from festivities initiating a project they would complete by sweat of brow and strain of muscle." While no evidence of similar protests exists on the Erie Canal, scattered reports suggest that workers on the Erie celebrated the Canal's completion in their own manner. When the first canal boat left Utica in 1819, a group of twenty workmen "sent up a shout of welcome, more cordial and contagious than ever before echoed through the woods of the Mohawk . . ." If hardly a true celebration, their cheers nonetheless suggest that they did not actively protest the celebration and the progress it championed.[35]

Like many other New Yorkers, laborers joined in cheering the Canal without marching behind banners or speaking publicly. Holmes Hutchinson, a prominent Canal surveyor, wrote in November 1822 from Schenectady: "The Canal is completed to this place . . . I anticipate seeing a good many drunken Dutchmen as great preparations are making for a celebration." Hutchinson's comment about Dutchmen, presumably a reference to the region's German immigrants, may have simply reflected his disdain for that ethnic group. It is more likely, however, that these workers had on previous occasions joined celebrations in ways that offended genteel mores. Commercial and middle-class New Yorkers thought of construction workers as a drunken and boisterous lot, as they could in fact sometimes be.[36]

For this reason, Canal sponsors may well have tried to exclude laborers from the official celebrations, which probably explains the separation of celebrations into two spheres: the outdoor, daytime ceremonies where workers joined other spectators, such as farmers and artisans, and the indoor, evening ceremonies where "ladies and gentlemen" heard toasts and speeches offered by their social peers. At these elite gatherings, toasts to popular contributions to the Canal took on the narrowest terms possible. In his official memoir of the Canal project, for example, Cadwallader Colden bragged that "every citizen deserves a share of the credit" for the new waterway. By way of explanation, he quoted the canal commissioners, who had written that "their labors could not have been perfected without the support of a wise foresight, and just liberality, in several successive Legislatures." Colden emphasized the labor of the commissioners, the foresight of the politicians, and the contribution of the citizens—who elected the politicians who had the foresight to support the commissioners. Such an interpretation was in keeping with ideal notions of how a representative republic should work. Virtuous citizens would protect the common good by electing their superiors to look after their interests. So even this mention of "every citizen" offered no recognition of the largely disenfranchised men whose labor had bored through the New York landscape. At the 1825 Grand Celebrations, a Colonel Stone offered a toast to "Genius and Enterprize—nature imposes no bounds to their march. They command mountains to move, and rivers to flow in dry places. The word is spoken, and it is done!" Had they been in attendance, the families of the workers who lost their lives blasting rocks or excavating canal beds could only have been puzzled by this explanation of how the artificial river came into being.[37]

Ambiguous at best in their recognition of labor, orators at the

Canal's official celebrations would probably have agreed with Webb Harwood's sentiments about construction workers. In 1821, when the section of canal in front of his farm had been completed, Harwood wrote: "We now just begin to rejoice in a retired life again—for 18 months our house has been thronged with men from 20 to 60 men & some of the roughest creatures, our life has been very uncomfortable, but 2 days ago they went away . . ." Permanent residents of the Canal region *could* find something to celebrate about canal diggers: once their job was completed, they moved on. The laborers left for other portions of the Canal, and when the Erie had been completed, they sought employment on projects in other states, where New York's success in canal-building had triggered a craze for similar projects.[38]

When Canal sponsors envisioned an era of material prosperity and moral improvement, they apparently assumed that common laborers would not figure into that picture in any substantial way. They did not toast canal laborers because those laborers represented neither the virtues of the republican past nor the prosperity of the commercial future. While laborers may have shared the "joy" of the Canal's ground-breaking ceremony, the next eight years had painfully demonstrated that their lives did not fit either the moral or economic visions of the Canal's promoters. By the time of the Erie's completion, the project's sponsors no longer claimed that the new commercial era could be launched without class tensions. Instead, they tried to convince themselves, and others, that the class of degraded workers they had come to scorn was a necessary—but temporary—evil.

In celebrating an early milestone in the creation of the artificial river, DeWitt Clinton emphasized how internal improvements would serve the ideals of nationalism and republicanism. Along with similar internal improvements in the states beyond the Great Lakes, the Erie Canal was destined to make

> the greater part of the United States . . . form one vast i[s]land, susceptible of circumnavigation to the extent of

many thousands of miles. The most distant parts of the confederacy will then be in a state of approximation, and the distinctions of eastern and western, of southern and northern interests, will be entirely prostrated. To be instrumental in producing so much good, by increasing the stock of human happiness—by establishing the perpetuity of free government—and by extending the empire of improvement, of knowledge, of refinement and of religion, is an ambition worthy of a free people.

Clinton spoke in 1819, in the middle of the national crisis over whether Missouri should be admitted to the Union with its constitution permitting slavery. As Americans worried that their country's fragile union might be severed by sectional disagreements, Clinton tried to assure them that the future looked brighter. By finishing God's work, by bringing distant parts of God's chosen nation into closer physical promixity, the Erie Canal promised to help eliminate those regional differences and allow the United States to continue on its march toward physical and moral improvement.[39]

Few Americans, it seems, would have argued with these sentiments. But New Yorkers did not agree on what made that artificial river materialize in the first place. While the Canal sponsors praised politicians and government officials, artisans paid honor to themselves and their workmanship. Laborers, meanwhile, gave a quick hurrah before moving on to another public works project. Although all praised the triumph of art over nature, they did so with different voices—and with different hopes for the future that such triumph would bring.

3

Reducing Distance and Time

T HE ERIE CANAL proved an immediate and extraordinary success. Before the waterway had been completed, politicians
began discussing its enlargement to accommodate the immense
volume of traffic. Horse-drawn boats, stacked high with bushels
of wheat, barrels of oats, and piles of logs, streamed steadily
eastward toward the New York City market. In the Canal's first
year of official operation, tolls collected on freight more than met
the interest on the state's construction debt; by 1837, the entire
loan on the original Canal was paid. Although the politicians
and engineers who envisioned and designed the Canal imagined
it primarily as a commercial channel for freight boats, passengers
also traveled on the Canal's long narrow boats, lured by the
affordability, smoothness, and convenience of canal travel. In
1825, the year that New Yorkers celebrated the Erie Canal so
fervently, more than forty thousand passengers traveled on the
new waterway, even though it had not yet gone into full service.
Other states, inspired by the success of New York's Erie and
Champlain canals, rushed to construct their own. The financial
accomplishments of the Erie, as well as the failures of subsequent
projects in other states, have been recounted in detail by previous
scholars.[1]

What remains to be told is what happened after residents of
the Canal corridor breathed a collective sigh of hope that their
transient workforce would head off to other states. Only then
did they begin to appreciate fully the ways in which the artificial

river would reshape their daily lives. Although they had joined DeWitt Clinton in praising the ways in which the Canal promised to keep the nation united, by 1825 their concerns were unabashedly personal. The Missouri Compromise of 1820 had removed the divisive issue of slavery from national politics at least for a time. As a result, New Yorkers were free to refocus their attention on what their state had hoped to do when it undertook Clinton's grand scheme: to defy nature by compressing distance and time.

In the decades after the Canal opened for business, millions of men, women, and children would flock through upstate New York. The artificial river provided inexpensive transportation for passengers whose journeys could not have been anticipated by its sponsors. Evangelical preachers made their circuits of the upstate region on the Erie Canal, exhorting residents, tourists, emigrants, and workers to seek salvation. In this period of evangelical reform, the Canal also served as the last leg of the underground railroad, ferrying runaway slaves from Syracuse to Buffalo, near the Canadian border. While some boat passengers sought to save souls or win freedom, others found canal boats to be convenient for running businesses. Entrepreneurs bought boats and outfitted them as groceries or, in the case of the *Encyclopedia*, as a museum and bookstore featuring "natural and artificial curiosities." Aspiring merchants of more modest means moved from boat to boat, peddling small items such as books, watches, and fruit. Confidence men, meanwhile, preyed on passengers, selling remedies for foot corns or offering counterfeit bills in exchange for items of value.[2]

None of these endeavors would have been possible without the Canal's steady flow of tourists, businessmen, and settlers. Together these travelers made up the vast majority of passengers on canal boats. The Canal's luxurious packet boats carried tourists on the "northern tour," a travel circuit that ultimately led to Niagara Falls, just north of Buffalo. Merchants used these same passenger boats for short trips to nearby towns or rode the waterway on their way to conduct affairs in New York City. Men and women living in the Canal corridor boarded packets to visit friends or relatives, to attend to business in other towns, or simply to have a relaxing excursion. Emigrants from Europe and New England, meanwhile, took passage on westbound freight boats, on which they also loaded their trunks and furniture. In exchange for cheap passage, they camped on deck or on top of crates. The Canal drew such a large number of passengers that a nineteenth-century observer remarked, "For about ten years after the opening of the Hudson and Erie Canal, in 1825, the man who had not voyaged upon those tranquil waters was considered a decided home body."[3]

Very few of these people would have ventured to western New York or points farther west had the Erie Canal not greatly eased transportation and communication between regions of the country that had just recently seemed extremely remote from one another. The Canal made distances seem short not so much with speed as with efficiency. Pulled by teams of horses, canal boats still moved relatively slowly, though methodically. Those catering exclusively to passengers reached speeds of up to five miles an hour, while freight boats moved at about two miles an hour. Yet canal boats cut nearly in half the travel time between Albany and Buffalo—a journey that now took between five and seven days—by offering what horse-drawn stages and wagons did not: a nonstop, smooth method of transportation. Canal boats could move day and night, and they ran at much more frequent intervals than stages. While passengers might wait days to catch the next stage, boats left even the most sleepy of towns at least several times a day. Moreover, because a single team of horses could pull much more freight over water than over land, the Canal dramatically reduced the cost of transporting goods; before the Canal, the difficulty of carrying commodities by wagon from Buffalo to Albany often increased their costs by five or six times the values of the goods themselves, which made the New York City market seem a world apart. Alleviating this obstacle to the nation's commercial development and westward expansion had been what DeWitt Clinton and others had stressed when they promoted the waterway. For reasons they did not anticipate, though, their artificial river would evoke feelings of ambivalence among many of the same people who celebrated the efficiency with which the Canal moved people and goods.[4]

In his 1828 satiric play *A Trip to Niagara*, William Dunlap caught this ambivalence. Scene 4 opens in front of the Little Falls aqueduct. Little Falls—with its massive stone aqueduct carrying boats over a series of majestic cascades—was one of the most popular stops for American and foreign tourists, who generally chose to travel by canal so that they could see a combination of artificial and natural sites. As the curtain rises on Dunlap's stage, the heroine, Amelia, begins praising the beauties of the surrounding natural landscape. She proclaims to Wentworth, her brother: "This is delightful, brother . . . The opportunity we so frequently have, of stepping from the canal-boat, and thus walking on the bank, adds to the pleasure derived from the ever changing scenery that is presented to us." Her brother's response is markedly less enthusiastic: "Pleasure! To be dragged along upon a muddy ditch, hour after hour, in constant dread of lifting your head above your knees for fear of having it knock'd off your shoulders by a bridge!" Amelia reminds her brother, in words similar to those DeWitt Clinton might have used, that he "must admire this great patriotic work—this union of the inland seas with the Atlantic Ocean." Amelia views the Canal as a vehicle for communing with nature and as a symbol of American ingenuity. It provides a means of taking in sublime surroundings, whether natural or technological. Where his sister sees sublime landscape, Wentworth sees only a filthy ditch upon which travel is tedious and potentially dangerous. These two points of view suggest that women and men responded to the Erie Canal in different ways, but the voices of the nineteenth-century travelers and settlers belie such generalization. Instead, individuals agreed with both Amelia and Wentworth, producing a complicated set of mixed feelings that evolved over time.[5]

The Little Falls aqueduct—representing the link between nature and
civilization—here used as a symbolic backdrop to depict
the 1825 Grand Canal Celebration
(Cadwallader D. Colden, *Memoir*, 1825, New York State Library)

Scholars have long realized that nineteenth-century Americans
felt equivocal about the role of technology in their lives. In *The
Machine in the Garden*, a cultural study of railroads and the pastoral ideal, Leo Marx uses the works of fiction writers, artists,
and philosophers to illustrate the tension between technology's
sublime and destructive consequences. In some ways, of course,
canals are not comparable to railroads; canal boats moved slowly

and were pulled by animals, while railroad engines raced through the countryside, powered by steam, clanging against their rails and sending sparks shooting through the air. Even so, the Canal's works of art—its locks and aqueducts—stood out as man-made structures among the natural. Social commentators of the age responded to these structures in much the same way as they did to the "iron horse." Nathaniel Hawthorne, for example, traveled on the Erie Canal in 1830 and objected to what he saw as the too-rapid, unthinking advance of progress.[6]

In one of his "Sketches from Memory," Hawthorne begins by claiming that he "was inclined to be poetical about the Grand Canal. In my imagination De Witt Clinton was an enchanter, who had waved his magic wand from the Hudson to Lake Erie and united them by a watery highway, crowded with the commerce of two worlds, till then inaccessible to each other." By recognizing the Canal's exceptional achievements—the ways it compressed distance—Hawthorne tries to create a bond of empathy with his readers, who he assumes view the artificial river as something to praise.

But then he changes his tune. After describing an unpleasant trip along the waterway, which he happily aborts short of his destination, Hawthorne lists a long series of complaints. Not only does he detest the means of travel, he also laments how the Canal gave rise to ill-developed towns where the extremes of wealth and poverty stand in stark contrast to each other. Finally, he decries what the works of art had wrought on the natural landscape. He writes about how the draining of swamps to provide water to feed the canal had caused vibrant forests to decay into what he paints as a ghostlike and disorderly cemetery. "In spots where destruction had been riotous, the lanterns [on the boat] showed perhaps a hundred trunks, erect, half overthrown, extended along the ground, resting on their shattered limbs or tossing them desperately into the darkness, but all of one ashy white, all naked together, in desolate confusion." Hawthorne concludes that this ghastly scene resulted from "the encroachments of civilized man." As in his criticism of railroads, Hawthorne ultimately viewed the Canal's technology as a threat to America's special geographic and moral destiny, as an encouragement of too much civilization.[7]

However, Hawthorne's portrait is at odds with those of more ordinary men and women who spent time in the Canal corridor. Like Hawthorne, most of these people initially perceived the Canal as extraordinary, as if a magic wand had been cast over nature's landscape. And also like Hawthorne, many of these men and women found their expectations disappointed. Remarkably few of them, though, would have concurred with Hawthorne's ambivalence about progress itself. Instead, their equivocal feelings were more in line with the less profound sentiments articulated by Amelia and Wentworth. Unlike Hawthorne, who hoped to convert his readers to his own worldview, Dunlap aimed to poke fun at ordinary people's sentiments. And in doing so, he exaggerated but did not misrepresent their basic perceptions.

Like Amelia, most tourists who traveled to Niagara Falls took the Erie Canal for at least part of their journey. Before the waterway's construction, the upstate region had remained inaccessible to all but the most hardy adventurers because of the difficulties confronting travel by stagecoach; visitors to Niagara Falls approached that "icon of the American sublime" from the south rather than the east—and in the process, they missed the other breathtaking falls of upstate New York. After the lavish Canal celebrations announced to the world that American ingenuity had been spectacularly successful, tourists from Europe and the eastern United States began flooding the region. The Canal provided a window on both art and nature. Stewart Scott, a Canadian student who visited Lockport in 1826, noted that "Lockport is itself a plain looking little village, but is rendered famous by its locks, of which there are 5 double ones upon the Canal, as close together as possible: as Niagara Falls are the greatest <u>natural</u> wonder, so Lockport, its Locks, and the portion of the Canal adjacent, are considered to be the greatest <u>artificial</u> curiosity in this part of America."[8]

Art and nature had a complex relationship. Although they worked in tandem, they also were implied opposites. One could be understood fully only in terms of the other, so tourists set out to experience the Canal as a juxtaposition of the two. The Canal was, after all, the "artificial river"; and the very phrase captures one of the central paradoxes in the attitudes of tourists and settlers alike. With the term "artificial," antebellum men and women emphasized the human resourcefulness behind the waterway and its alteration of the physical landscape. This triumph of art represented progress, the ability of humanity to subdue nature and craft a civilized society out of wilderness. Yet by clinging to the notion of a "river," they also suggested that the waterway belonged to an older way of life, one in which nature, not humans, determined the shape of the physical world. They thus revealed their seemingly contradictory impulses to welcome the Canal as at once a symbol of progress and a link to the past.[9]

From the moment tourists stepped on canal packets, they saw evidence of ingenuity. Measuring no more than seventy-eight feet in length and fourteen and a half feet across, packets made clever use of space to accommodate up to forty passengers at night and more than three times that number in the daytime. During waking hours, packets' central cabins served as sitting rooms, with carpeted floors, stuffed chairs, and mahogany tables stacked high with newspapers and books. Some boat captains hired musicians to serenade their passengers, who danced on the deck. At mealtimes, the crew transformed the boat's cabin into a dining room and served up plentiful and even elegant meals, with delicacies like roast beef, ham, plum pudding, and liqueurs. After the evening meal, servants converted the cabin once again, this time from a dining room into sleeping areas. They began by drawing a curtain across the width of the room to divide the cabin into ladies' and gentlemen's quarters. From the cabin walls they then pulled down tiered berths, three or four deep, outfitted with linens and blankets; they attached additional cots to hooks in the ceiling. A Scottish farmer who traveled on the Canal in the early 1830s exclaimed, "Few things in America seem more extraordinary than the sleeping accommodation of the packets." Some people traveled on the Canal merely to experience the novelty of the boats' arrangements. Along with the waterway's locks, aqueducts, deep cuts, and massive embankments, the packets exposed passengers to the works of human innovation.[10]

As seen from the deck of a canal boat, the upstate region's varied landscape highlighted the ways in which the Canal had brought civilization into the wilderness. The waterway carried passengers past deep forests and seemingly endless swamps as well as mushrooming towns. The long stretches of untamed nature along the Canal reminded tourists of what had existed in the region prior to the boom in town development set off by the Canal's opening. Basil Hall, a famed British traveler, drew a contrast between the town of Camillus and the surrounding countryside: "At the next crack of the whip—hocus pocus! all is changed. [An English tourist] looks out of the window—rubs his eyes, and discovers that he is again in the depths of wood at the other extremity of civilized society . . ." Nature stood for the opposite of civilization—it existed where humans, and art, had not yet made their impact on the landscape. And unlike Hawthorne, most tourists liked this contrast. Traveling in the same year as Hawthorne, Sibyl Tatum commented on the village of Canastota: "There are some beautiful farm houses here around the village, which forms a striking contrast with the wild uncultivated land we have been passing all day." While Hawthorne preferred the wild, Tatum saw villages—with their farms, churches, schools, and factories—as representations of progress. When travelers saw stretches of untamed nature from their canal boats, they were reminded not so much of the region's former wildness but rather of its progression from savagery to civilization. The wilderness (and nature) represented savagery, as it had for generations of Americans. Viewed this way, nature was something to be conquered rather than preserved.[11]

Yet, at the same time, the Canal provided a healthy escape into nature, a place enticing precisely because it remained untouched by "civilized" human beings and progress. Tourists saw the Canal not only as an artificial wonder but as a way to gain access to the upstate region's "sublime" and previously remote landscape. The Erie Canal reminded tourists of a time when God, not human progress, had formed the world. The region's natural wonders reacquainted tourists with the powers and gifts of nature. When Clarissa Burroughs visited Little Falls in 1835, she remarked: "Here the smooth waters of the Canal wind round this tumultuous current, producing a pleasant association of the beauties of nature with the works of art." Another traveler commented that "this is a ragged cragged place, yet affords many natural curiosities, which together with the stupendious works of art in the structure of the Canal renders it one of the greatest curiosities of the whole line of the Canal." Nature could be powerful, potentially dangerous, but also awe-inspiring, beautiful, even benevolent. Sibyl Tatum's trip to Little Falls led her to observe that "such scenery is too sublime for my dull pen." So awe-inspiring was nature that it defied human description. A trip along the Canal reminded these tourists of the relative impotence and insignificance of human achievements.[12]

If boat crews drew a curtain between male and female tourists at night, during the day men joined women in seeing art as ultimately less significant than nature. The editor of *Atkinson's Casket* described Little Falls in similar terms: "In this scene, where the rude, but magnificent works of nature are so profusely displayed, the imagination is overpowered in their subliminity, and the proudest works of man, and man himself, lose their importance." Nature stood grand and godly; humanity and humanity's creations seemed insignificant. By offering an escape into the sublime landscape of upstate New York, the Erie Canal allowed tourists to reaffirm the superiority of God and God's pristine creations. Theodore Dwight, who traveled on the Canal in the early 1830s, did not understand why some people found traveling through the Canal's long stretches of wilderness "so wearisome and destitute of interest." Dwight himself saw the Canal as a vehicle for communing with nature. The canal boat, he wrote, "had brought me into a beautiful grove of forest trees, whose numberless stems, like the innumerable columns of some extensive temple, were faithfully reflected below." Nature was like a temple, a place to commune with God. Hawthorne and Dwight would have agreed on this point. But while Hawthorne emphasized the Canal's encroachment on nature, Dwight approached canal travel as a spiritual escape from the earthly concerns of human civilization.[13]

Tourists used what was a great symbol of technological progress—the Erie Canal—to carry them to a place that suggested that technological and moral improvement need not be at odds. They still saw the Canal's structures as reminders that art had triumphed over nature, that humanity had tamed the wilderness. They congratulated humanity on this progress. After passing up a lock, Clarissa Burroughs—who had also praised the natural beauties of Little Falls—declared that the experience "exhibits the powers of mind, the enterprize & industry of man." But at the same time, romanticism—also a product of this era —reminded Americans that progress did not satisfy all their needs. Where nature was sublime, where its strength and beauty combined to remind tourists of God's power and generosity, the Canal offered a foray into what seemed to be an older way of seeing the world: a place where God and nature dwarfed humanity and its quest for material progress. For those tourists who saw a trip down the Canal as a retreat from the commercial bustle of the increasingly urban Atlantic coast, the artificial river's juxtaposition of art and nature reaffirmed what they wanted to believe: that it was not necessary to choose between material progress and a godly society.[14]

If tourists traveled to the upstate region in part because it provided a temporary respite from the cares of urban life, settlers welcomed the Canal precisely because it brought them the comforts of civilization. DeWitt Clinton and his fellow Canal sponsors tended to stress how the waterway would provide a market

Passing through a lock
(Jacob Abbot, *Marco Paul's Travels on the Erie Canal,* 1852,
New York State Library)

for the bounty of the West, and thus promote the nation's long-term commercial development. But settlers in the Canal corridor put equal emphasis on how the waterway would allow them to procure highly desired eastern manufactures and luxuries. To them, the market revolution was as much about purchasing comforts as it was about selling raw materials. At a local Canal celebration in Brockport, a farming village outside Rochester, a local resident offered a toast in 1823 to "Our Internal Navigation—Pork and Flour coming down—Tea and Sugar coming up. Things are as they should be; some up, some down." Farmers wanted to sell their pork and their flour in the East, but not necessarily because they wanted to contribute to the nation's moral and economic progress. Instead, they wanted to buy comforts like tea and sugar—what some would call luxuries, and foreign ones at that. Like all upstate towns with its suffix, Brockport was established after the Canal promised to make it an interior "port." Its residents had moved west because the new waterway promised to link them to markets as both producers and consumers. They expected that internal navigation would help them to secure a comfortable, if not extravagant, life off the land.[15]

Emigrants moved west generally not to escape civilization but to take advantage of economic opportunities. The difficulty and expense of transporting the necessities and pleasures of home—stoves, plows, furniture, keepsakes—had discouraged families from migrating in the early years of the Republic. Their new homes often proved scary as well as sparse. Isolated from neighbors, settlers felt threatened—in reality or imagination—by Indians; distant from sources of help at times of birth, sickness, and death; wanting in companions with whom to share news about crops and tales about home. To encourage western settlement after the Canal opened, the state exempted emigrants' personal belongings from tolls, offering them an inexpensive way to transport their familiar furnishings to new and forbidding surroundings.[16]

Once in those new communities, settlers looked to the Canal to bring them additional comforts from the East. In 1828, Everard Peck, a Rochester editor, remarked that "the artificial river is thronged with vessels bearing to market the products of our highly favored country & returning to us the luxuries and comforts of other climes." Far from repudiating the luxuries of home, emigrants craved them. After reporting the arrival of a shipment of oysters and clams in Buffalo, a newspaper in that city observed in 1825: "The late emigrations to Ohio and Michigan have created an unusual demand for the necessities and luxuries of life in those regions." Settlers did not take those luxuries for granted; they gave credit to the Erie Canal. The residents of Batavia congratulated DeWitt Clinton for bringing them fresh oysters because nothing better symbolized their connection to their former homes. During an illness late in life, Mary Ann Archbald adopted a diet rich in fresh seafood. After mentioning her new diet to a relative in Scotland, Archbald added, "We are 200 miles from the sea but distance you know is reduced to nothing here . . ." While she had written earlier in life of her quest for independence and her admiration for Jefferson, she clearly did not believe in a Spartan version of republicanism. Like so many residents of upstate New York who, as we will see later on, would also borrow the language of republicanism, Archbald welcomed the luxuries that progress afforded her.[17]

Unlike the Archbalds and other families who had settled the Mohawk Valley after the Revolution, settlers who moved to western New York after the Canal's completion often had, by necessity, more modest aspirations. They, too, wanted access to markets, which was why they moved west in the first place. An 1823 advertisement for "Canal Lands" in Jefferson and Oswego counties emphasized: "Every part of the tract is within one day's easy drive of the *Erie Canal*." The proprietor of the land—a New York City developer and speculator—tried to appeal to potential settlers who did not have cash to purchase land. He offered to accept their "ashes, grain, pork, butter &c" as payment on the land. Like Mary Ann Archbald, these settlers must have set their initial goals on independence. Yet they likewise wanted the minimum comforts of home from the outset. The advertisement also assured them that they would find nearby "most of the advantages of old countries, as to schools, public worships, mills, distilleries, mechanics, manufactories, &c." These settlers would not have had the spare cash to buy luxuries, but they still shared Archbald's basic impulse to feel connected to the "advantages of old countries."[18]

Settlers who took advantage of the Canal to move west often found themselves connected to markets yet isolated socially. Joseph and Ann Webb, who settled near Rochester in the early 1830s, wrote to friends in England that "we was almost afraid to live in the house we are now in at first its a lonesome place

no house nearer than 2 Miles & the Woods comes down close
to it, not see two people all day somettimes . . ." The fast pace
of settlement usually eased physical isolation rather quickly, but
the mere ability to see other people did not necessarily provide an antidote to a sense of social detachment. After moving
from the southern part of the state to a farm near Syracuse in
1837, William Harris complained of loneliness even though
he had neighbors living nearby. "I hope that in another year I
may be known [and] no longer distrusted as a stranger." Even
though Harris interacted frequently with his neighbors, he
would repeat his wish several times. The exchange of goods and
services did not, in his case at least, foster a broader sense of
community.[19]

While such feelings of isolation may have partially diminished
after a few years of settlement, the booming cities of the Canal
corridor, in particular, seemed especially impersonal because so
many people moved in and out of them. When his sister died
in Rochester in 1837, Eleazor Conkey lamented, "It was a trying
time to be among strangers in a strange city, I only having
moved there last spring." The Canal, and other transportation
innovations, may actually have contributed to these feelings of
isolation. In 1828, for example, Samuel Porter moved to Rochester, a place that he extolled as representing the "wonder of
Nature and Art." Yet he had mixed feelings about the compression of distance made possible by the works of art. He informed his grandfather, "I am now a Citizen of Rochester or
rather I may say a Citizen of the World for my locomotive fac-
ulties have been so many times put in practice during the last
20 Years that I am hardly entitled to call myself a citizen of any
particular place." As Porter made clear, Americans enjoyed geographic mobility long before the Erie Canal crossed the state of
New York. But geographic mobility took on unprecedented proportions in the years after the waterway opened. While many
people eagerly took advantage of these opportunities—including
Harris, Conkey, Porter, and the Webbs—they also yearned for
homes left behind, homes nestled, whether in fact or imagination
alone, within secure and supportive communities.[20]

At the same time that the Erie Canal exacerbated the impersonality of life in the upstate region, it also lessened the emotional and material strains of everyday life on the frontier. The Canal provided a connection between the West and homes left behind in New England or even Europe. In 1821, before the Canal had begun to carry emigrants along the whole route from Albany to Buffalo, the *Connecticut Herald* observed, "When it is considered with how much ease families can remove to the land which they own in the west, and with what facility and delight emigrants thither can occasionally revisit their friends and the spot of their nativity, the mind is at once impressed with the magnitude and importance of this great inland communication." The idea of occasional visits, almost as much as the visits themselves, could ease the burdens of separation. Mary Ann Archbald wrote with excitement to her friends in Scotland to announce that the Canal would allow them to visit one another "without stepping foot on dry land." If Archbald overstated the ease with which immigrants could visit Europe, the very possibility of such travel made her feel more connected to her former way of life.[21]

Even when settlers did not visit their relatives and friends, they still used the Canal to reinforce ties with their earlier lives. Mail traveled quickly along the artificial river, bringing news from home. Mary Ann Archbald praised the Canal for bringing her a letter from New York City in one day; her farm was more than 50 miles west of Albany, itself about 150 miles from the port city. While Archbald clearly exaggerated how quickly the letter got to her, she nonetheless revealed her perception that the Canal brought news very quickly. Since Archbald had settled in the region before the Canal's construction, the compression of distance came as unexpected good fortune.[22]

But settlers who moved to the region after 1817 showed no less delight in the Canal's artificial accomplishments. After spending a cold Sabbath day in 1838 writing to old friends, William Harris jotted down in his diary, "It is truly one of the greatest blessing[s] confered on man in that he is able to communicate his thoughts and a knowledge of his situation to his friends at a distance and to hear from them in the same manner."

Abigail Marks agreed that the Canal provided a remedy for isolation. In 1840, she moved from Connecticut to Lockport to join
her new husband, who had recently set up a business in that
burgeoning canal town. When Marks decided to marry, she recognized that doing so meant moving to western New York. Yet
her role in making that decision did not make her feel less isolated. Marks longed for the company of her family, particularly
her sisters. Her husband frequently had to work late in the evening, leaving Marks alone at home, a striking contrast to the
lively family and social life she had led in Connecticut. She found
partial relief from her solitude in the Canal's regular transportation of people and mail. "I cannot realize when I think of it,"
she wrote home in 1840, "that I am nearly six hundred miles
from all my friends, and it is indeed a great distance but then
the mail accommodation and our facillities for traveling at the
present day are such as it is indeed consolation." Whatever drew
them to western New York in the first place, a variety of settlers
appreciated the artificial river for keeping them in contact with
what they still considered home.[23]

The Canal's reduction of distance did much more than set in
motion a commercial revolution. It encouraged people to move
west, people who saw themselves not simply as producers of raw
materials but as human beings longing for certain comforts, material and otherwise. The Canal brought them consumer goods,
luxuries, visitors, and mail. It provided residents of the Canal
corridor, and emigrants farther west, with a vital link to the
worlds they left behind. Such emigrants cheered the triumph of
art over nature—progress—not only because it provided them
with economic opportunities. They also welcomed progress because, paradoxically, it reinforced their ties to the past. They
embraced the changes of the transportation revolution, in part,
because those very changes provided continuity in their lives.

Tourists and settlers alike generally agreed with the fictional
Amelia's praise of "this union of the inland seas with the Atlantic

Bedtime on a packet; passengers choose berths
(Jacob Abbot, *Marco Paul's Travels on the Erie Canal*, 1852,
New York State Library)

Ocean." Yet, like her brother Wentworth, they also complained about the shortcomings of the Canal's engineering, or its works of art. Criticisms of the Canal usually involved the mundane details of travel. While tourists admired the clever organization of packet boats, for example, many also criticized those same accommodations, especially once the novelty had worn off. An excess of passengers on packet boats meant that some travelers whose fares supposedly included the price of berths had to spend the night on the floor. Even those with beds had difficulty sleeping; people tumbled out of their narrow berths; entire berths collapsed onto unsuspecting passengers sleeping below; babies cried, adults snored in the damp, stagnant air; mosquitoes bit;

the entire boat rocked back and forth as it passed oncoming boats or entered and exited locks. After describing the over-crowded conditions—and the "stench and effluvia from such a collection of human beings"—one Scottish traveler commented, "In taking notice of this mode of conveyance, it is merely to guard my countrymen from travelling much by canal in the States."[24]

As Wentworth suggested, nothing better represented the nuisances of Canal travel than the peril caused by low bridges. Farmers fervently fought for bridges to reconnect their canal-torn property, but boat passengers found these bridges at best annoying and at worst deadly. In heavily populated areas, bridges appeared at intervals of about one-quarter mile. Virtually every travel account from the period contains a reference to low bridges, and travelers delighted in describing their personal brushes with disaster. Yet not all were so fortunate. Newspapers carried reports of unwary (or intoxicated) passengers smashed to death against bridges, and even DeWitt Clinton worried that bridges "occasioned the loss of several valuable lives" while also threatening to impede the transportation of freight piled high on boats. Passengers, moreover, also found bridges to be regular obstacles to enjoying the "works of art and beauties of nature." In nice weather especially, passengers preferred to view the surrounding landscape from the decks of their boats. As they approached bridges, though, passengers had either to fling themselves flat against the deck or to scramble into the cabin. Finding this routine wearing, many passengers abandoned their hopes of enjoying the surrounding countryside from the deck— at least as they passed through sections of the Canal most thickly laced with bridges. The cabin provided shelter from bridges, but it also stood between passengers and the scenery with which they had hoped to commune.[25]

While bridges made it harder for Canal travelers to experience the landscape, locks—those great symbols of ingenuity—often stood in the way of the rapid transportation of passengers and merchandise. Crowded and improperly functioning locks significantly increased the duration of canal trips. The dramatic success of the Canal combined with its modest dimensions to create vastly overcrowded conditions. Before the Canal had even been completed, New Yorkers began petitioning the state to build extra sets of locks in certain busy locations along the Mohawk River. The state ultimately responded with an enlargement project, approved in 1835. But in 1842, before most of the work

As a packet passes under a farm bridge, passengers fling themselves on deck
(Jacob Abbot, *Marco Paul's Travels on the Erie Canal,* 1852, New York State Library)

on this enlargement had been completed, boats traveling between Albany and Buffalo endured an average delay of thirty-six
hours because of long lines at the locks. Some tourists agreed
with Amelia that these delays provided travelers with an opportunity to descend from their boats to luxuriate in nature. But
most passengers grew impatient when these contrivances length-
ened their journey, even though it was art's very success at triumphing over nature that caused certain of these problems in
the first place. The waterway stimulated agricultural and urban
development in the western end of the state, creating the need
for bridges connecting cultivated pieces of land that had been
wilderness only a few years earlier. The heavy volume of passenger and, especially, freight traffic on the Canal caused delays at
locks. But to tourists and settlers, these nuisances did not appear
to be signs of progress.[26]

Passengers pressed for time, especially businessmen, trans-
ferred to stages to avoid the stretches of the Canal with many
locks. Because the section of the Canal between Albany and Schenectady contained twenty-seven locks, many passengers took a
stage—or, later, a train—between those two cities. When Mary
Ann Archbald journeyed to New York City in 1828 with her
daughter and son-in-law, Archbald and her daughter took the
Canal all the way to Albany so that they could pass through
mountainous and "romantic" countryside. Archbald's son-in-law,
who had business to conduct in New York, did not accompany
the women for the entire trip. Rather, in Schenectady he trans-
ferred from the Canal to a stage. By doing so, he saved a day's
travel. While the Archbald women seemed to share Amelia's
desire to use art as a vehicle to admire nature, their male com-
panion wanted to perform his business as expeditiously as possible. Yet these distinctions did not arise from gender alone.
When Mary Ann wanted something quickly—either goods or
mail—she could be just as impatient as any businessman. Most
of the time she was a settler who wanted quick ties to New York
City; at other times she was a tourist who wanted to admire in
a leisurely fashion the surrounding landscape.[27]

Despite the Canal's success, it had its shortcomings. Aqueduct walls crumbled; locks malfunctioned; and canal banks burst open. The resulting delays to navigation could be severe. Lyman Spalding, a Lockport miller, complained in his diary in June 1847 that he could not get his flour to market, since a hundred boats lined up "all the time" at the Lockport locks after one of the two tiers of locks stopped working. Clarissa Burroughs, who had praised the "powers of mind" visible in the locks, regretted having to take another meal in "this dirty place" when a broken lock delayed her boat at German Flats. Breaches in the Canal banks sent water gushing out with tremendous force, shutting down the Canal for as much as two weeks at a time. In 1850, a breach near Rochester required 2,400 workers around the clock for ten days to repair the damage, and one near the town of Frankfort in 1839 caused boats to line up for ten miles.[28]

Navigation could take weeks to return to normal after such congestion, because all those boats would then arrive at the next lock in succession. While passengers generally abandoned the Canal for land travel in such frustrating circumstances, breaches trapped boat crews and freight for the duration of the repair work. Failures of engineering, construction, or maintenance led to a variety of other problems as well. Since the Canal originally was only four feet deep, heavy freight boats ran aground when the water level was improperly maintained or when silt collected on the canal bed. The Canal's narrow width led to periodic crashes, since boats barely had room to pass one another. Towpaths caved in, tripping horses and sometimes breaking their legs. Obstructions in the Canal—rocks, pieces of fallen bridges, and sunken boats—crippled passing boats and delayed those following behind.

The failures of art not only delayed navigation; they also threatened middle-class understandings of social order, calling into question whether the Canal was really a symbol of progress. While New Yorkers wished their problems with unruly workers would end with the construction of the artificial river, they would soon be sorely disappointed. Folklore suggests that virtually unceasing brawls erupted at locks, as swearing—and often

drunk—crews vied to reach the front of the lines of boats waiting to pass through the locks. These stories would have rung
true for at least some antebellum residents of the Canal corridor.
In 1827, a group of residents in the Mohawk Valley petitioned
the legislature to construct a second canal parallel to the original
one in order to alleviate long delays at the locks. The Canal's
crowded conditions, the petitioners complained, did much more
than simply detain passengers and goods.

> In addition to the trouble and expense of delay, and of
> frequent damage to boats and merchandize occasioned by
> the anxious press for preference at the locks, the same cause
> produces contention, strife, and lawsuits, not only injurious
> to the person concerned, but the citizens of the vicinity of
> the Canal are greatly annoyed by frequent calls as jurors
> and witnesses, to determine these endless controversies.

The accumulation of large numbers of workers, irritated and
bored by their inability to proceed more rapidly, inflamed tem-
pers that triggered fights among boatmen. In 1837, the *Rochester
Republican* reported that during a delay caused by a breach near
Rochester, boat workers "had a row" with state repair workers.
A decade later the directors of the American Bethel Society, an
organization interested in reforming boat workers, commented
in its annual report that although the previous year had seen a
large number of breaks in the Canal, workers had remained unusually orderly. After a breach trapped several hundred boats and
twelve hundred men near Rochester, according to the society,
the workers' restrained conduct elicited complimentary remarks
from local newspaper editors. That editors made such comments
at all, however, suggests that previous breaches had encouraged
what they deemed less-than-orderly conduct among boat crews.[29]
   The Canal's failures impeded commerce, tourism, and even
social order. Merchants and farmers had come to expect that their
products would travel rapidly to market. For people living directly along the Canal's banks, delays in navigation meant
trapped workers and calls to offer testimony in seemingly petty

legal disputes. When Hawthorne wrote his critique of the Canal, he mentioned similar nuisances. But while his conclusion was to condemn rapid progress, ordinary people felt quite differently. Their disappointment stemmed from the Canal's becoming at times more of an obstacle to progress than an example of it.

The greatest impediment to the Canal's success, however, came not from the shortcomings of art but rather from nature's stubborn insistence on turning water to ice in freezing weather. The frigid temperatures in upstate New York shut down the Canal for up to five months every year. From the Canal's earliest years of operation, entrepreneurs from around the country wrote to Canal officials offering their fail-safe inventions for keeping the Canal free from ice. But nothing could keep the Canal open between mid-December and April. The Canal's annual wintertime closing disappointed settlers who for much of the year built their daily lives around the Canal's rapid conveyance of goods, people, and news. While they had been used to natural rivers freezing, New Yorkers expected more from their artificial river.

The onset of winter could be dramatic. Sudden freezes trapped boats mid-journey, along with their workers and freight. Sometimes the Canal would temporarily thaw, allowing boats to advance. The merchant Horace Wheeler spent two weeks on the Canal in December 1825 creeping along the thirty miles between Schenectady and Albany, a journey that normally would have taken one day. Without a thaw, merchants had either to transport their stranded goods by costly land routes or to abandon their freight until spring. Silas Marks, the Lockport merchant married to Abigail Marks, expressed relief in 1842 when all his goods arrived before the Canal's freezing. "Most of our Merchants," he wrote, "had thiers freeze up on the Canal from 60 to 100 Miles East and it was quite expensive getting them by Land." Since merchants passed along at least part of those expenses to customers, virtually all upstate New Yorkers suffered materially when the Canal froze, often literally overnight.[30]

A sudden thaw of the Canal in spring could have even more

devastating consequences than the troublesome and expensive wintertime freezes. Thaws sent huge quantities of melted snow into the rivers and streams that fed the Canal. Although some excess water could be released through the Canal's waste weirs (gates that emptied water into tributary creeks), severe freshets could overflow or sweep away the canal bed. Sometimes they took canalside property with them. In a particularly bad flood in 1832, one upstate resident reported that raging water took a "large quantity of Lumber and Buildings off the pier at Albany . . . People went to their stores on the wharf at Albany in Boats and landed in the Second Stories." Nature could undo human efforts to make the physical landscape more accessible and dependable.[31]

But nature primarily influenced the Canal's operation with its regular closing of the waterway for four or five months of the year. Nothing—and nobody—moved on the Canal during its closed season. Although few tourists would have found upstate New York an appealing wintertime destination, emigrants would have liked to plan their journeys to arrive in time to be ready for the spring planting. But as Joseph and Ann Webb counseled their family and friends in England, "If anyone two three or more should feel inclined to come [we] should advise you not to start before March or April for the Canal will not be thawd before May and it would be expensive traveling by land . . ." Men and women in the upstate region had to plan their visits with friends and relatives around the Canal's open season. When corresponding about visits, New Yorkers and their families often qualified their plans with phrases like "if navigation permits."[32]

The Canal's closed season also slowed down mail between upstate New York and the eastern seaboard. Thanking her cousin for sending her a package of books, Mary Ann Archbald wrote in 1832 that the parcel "had long been detained, no less than a month between New York & this. at least had lain a month in Albany owing to the stopping of the canal breaking up of the roads etc. I knew it was in Albany & had to exercise all my little

stock of patience." The Canal had encouraged upstaters to become impatient, to expect mail to arrive quickly. Abigail Marks
also found the Canal's wintertime closing frustrating. On Christ-
mas Day 1840, she wrote to her family: "Let me urge you . . .
to be more punctual in writing me often for our mails this season
of the year are detained which will make intercourse more irregular and difficult and for friends so distantly seperated is I think
extremely unpleasant." In the warmer months of the year, both
Marks and Archbald had praised the Canal for keeping them in
close touch with their distant relations. Having experienced the
advantages that art afforded, upstaters felt disappointed when
nature cut off those same opportunities.[33]

New Yorkers conceded that nature held more power than humanity when it came to regulating the Canal's season of operation. A Rochester newspaper reported in 1842 that canal workers
had been making very slow progress in clearing paths for ice-
bound boats. Then "the weather last evening, bid fair to do what
the State Scows could not—melt the ice, and give a week or two
of uninterrupted navigation." But nature's malevolent side pro-
voked more frequent—and strident—commentary. *The New
York Times*, for example, reported in 1832 that "forty thousand
barrels of flour, on their way to this city, have stopt [on the
Canal] by the recent embargo placed on them by the relentless
despot, Jack Frost." American inventiveness could not outsmart
the despotic ice that interrupted commerce, travel, and communications.[34]

The Canal had raised people's expectations. They hoped to
travel easily and quickly, to ship and buy goods inexpensively,
and to communicate at will with their distant relatives and
friends. They grew impatient when goods stalled on the Canal
or when the exchange of visits and mail grew irregular. New
Yorkers' most persistent complaints about the Canal stemmed
from the irregularity of the compression of distance, from the
failures to triumph over nature. Their ambivalence about progress arose from their inability to take full advantage of the ways
it promised to improve their lives.

The Canal's weaknesses would ultimately lead many New Yorkers to embrace railroads, which succeeded where the Canal could not: at running all year round. But in the meantime, New Yorkers continued to emphasize the "artificial" aspects of their artificial river. People had built the Canal, and—within the limits set by nature—people should still be able to control it. They should be able to use this work of progress to satisfy their goals and values, even if those aspirations differed from those of the Canal's sponsors. With this same sense of power, different groups of New Yorkers would look to their government to further their own interests within the expanding commercial economy.

4

The Politics of Land and Water

IN CARVING a commercial corridor through the upstate region, the State of New York had tampered with a sacred element of American society: property. If the Canal's sponsors liked to portray the artificial river as appearing almost magically, people living along the new waterway would tell a different version of the story: laborers, working in gangs of twenty or thirty, had torn down fences, trampled crops, rechanneled streams, relocated buildings. To owners of land along the Erie Canal's banks, the triumph of art over nature could seem more like plain and simple destruction of property.

The extent of property damage varied along the Canal's length. In the western part of the state, a region that had been only sparsely populated before 1817, the Erie passed mostly through "unimproved" land, only occasionally cutting through a cultivated field or diverting water from a mill. At its eastern end, though, the new waterway paralleled the Mohawk River. Back when the Canal remained just a fantasy in most people's minds, Mohawk Valley farmers cleared land and planted crops, while millwrights tapped the region's natural water flow. These settlers, people like the Archbalds, coveted property directly along the river's banks, a location from which they could easily cart their produce to river-going boats bound ultimately for the Hudson. When the state constructed the Erie Canal—when it tried to follow through on its promise to "bring a market to every man's door"—it damaged the productive worth of these earlier settlers' property. To these people, the value of "nature" lay less in its subliminity than in its practical ability to grow food and commodities. And because the digging of the Canal turned out to be an extended process, rather than a momentous event ending in 1825, the state repeatedly appropriated or damaged property belonging to citizens along the entire route from Buffalo to Albany.[1]

Many New Yorkers did not accept their property losses passively but instead turned to the state government for redress. Although farmers generally welcomed internal improvements, many of them nonetheless clung to the notion that their agricultural pursuits should take precedence over mercantile ventures. They therefore viewed economic progress with at least a touch of ambivalence: although they looked forward to loading their wheat and apples on the eastbound boats that docked in front of their doors, they feared that the state's attempts to encourage the building of commercial mills and warehouses would jeopardize yeomen's economic investments and legal standing. This tension posed vexing problems for progress-minded landowners throughout the United States. In articulating understandings of their rights to land and water, upstate farmers thus also made clear their broader feelings about the nation's political economy, sentiments that would evolve significantly over the antebellum period.[2]

The American legal community in the early nineteenth century tried to mediate between these opposing impulses to preserve the sanctity of property and to encourage economic development. To most of the Founding Fathers, the ownership of agricultural land was a natural right. The health of the Republic, moreover, depended on the liberty of white men to acquire such property. Land ownership would allow them to become independent and virtuous citizens who voted with an eye toward fostering the common good. By the turn of the century, though, it became clear that property rights sometimes interfered with the young nation's imperative to develop economically. Roads and canals had to run across what had been private property; new mills and factories diverted the natural flow of water, upsetting established practices of agriculture.

To justify their states' active promotion of economic development, Northern governments provided compensation for the taking of private property designated for enterprises that served the "common good." Judges, too, rendered common-law decisions—judicial interpretations that adjusted the principles of long-standing precedents to new circumstances—that increasingly paid homage to the "common good" or "public interest." No longer was a man's land his exclusive domain, one which only he, the state, or God could alter. Instead, judges allowed landowners—often corporations—to alter their property in ways that might upset another person's property, as long as they compensated the neighbor for the losses of the land's productive worth. With these shifts in legal precedent, for example, a landowner living upstream could divert water to run his mill even if that meant a downstream farmer found himself with less water with which to irrigate his crops. Such legal decisions generally promoted the interests of newly emerging commercial classes over those of established agrarian classes. In both statutory and common law, property in real estate lost some of its inviolable character.[3]

But what did property mean to the people themselves? The Erie Canal region offers a rare opportunity to see how ordinary men—and, to a much lesser extent, women—understood the significance of property. By looking at surviving records of New York's administration of its canal system, we can recover the voices of property owners living in the Canal corridor—thanks to New York's novel approach to running its internal improvements. Unlike many other states, New York did not charter private corporations to build and operate its canal system; instead, state officials themselves oversaw the artificial waterways.

In 1826, the legislature created the Canal Board, an agency designed specifically to handle issues related to the state's arti-

ficial waterways. While responsible to the legislature, the Canal
Board made most of the decisions about building, funding, and
managing the Erie Canal. Before 1844, its members included
five canal commissioners, appointed by a joint legislative committee, as well as officers of the Canal Fund, made up of six of
the state's highest-ranking elected officials. In 1844, the legislature passed a law providing that general elections would determine all positions on the Canal Board, including the
commissioners. These commissioners, along with the Engineer (a
position created in 1844), oversaw the daily administration of
the Canal, while the officers of the Canal Fund guided the finances. Although the legislature still maintained responsibility
for establishing canal laws, it generally did so at the recommen-
dation of the board. Since the Erie Canal was the first state-run
enterprise of such an enormous magnitude, no one could foresee
all the issues that the endeavor would generate, leaving the Canal
Board to interpret various situations as they presented themselves.[4]

Of all the arms of the legal system, the Canal Board was the
most accessible to ordinary men and women—an ironic consequence of what was probably an attempt to keep power out of
such people's hands. During the early nineteenth century, juries
had become well known for making generous awards for property
damage, undoubtedly out of empathy for the plaintiffs. While
New York's motives for establishing the Canal Board have been
obscured over time, it seems likely that the legislature wanted
decisions about property damage, especially, to be made by public officials sympathetic to the need for development, rather than
by juries made up of small landowners. In creating the Canal
Board, though, the legislature inadvertently gave ordinary people
an extraordinary method for making their voices heard.[5]

Even though the board frequently did not award freeholders
the damages they claimed, it nonetheless made itself available to
a wide variety of petitioners, people who might not have readily
sought hearings in other branches of the government, such as
the legislature or the courts. While the business of the New York

State Legislature did revolve largely around the consideration of private bills, including many that involved the Erie Canal, relatively few small landowners had the political connections to receive a sympathetic hearing in that body. Some of them sought redress through the courts for canal-related issues, but state law channeled most of their property claims through the Canal Board. Like the legislature, the Canal Board was located in Albany—and men with political connections stood a better chance of having their grievances heard. But the appraisers—the men in charge of establishing the extent of property damage—held hearings around the state, calling on local witnesses to testify about the ways in which specific parcels of land had been damaged. Newspapers published the time and place of these public hearings, making the board a more accessible state organ to people without the time, money, or connections to make their cases heard in Albany. In some ways, the appraisers acted as roving agents of the state, riding circuit to make judgments that sought to balance individual property rights with a communal commitment to economic development.[6]

Even when they did not appear personally before the Canal Board, people from all around the state corresponded with this administrative body. Thousands of these New Yorkers, perhaps close to ten thousand, sought redress for a variety of canal-related problems. If most of these people were male property owners, their economic standing—unlike their gender—did not alone make them an unusually privileged group. Many of them were quintessential freeholders who throughout the pre–Civil War era constituted a larger share of the male population than did the semiskilled laborers who dug the Canal or who made their livings in mills and factories.[7]

Most people who addressed the Canal Board sought compensation for appropriated or damaged land. Sometimes they addressed the board through their lawyers, sometimes without the aid of legal counsel. Either way, their words have survived in records of their testimony during investigative hearings, or in handwritten appeals ranging in length from a single paragraph to dozens of pages. Since these records do not consistently indicate how state officials responded to the claims of their citizens, they unfortunately tell us relatively little about the formulation of administrative law. But they more than make up for this limitation by offering rich details about the everyday impact of rapid economic development and by recording how people articulated their views of their rights and responsibilities within a swiftly changing political economy.

It is nearly impossible to generalize about the economic activities and aspirations of the people who sought a hearing before the Canal Board. Even individuals are not easily categorized. Jamie Archbald provides a poignant example. In 1826, Jamie and the rest of his family received a settlement from the state for land that had been damaged during the Canal's construction. But it would be difficult to give Jamie an occupational label. In just the eight years during which the Canal was under construction, Jamie had engaged in at least four occupations. He farmed, tried his hand at commercial speculation (and failed), opened a small shop, and helped to dig the Canal. After the Canal opened, he would hold several more positions, ultimately becoming an engineer on the Erie Canal Enlargement. Was Jamie a farmer? A commercial businessman? A small merchant? A laborer? An engineer? Occupational mobility was commonplace during the antebellum period.[8]

People also frequently held more than one occupation at once: a farmer might own a grocery; another might own a mill; still another might work on the Canal for part of the year. Moreover, the terms "landowner" and "miller" could be applied to a very wide range of people. Some landowners owned as few as two or three acres, while at the other extreme speculators might own more than one hundred thousand. One miller could operate his mill alone, grinding the wheat he and his neighbors grew, while another could employ fifty or seventy-five workers and have hundreds of customers. For the sake of simplicity, though, the term "modest landowner" will refer to anyone who farmed or milled with the help of no one but family members and an occasional hired hand. If these people sometimes wore a merchant's hat or a laborer's cap, they will also appear in other places in the story. "Substantial landowners" could also occupy more than one professional space, but they will be defined as people whose property required the regular labor of numerous tenants or employees to maintain its normal state of productivity.

By looking at the ways in which a range of property holders addressed state officials about their property claims, we can see how they cast their pleas in what they thought would be persuasive rhetoric. In the nineteenth century, rhetoric was an important tool—a "practical art"—essential to a political system in which people could not be coerced and so had to be convinced. The emphasis on persuasion was reflected in the public meetings and orations so central to antebellum political culture; it also helps to explain why many of the era's leaders, men such as Daniel Webster, Henry Clay, and, later, Abraham Lincoln, expended so much effort to cultivate eloquence in the spoken and written word. Yet politicians did not have a monopoly in the art of persuasion; nor was it the exclusive domain of the highly educated. Ordinary citizens also turned to carefully crafted rhetoric in their attempts to influence the state's canal policy. Whatever the actual merits of their cases before the Canal Board—and many surely exaggerated their claims in an effort to gain a favorable settlement—the Canal Board Papers offer an unusual view of ordinary people's ideas about the relationship between the individual, the state, and economic development.[9]

The Erie Canal was a public enterprise, an unabashed effort at state-controlled economic development. After both the federal government and neighboring states rejected New York's requests for financial assistance, the state had taken sole responsibility for funding, constructing, and operating its artificial river. New York also undertook several additional canal projects in the years after 1825. Following the completion of the main Canal, the state constructed small channels linking land-bound communi-

ties to the main waterway; built the eight lateral canals running
north or south from the Erie; and enlarged and rerouted the Erie
Canal itself. More canal digging took place after the opening of
the Erie Canal than before.[10]

While a wide variety of New Yorkers joined in celebrating
the Canal's accomplishments, many of them also knew from personal experience that the business of creating and then enlarging
a canal might damage a property owner's land or buildings in a
number of ways. Before laborers had even picked up their axes
and shovels, the state legislature had taken for public use a strip
of private property extending across the width of the state.
Where the government did not receive outright property grants
along the route, it appropriated land—without always paying
for it. An important piece of canal legislation did require the
state to compensate individuals for any appropriation of private
property. But, in keeping with a general trend in legal reasoning
across the country, that piece of legislation provided that if the
state's appraisers deemed that the benefit a landowner would
receive from proximity to the Canal outweighed the value of the
land appropriated, then the state did not owe the proprietor any
financial compensation.[11]

Land had become a commodity whose value could be measured
in terms of relative market value. The appropriation of farmland
clearly constituted an "injury." But the Canal also increased the
value of the owner's remaining contiguous property, conferring
a certain "benefit." If, to take a typical case, an appropriated
piece of a farm bordered on the site of a canal lock, where grocery
stores and other businesses would thrive from the congregation
of boats at that spot, then the appraisers usually argued that the
increased value of the owner's remaining land was greater than
the injury caused to the owner by the appropriation. Given that
many farmers in the Mohawk Valley already feared that their
relative market advantage would decline once the Canal provided
easy access to less expensive western lands, these New Yorkers
did not always accept the state's arguments that access to the
waterway would compensate them for the loss of their property.

Landowners' discontent only intensified once construction got under way. Laborers did not restrict their canal-building to lands that had been ceded or appropriated. While workmen usually destroyed farmers' property because they needed to clear a path to the actual canal site, they also cut down trees or tore down fences to provide themselves with fuel for cooking or heating. One farmer even complained that laborers had ripped down his fences simply to amuse themselves. The trampling of workers' feet flattened crops and churned up mud. Even when construction workers moved on to begin digging the next strip of canal, landowners did not see an end of their problems. The Canal frequently cut property holdings in two. Then, once the state let water into the Canal, spring freshets, poor engineering, shoddy workmanship, or nesting muskrats caused breaks in the canal bank, sending water streaming out—flooding fields, injuring gardens, drowning livestock, filling cellars, and accumulating in stagnant pools that became the breeding ground for mosquitoes and disease. A lack of water could prove just as economically disastrous for people who depended on the region's natural water supplies to propel their mills; such shortages resulted from the diversion of streams to fill the Canal, the draining of the Canal in winter for repairs, or the shifts in freezing patterns of existing waterways because of the restructuring of the landscape. If too much water could flood a mill, too little could stop operations for months at a time. Rural people had long dealt with the vagaries of nature; the Canal project added the mistakes, neglect, and whims of state employees to the list of forces which they faced.[12]

The extent of property damage caused by the Canal varied greatly, but even minor "injuries" upset people's daily routines. Rebuilding a section of fence diverted energy away from planting crops. Walking across a neighbor's fields to reach a bridge over the Canal was a time-consuming and repeated nuisance. One farmer explained that "these things though they may appear trifling in representation, yet, are of considerable importance to those who feel the daily inconveniences of them." Few people questioned that the Canal had enhanced the overall quality of life in the upstate region. But they did question why—especially in light of the technological feats of the Canal project—they had to suffer even petty annoyances and damages. If the Canal's engineers could design locks that would lift boats over a sixty-foot cliff, why could they not prevent water from leaking into someone's cellar?[13]

The possibility of owning land, as we have seen, is what lured such large numbers of people to the upstate region in the first place; property offered economic security as well as political rights and social status. Few upstate farmers could afford to buy land outright, but rather gradually paid off their mortgages by selling produce on the market. By necessity, if not choice, these farmers' immediate aspirations were modest. They first had to clear their land—an arduous and labor-intensive task. The simplest way to remove trees was girdling, which meant killing a tree by cutting deep notches around its trunk with an ax. A few weeks later, the trees would lose their leaves, allowing sun to shine through on what would become fields. As soon as enough light shone through the remaining limbs, settlers would plant wheat or corn to feed their families for their first year on the frontier. After chopping down the trees during the off season, farmers planted their crops around the stumps. Thus, the average farm family could clear only between five and ten acres per year, depending on the number of family members who could girdle trunks, chop limbs, burn leaves and stumps, rake ashes, pull up roots, and remove rocks. With so much of their time and energy invested in their land, modest farmers understandably resented the ways in which the state's improvements damaged their property.[14]

When farmers' land was damaged by the works of art, they expected the state either to fix the damage or to compensate them for their losses. Among upstate farmers who had begun improving their land before 1817, the most common complaint about the artificial river was that it divided their property in two by running through it. Some yeomen had to walk substantial distances, even over a mile, to the nearest bridge across the waterway, a trek that usually involved trespassing on someone else's fields with horse and wagon in tow. Hundreds of settlers appealed to the Canal Board to repair the property damage by building bridges across the waterway, or by reimbursing them for building their own bridges. The same structures that sent passengers flinging themselves onto the decks of canal boats also served a crucial economic purpose to farmers. Bridges allowed them access to fields and mills that had once been attached to the main part of their property but that now stood on the opposite side of a forty-foot-wide canal. Other damage caused by the Canal could not be repaired, leading property owners to demand financial reparations instead. Sarah Beaston, who owned property along one of the lateral canals, accepted that the waterway had to run through her property. But when laborers cut down trees on her remaining land, she argued that the canal project threatened her ability to eke out a basic living from the land. "The destruction of my timber every day, Is more than I am able to loose . . . , " she explained to her lawyer. "[I] do think [it] hard that myself and children must be deprived of our small support and not rewarded in any way for It . . ."[15]

Settlers who bought land after the Canal's route had been laid out believed that the value of their property lay in a combination of its productive worth and its proximity to markets. The closer a piece of land was to the Canal, the simpler it was to reach markets. As Cadwallader Colden noted in his official memoir of the Erie's construction, "Now, that the Canals are open, the distance from market may be almost computed by the distance from the Canal, or the distance from the water communications with it . . ." Land along the waterway's route fetched a higher selling price. When farm families decided to move to western New York in the years after 1817, they calculated whether the expense of land along the waterway would be balanced by the benefits they would derive from such proximity. Because these farmers often knew where the Canal would flow before they began clearing their land, they planned their improvements to the land to avoid or minimize construction damage. As a result, few of these property holders petitioned the state for compensation for damaged land.[16]

Instead they argued that the state had the obligation to help them take advantage of fresh opportunities the Canal had opened. Such arguments commonly emerged in requests for use of so-called surplus water, water that state workers released from the Canal to prevent an excess from weakening the banks. In 1825, the legislature passed a law permitting canal officials to lease the right to these waters to private concerns. When in 1827 inhabitants of the Genesee region petitioned the Canal Board to channel such surplus water to the village of Holley, where they would establish mills, they argued that such a policy would benefit the population's struggling new settlers. "When it is remembered that most of the inhabitants . . . are new settlers & with very few exceptions yet indebted for their land that a majority of them are indeed, & in truth poor . . . ," the farmers of Holley remonstrated, "it must be obvious that those severe privations & expences incident to their remote situation from Mills necessarily come home to them with superadded calamity." Without water to propel a mill near their farms, the petition continued, settlers would have to rely on "a more fortunate neighbor"—one with a wagon team or riverboat—to transport their wheat to mills. If the state granted surplus water rights to the town of Holley, it would allow these poor farmers to realize their property's productive worth while relieving them of any dependence on wealthier neighbors.[17]

Poor people were not alone in thinking that the state had an obligation to foster their prosperity. In 1831, a group of prosperous farmers insisted that the state build a lock that would allow them to move their produce around a dam blocking their easy access to the Canal. One witness for the petitioners told the Canal Board that "there are many large farmers who raise grain to a great extent, and they would be accommodated by this work." John Stainton explained that when the Canal divided his property, it burdened both his tenant and himself. The tenant now had to carry his grain half a mile on his back to get to a mill. But Stainton had also suffered, since the tenant's inconvenience in getting to a mill meant that the farm commanded only half the rent it might otherwise. The government, Stainton explained, must take responsibility for building a bridge across the property so that he could profit fully from his land's potential market value. Whether "poor" or "large"—and whether they measured their losses in terms of the productive or the market value of their property—farmers thought it reasonable to expect the state to promote their private economic interests.[18]

Although New Yorkers regularly filed petitions with the Canal Board to serve their private interests, farmers (modest and substantial) tried to bolster their arguments by telling state officials that their own interests coincided with the public good. From the Canal's inception, its promoters had referred to its promised impact on the public welfare, a central component of both republican and liberal approaches to political economy. Perhaps remembering that the Canal corridor had been touted as a sort of middle landscape between the extremes of civilization and savagery, New Yorkers sometimes argued that the state should use its regulatory powers to shield the public from some of the potentially harmful forces of the expanding commercial world. Some of them accordingly asked the state to intercede to prevent the excesses of unfettered market competition as well as the contamination of nature.

Antebellum Americans generally feared that market expansion would intensify class stratification, which helps explain, as we have seen, the symbolism of the official Canal celebrations. Yet symbolic gestures represent what people want to happen and not what is actually happening around them. If small and large property owners did indeed join forces in 1825 in wishing that construction workers would quickly move on to Ohio, they nonetheless found themselves vying with one another for access to state-regulated largess. In trying to convince the Canal Board to adopt their own preferred policies, people of modest circumstances often made appeals based on what they articulated as the government's obligation to control the greedy intentions of wealthier members of society.

The Genesee farmers who petitioned for surplus water rights, for example, tried to bolster their case by pointing out that without the state's intervention they would be deprived of equal access to economic opportunity. When the villagers traveled to distant mills, they explained, they were often "compelled to return without their grist, those mills being in most cases too exclusively <u>Merchant</u> mills to perform <u>custom</u> work promptly . . ." Merchant mills ground large quantities of grain for their customers; they would not stop a well-paying job to grind a farmer's small load of wheat while he waited. By granting water power at Holley and thus allowing its residents to construct their own mills, the petitioners argued, the state would be acting both with equity and with the public interest in mind:

> far greater difficulties . . . have not deterred your Honorable Board from <u>controlling</u> & <u>dispensing</u> the surplus waters at all other points upon the canal, in such a manner as best to promote <u>public revenue</u> & the <u>greatest amount of accommodation</u> to the <u>inhabitants,</u> without regard to <u>individual cupidity,</u> or <u>sectional influence</u>.

While the market's invisible hand favored merchant grinding and "cupidity" on the part of commercial millowners, the petitioners demanded that the state intervene to protect its citizens' access to family grinding by channeling water to Holley; this, in turn, would promote the common good in at least two ways. Since residents paid the state for access to surplus water, the citizens of Holley would be contributing to the "public revenue." And because that water would serve more people, and less selfish ones, it would contribute to an abstract sense of good as well.[19]

For the first decade or so of the canal era, other modest property owners joined the farmers of Holley in thinking that the Canal Board would dispense artificial resources more equitably than would uncontrolled market competition. While these petitioners may well have molded their rhetoric to appeal to what they thought state officials would like to hear, they nonetheless chose to turn to the state for help in the first place, which suggests that they believed they would personally benefit from governmental intervention in distributing resources. Their faith in the Canal Board stemmed in part from the belief that the members of that agency represented the entire state and not just a single locality or "section." Unlike the legislature, then, the Canal Board—in theory—should have been better able to dispassionately balance the needs of various constituencies within the public.

Drawing on this same belief that state officials would see themselves as having an obligation to stave off the negative consequences of the market expansion they had promoted, New Yorkers regularly argued that when the Canal damaged their property, it also threatened the public health. They complained about how the accumulation of water on their land allowed disease to fester in stagnant pools. They detailed their bouts with fever and ague and provided supporting testimony from local physicians. Stagnant water did in fact pose health risks, especially in summertime, and the state usually acted quickly to remedy such problems.

Some people, though, apparently took advantage of this genuine concern about the public health to bolster their claims of financial loss. William DeZeng, for example, combined a claim for a ruined investment with an appeal for a remedy to a public problem. A prominent farmer in the town of Clyde, DeZeng also speculated in real estate bordering the Canal. In order to increase the value of his village lots, he had cleared streets between them. He claimed in 1828 that because of the faulty construction of the canal embankment, water had seeped out of the waterway and onto his land, where it formed stagnant pools and flooded streets, making the roads "entirely useless" to the public and himself. Admitting his own interest in having the water drained, DeZeng insisted that his problems hindered the public as well; not only were certain streets impassable, but they were also "injurious to the health of the inhabitants." Even if the state did not want to protect his investment by draining the land, he argued that it still had the unquestionable duty to correct a situation that, as a result of the artificial reshaping of the landscape, endangered the health of its citizens. DeZeng berated the "studied neglect of every interest relating to the village of Clyde by the [Canal] Superintendent and his Agents." DeZeng's claim provides an early hint of what would become a growing distrust—and condemnation—of the state.[20]

In the first decade after the Canal's completion, though, direct criticism of the state was unusual. Most Canal Board petitioners maintained faith in the government that had built the triumphant Erie Canal. One of the state's greatest mandates, they believed, was to protect their property rights. In this assumption, they had the support of legal decisions and treatises. No longer a natural right—one governed by God—property was clearly a civil right—one managed by the state. Writing an encyclopedia entry on natural law in 1836, Joseph Story, an influential Supreme Court justice, explained, "[W]hatever . . . the origin of the right to property, it is . . . now . . . a creature of civil government." As their appeals to the Canal Board suggest, even settlers who arrived in the upstate region before 1817 shared this basic understanding. While they often felt very real losses in the value of their property, they believed that the state—with proper guidance from its citizens—would pursue its artificial remaking of the landscape in a just and equitable way. Whether they appealed to the state to protect or to promote their property investments, they felt that the state had the power to do so—and that it would use its power fairly.[21]

By the mid-1830s, the landscape of upstate New York barely resembled its earlier appearance, complicating the state's efforts to promote internal improvements. Largely because of the influences of the Erie Canal, New York was now the Empire State. With each passing year, more and more western produce flowed through central New York on its way to the Hudson, helping to make New York City the nation's leading port. The western section of the state had been transformed into a thriving commercial and manufacturing corridor, with its population already more thickly settled than that of the Mohawk Valley. The waterway nurtured several of the state's largest cities, in areas that had been swamps or woodlands just decades earlier. Warehouses and mills dotted the Canal's banks, and wheat sprouted where formerly pine needles had collected on the forest floor.[22]

This prosperity signaled the transformation of the "wilderness" into "civilization," and New Yorkers still had reasons to believe that they could avoid some of the corruption of older civilizations. Theirs seemed to be a land of social mobility, where a resident of Rochester could exclaim, "The Labourer feels himself as independent as the Esqr. we bow our heads to Nothing nor Nobody excepting the Lord above & the canal bridges as we pass under." Most white men could continue to aspire to economic independence as well, by mustering the cash either to purchase land or to become a workshop master.[23]

With so many visible signs of progress, many New Yorkers actively campaigned to make the Erie Canal bigger and, they hoped, even better. In 1835, the state passed the Enlargement Bill, designed to widen the waterway to seventy feet from forty feet and to deepen it to seven feet from four feet (a tripling of volume.) By allowing larger boats to travel the waterway, the new construction would cut transportation costs even further by taking advantage of the economies of scale. It would allow farmers to market their produce more competitively while also decreasing the price of luxury goods imported from the East. Few farmers objected in theory to an enlarged Canal, though they certainly hoped the waterway could be widened without damaging their own buildings and land—property whose market value had increased along with the Canal's success.

This new Canal would cut through not just a more settled

and "civilized" landscape but one that was also much more complex. In the commercial world that the Canal had helped to
foster, everything took on a different meaning. When they appealed to the state to build them bridges, for example, farmers
now chose to explain to members of the Canal Board just what
trespassing implied. Farmers in the 1820s had assumed that
members of the Canal Board had an implicit understanding of
the inconvenience of being forced to trespass, so they had not
elaborated on the term. But in the 1830s farmers began offering
explicit explanations of the serious economic and legal consequences of not having their own bridges. Complaining in 1837
that his farm in Palmyra had been cut in two by the enlargement, William Wilcox noted that the nearest canal bridge lay
across someone else's land. His neighbor might "at any time
from whim or Caprice prevent his goeing over his said land thus
leaving your petitioner without means of access to his said land."
Anson Cary argued that when the enlargement divided his
twenty-acre farm, it forced him to walk over someone else's land
to get to a bridge to reach his own property and subjected him
"to a trespass suit from the Owner who knows his advantages &
may or will make use of it when he thinks propper to haris me
untill he brings me to his own terms or one half of its value."
Refusing a right-of-way in order to lower a neighbor's property
value, Cary explained, "is not very uncommon in these days of
spekulation." By forcing a neighbor to sell his land at below-
market prices, a speculator could purchase the land himself, offer
potential buyers access to his nearby canal bridge, and then sell
the land at market value—and at a substantial profit to himself.
Such caprice and greed, such sharp dealing, made some residents
long for what they perceived as the less rapacious economic order
of their earlier lives.[24]

Yet if they lamented some of the consequences of market expansion, farmers did their part in helping to transform the economic landscape. In a region where nothing seemed to carry
the same meaning anymore, not even a tree was just a tree. When
construction workers felled trees to clear a path for the enlarged

Canal, they no longer simply deprived a widow of timber for her family's support. As Abraham Lansing explained to the Canal Board, he "grows his trees for the purpose of selling the fruit they yield him and not merely for his private use." Lansing and other farmers did not merely sell the fruits of nature; instead, they consciously invested in market production. Their trees had been grafted to improve their yields. Now farmers complained that when the state cut down their trees, it destroyed more than their God-given gifts. The loss of such improved trees, farmers argued, constituted a greater "damage" than canal appraisers recognized; farmers, too, had made commercial investments.[25]

Upstate farmers' active participation in market-oriented production enmeshed them in a complex economic web that made international economic crises reverberate on even the most local level. A waterway that brought exotic goods to the hinterlands also created interdependent credit relationships among a vast network of economic actors. When financial panics hit the country in 1834, 1837, and again in 1839, they exploded New Yorkers' notions of inevitable economic growth. Shortages of cash almost halted business activity, casting many farmers back into debt and bankrupting others. When international merchants did not have cash to pay the forwarding merchant, that entrepreneur could not pay the local merchant, who, in turn, could not buy the farmers' apples. Everyone from farmers to speculators began to realize that economic mobility could move downward as well as upward.[26]

Property owners feared slipping down the social ladder, a fear that the enlargement project exacerbated. While before they had snatched glimpses of what lay below them, now they looked more closely at where they could possibly land—and they did not like what they saw. By 1840, more—not fewer—New Yorkers worked for other people, and the Canal corridor provided tangible and daily reminders of this shift. With the start of the enlargement project, construction workers again overran the landscape, and this time they were more visible. Whereas much of the original construction had taken place in wilderness, the work on the enlargement was centered in heavily populated areas. And unlike the previous generation of canal diggers, this later group occasionally joined together to strike for higher wages, reminding residents of the class strife that Americans feared would accompany economic growth. If in the 1820s property owners believed that wage laborers would disappear once construction came to an end, by the 1830s they had too much evidence to the contrary.[27]

Not only did businessmen set up large manufacturing and milling establishments right along the Canal's banks, but the operation of the waterway itself required the labor of tens of thousands of semiskilled wage earners. The boatmen had replaced the original canal diggers, and they seemed no better fit to become productive members of society than had the construction workers. Worse yet, their numbers promised to increase once the enlargement was completed and began carrying larger boats requiring additional hands. By the late 1830s, it became obvious that—promises of the Canal's sponsors notwithstanding—the artificial waterway had helped bring into being a more divided society, one that even state-funded canal bridges could not mend.[28]

As the state's finances became more strained over time, reaching a true crisis in the early 1840s, residents of the Canal corridor grew increasingly suspicious of the state's ability to satisfactorily reconcile competing claims to its resources. This shift in popular mood did not arise from doubts about the state's ability to play a useful role in economic development. To the contrary, thousands of New Yorkers continued to petition for lateral canals that would be poor financial investments for the state but that petitioners justified as means to spur local enterprise. People's growing distrust of the state registered instead the fear—especially among Jacksonian Democrats—that scheming interests might too easily corrupt the state for their own selfish ends. If farmers and millers continued to welcome opportunities to participate in an expanded market economy, they came to fear that the state favored commercial over agrarian interests and well-connected politicos over ordinary citizens.[29]

While many New Yorkers borrowed the language of the Jacksonians, political parties in the upstate region tended not to entirely share their national leaders' views on economic development. Andrew Jackson had led the Democrats in opposing government intervention in the market economy, using his veto to prevent federal funding of Kentucky's Maysville Road and to deny the Second Bank of the United States a renewed charter. Jacksonians harked back to Jeffersonian notions that the country should expend its resources primarily on geographic expansion rather than on commercial development. Members of the Whig opposition—who portrayed themselves as the "loyal opposition" to what they called King Andrew's abuse of executive power— saw government-sponsored internal improvements as crucial to the nation's economic growth and cultural maturation. They borrowed their ideology in part from the Federalists, while pushing the "American System" that was first articulated by Henry Clay during John Quincy Adams's Republican administration in the 1820s. The American System would encourage American commercial growth through internal improvements, a national banking system, and a protective tariff.[30]

While the second party system of Democrats and Whigs did not always follow such neat divisions over policy, the lines between them became particularly blurred in regions of the country—upstate New York, for example—where internal improvements played such an immediate and direct role in the economy. In the Canal corridor, many Whigs opposed federal support for internal improvements; if New York had to pay for its own transportation system, then so, too, should other states. Democrats, for their part, had overseen the building of the original Canal, and they had been in power when the Enlargement Bill became law. They did not oppose the expansion of their commercial highway, but they would later encourage the state to adopt what they saw as more responsible and equitable fiscal policies. Political lines in the upstate region were made even more murky by the popularity of the Anti-Masonic Party, which appealed to voters who distrusted party politics generally.[31]

As we have seen, whatever their party affiliation, New Yorkers often used the rhetoric of republicanism when they addressed state officials. Yet by the 1830s the meaning of republicanism had evolved even beyond the ideas articulated by the Canal's sponsors. After 1825, property owners no longer had an exclusive claim on voting rights, thanks to a change in the state constitution. The deference that DeWitt Clinton had extolled had also died; the laborer bowed his head to nobody but God. People still spoke of their republican rights, and they still lauded the common good or public interest. But to many of them, republicanism had come to mean "fairness." "Now I ask the State to build me a Brige," demanded one farmer whose lands had been cut in two by the enlargement. "[I]f they say they will not because it is there rules, I am a Jackson man & Will Try to Git my rites in a free republicking Govrment." More and more farmers began to question whether the government could be trusted to ensure those republican rights, their right—as this same farmer put it —"to have the State deel farly with me."[32]

Perhaps because many landowners had begun by the 1830s to take the original Canal's benefits for granted, they ardently protested the state's attempts to deny them compensation for land appropriated for the enlargement project. They showed less inclination than they had a decade earlier to accept the appraisers' arguments that the benefits brought by the waterway counterbalanced the injuries it caused. Their acceptance of progress had led them back to a much earlier understanding of property, one in which agricultural land was seen as a natural right. This idea, of course, only added fuel to the fire of their republican rhetoric. Anson Cary, for example, drew on Patrick Henry's "Give Me Liberty or Give Me Death" speech when he blasted the Canal Board for devaluing his farm. "I am wronged, defrauded or give it what name you please . . . ," he thundered, "from the mistaken & delusive Idea of Benefits yet when I prove to [the appraisers] my property was Injured $1000 in the Intrisick vallue of it to repair this loss they sing the Syrin Song Benefit-Benefit—it is crying Peace-Peace where there is no peace." By borrowing from Patrick Henry, Cary did more than associate property rights with natural rights; he also linked the state's attempts to deny those rights to the despotism of British kings. The state, in other words, had become the agent of the aristocracy, threatening the God-given rights of hardworking men like himself.[33]

To Cary, the state had failed at more than protecting his property rights. Rather than treating citizens fairly, the state had come to represent the interests of the commercial elite. Cary argued that the state favored merchants at the expense of farmers; "there is merchants in the Village of Oxford who have Benefited Thousands of dollars who have not had one foot of their land injured while the farmer who has had his farm & prospect distroyed is taxed with benefits . . ." While the Revolutionaries had decried taxation without representation, Cary showed disgust for uncompensated property damage (which amounted to a form of indirect taxation) without genuine benefits. Even without the advantage of hindsight, Cary apparently realized what the legal historian Morton Horwitz has pointed out: that a genuine tax on property values would probably have been a more progressive way of funding internal improvements.[34]

Since these farmers wanted the state to protect their property rights, they probably took little comfort from the U.S. Supreme Court's ruling in the *Charles River Bridge* case. Although the contract issues raised by this well-publicized case did not bear directly on their predicament, the Court's ruling had broader implications about the relationship between property rights and economic development. In Boston, where the case arose, the immediate issue was whether the Commonwealth of Massachusetts could grant a charter to the Warren Bridge Company, even though the company's proposed bridge would compete for business with the Charles River Bridge; the latter company had held a state-granted monopoly on traffic over the river since the colonial era and argued that Massachusetts should protect that privilege. Writing for the majority, Chief Justice Roger B. Taney—a Democrat—held that when the privileges conferred by corporate charters conflicted with economic development, the state could favor development if doing so promoted the "common good" and "progress." In Massachusetts, the immediate impact of favoring venture capital actually served people of modest means; the competing bridge offered them a cheaper route to and from work. But while farmers along New York's Erie Canal also identified their interests with the "common good" and "progress," these landowners had a stake in protecting established property rights—rights they saw as inviolable—since the property in question was theirs. They therefore adopted the language of the "common good" in their appeals to the state, but they saw that good as being intimately connected with their own property investments.[35]

Farmers increasingly distrusted the state's commitment to their visions of the common good in part because canal appraisers made damage assessments with a merchant's view of the world, one that assumed that property's worth lay in its potential as a commercial site or a speculative investment. They failed, in Cary's words, to consider the "intrinsic" value of the land, the property's productive worth. As a seventy-eight-year-old farmer who would have been twelve years old when Patrick Henry stirred the American public with his rousing words, Anson Cary may not have been completely typical in how he defined property's value. But other farmers, including those who actively engaged in commercial farming, shared his sense that the state favored merchants over producers.

Abraham and Levinus Lansing, for example, did not just complain that the state's appraisers failed to recognize a grafted fruit tree when they saw it. They also argued that the state's more general definition of "benefits" demonstrated an eagerness to promote mercantile activity over agriculture. In assessing the damage awards owed the Lansings, the state's appraisers had ruled that the farmers stood to accrue benefits outweighing any damage done, and thus the state owed them no remuneration. The appraisers reasoned that the farmers' remaining land, now bordering on a newly built lock, had appreciated in value because it offered an ideal site for tavern stands to serve boatmen and travelers. Although the Lansings' land had been damaged for farming, their chosen and established occupation, it was arguably greatly enhanced as commercial real estate. The appraisers emphasized the land's commercial potential over its past productive capabilities. Most farmers did not object to the marketing revolution per se, but they did object to the ways in which it seemed ever more likely to encourage trading and speculation over the growing of crops or the raising of livestock.[36]

No one felt more strongly about this issue than the farmers of Dansville in Livingston County. Although the original Canal had bypassed their town altogether, in the late 1830s the state had completed the lateral Genesee Valley Canal, a branch of which ran three-quarters of a mile from the center of their village. For years, the residents of Dansville petitioned first the legislature and then the Canal Board to remedy their lack of access to the lateral waterway. They offered to bear the cost of constructing a channel to that canal if the state would secure them a right-of-way to the land. Adopting the language of Jacksonian Democracy, they argued that the interests of the "many"—*their* interests—should take priority over the interests of the "few." They couched their own interests in terms of the common good. Meanwhile, the "few" had seen opportunity in the villagers' misfortune. Speculators purchased the land that lay between the village and the feeder to the Genesee Valley Canal, hoping that the village would expand toward the canal in order to take full advantage of its trading opportunities. Were that to happen, the market value of property that lay between the town and the canal could be expected to appreciate greatly. In order to protect their investments, these speculators refused to grant a right-of-way through their property, even though the farmers had already dug a slip to within a few hundred yards of the lateral canal.[37]

When the farmers of Dansville brought their claim to the legislature in 1844, the assembly voted in favor of a bill granting them a right-of-way. But the bill did not pass the senate, and so did not become law. As it happened, Senator Faulkner, the state senator from Dansville, owned a portion of the land in question. According to the *Albany Evening Atlas*, he convinced some of his colleagues to vote against the bill and, as a result, the measure lost by a narrow margin. In this case, the farmers of Dansville could not trust even their own representative to avoid the temptations of greed.

The farmers now made their dissatisfaction known through action rather than rhetoric. When the state twice sent workers to fill in the farmers' slip, the villagers drove them away with raised shovels and spades. After the second rebuff, according to the *Atlas*, the farmers "proceeded to aggression, and assembling some three hundred strong, cut through the corner lots of the Senator, and made a union between the canal and their basin and slip." The newspaper labeled the farmers' actions "a riot." When the citizens of Dansville realized that all the rhetoric in the world could not make the state fulfill its mandate to represent what they saw as the common good, they took the law into their own hands. The state might need them to build its artificial river, but *they* did not need the state to build theirs.[38]

Two years after the Dansville riot, the Democratic-controlled legislature issued a 866-page report outlining the frauds that state employees had committed while managing the Canal's construction and maintenance. These deceptions usually involved state employees and contractors charging the government for work they did not perform or could have performed more efficiently. Very much aware of such dishonest deals on the local level (deals that tempted members of all political parties), many New Yorkers submitted lengthy petitions to the Canal Board demanding that the state official in charge of their section of the Canal be dismissed. Evidence of widespread dishonesty, designed to line the pockets of men who had gotten their jobs through political patronage in the first place, only increased farmers' perceptions that the state disregarded their interests in favor of the wealthy and powerful. Many small landowners had come to see the state's failures as moral in nature.[39]

When they pointed to the state's moral failings, most Canal Board petitioners concentrated on what they called violations of the public trust. These New Yorkers' willingness to risk offending the very officials whom they sought to persuade suggests that they may well have believed what they said. Such harsh rhetoric also reflects a more widespread decline in deference-based politics, but even so it is telling that people took the risk of insulting the state officials who most easily wielded immediate, tangible power over their lives. It is one thing to say that a Presidential candidate won office through a "corrupt bargain," as Jackson's supporters accused Adams of doing in 1824. It is quite another issue to insult the person charged with the responsibility of making sure that canal water does not destroy your crops, especially since a certain amount of canal damage was known to result from neglect and even vandalism.[40]

Even if we remain skeptical of the farmers' rhetoric and assume that they chose to couch their claims in moral terms to strengthen their appeals for policies in which they held a self-interest, their rhetoric is nonetheless revealing. Their insistence that the government maintain a certain moral standard in a time of market expansion suggests a great deal about their broader conceptions of the state's obligations to its citizens. Whether or not they genuinely believed their own words, property owners cast their Canal Board claims in logic that they thought state officials would find compelling.

Levinus and Abraham Lansing were among those who used a combination of harsh language and moral reasoning in their attempts to win greater compensation for their damaged land. When the state argued that their land now held increased value as a potential tavern stand, the Lansings retorted that they did not want to open businesses, and surely, they insisted, not businesses profiting from "immorality." Taverns sold alcohol, which was consumed in tremendous amounts by antebellum Americans. Yet in reaction to what one historian has called the "alcoholic republic," other antebellum Americans considered the consumption of alcohol, and certainly its sale, a vice. "At the present day," Levinus Lansing contended, "it seems a libel upon the character of the State to say that a tipling shop is such a benefit to an individual or to a community that the State ought to compel persons to resort to the establishment of such places of immorality & vice to get pay for the land taken from them for the use of the public." While we have no way of knowing whether the Lansings truly believed that taverns were immoral, they did make their claim near the peak of the antebellum temperance campaigns. Either they truly believed that the state should not encourage immoral behavior, or they thought that state officials would be swayed by an appeal to their responsibility to uphold public morality.[41]

The state risked further violating its mandate, some property owners argued, by ignoring democratic judicial procedures for determining individuals' claims for damage awards. One resident complained that the state appraisers had "made themselves both the witnesses and the judges"; another that "the benefits (if any) are merely a matter of speculation & fancy"; and still another that "the privilege of being heard in defending individual right seems to be guaranteed by the laws and Constitution of our Country . . ." Ephraim Beach similarly protested what he saw as an abuse of official power. Not only did the state "arbitrarily" take his property; its agents awarded more in damages to his neighbors than to him. "I am but a single individual upon one side, claiming nothing but Justice & equity from the great State of New York upon the other," Beach pleaded. "I appeal to you with great confidence; that you will not suffer the imputation to exist; that the State of New York, because she had the power, deprived an individual of his property, leaving him remediless and without adequate compensation." The state had an obligation to treat its citizens equally under the law and to grant its citizens due process. Since American governments were by definition governments of the people, they could be accused of nothing worse than abusing their power over their citizens.[42]

Few seemed to doubt that the state had a right to appropriate property for a project that served the common good; legal precedent amply supported the right of eminent domain. But property owners did insist that the state follow through on its obligation, also legally mandated, to compensate them fairly for their economic losses. Jacob Sanders, who had bought land along the Canal in Schenectady expecting to rent it to merchants, had his land appropriated for the Canal enlargement. In 1841 he declared that he could not "conceive why individual property should be appropriated for the use of the State, and great damage caused thereby and not the least compensation allowed . . ." This uncompensated appropriation of land went against Sanders's view of how political economy should work, prompting him to add in disgust that "if this is public justice he would hereafter crave to be delivered from it."[43]

People who hoped to use their land for agricultural purposes felt even more strongly. Some individuals, particularly members of the Democratic Party, began to argue that the state could no longer be trusted to regulate internal improvements. In 1846, the *Rochester Daily Democrat* reported that the state had appropriated water from the Genesee River for use in the Erie Canal, which deprived local millers of an essential source of power to run their mills. The newspaper's editor accused the state of "one of the most outrageous acts of oppression ever known in a country not an absolute despotism." Democrats throughout the country used such vigorous language to show their disapproval for the government's seemingly inequitable intervention in economic development. In the Canal corridor, many Democratic farmers adopted this language despite their firm belief that the state had a valuable role to play in internal improvements. If they sometimes used the language of laissez-faire, it was because they believed the government itself had been corrupted.[44]

Some New Yorkers sensed that the state had violated its mandate not just by favoring the wealthy and well-connected but also by failing to follow through on its more general commitment to use internal improvements to promote its citizens' welfare. Property owners' distrust of the state government increased after the Democrats cut back on canal spending in a process that culminated in the 1842 "Stop and Tax" law. With this law, the legislature halted further work on internal improvements until adequate funds could be raised through taxation to support the work. Under severe financial stress, state officials decided that they could no longer finance internal improvements through loans, as they had done up to this point. Given the burden of the debt, the legislature voted to place property taxes on residents throughout the state to fund improvement projects. In theory, small property owners along the Canal's banks should have welcomed this shift in policy. In their eyes, they had been unduly "taxed" for the Canal all along, and the new law promised to spread the burden more broadly.

While most newspapers in the region endorsed the new policy, believing it necessary to maintain the state's solvency, they did not always speak for those who lived directly on the waterway's banks. These property owners objected not to the "tax" part of the bill but to its "stop" provision. For them, the abrupt stop in improvements caused them to lose additional faith in the state's willingness to meet its obligations to its citizens. Once the state began making changes in the landscape, it needed to carry through on them. If not, then, like Jacob Sanders, these residents would crave to be delivered from public justice, not because they doubted the state's ability to play a beneficial role in the economy but because they had misgivings about its abilities to be just.[45]

Internal improvements were not supposed to disappear as quickly as they had sprung up. From the outset, the Canal's promoters had bragged about the durability and permanence of its structures. And in the intervening decades, the artificial river had in many respects become part of the natural topography. Having already had their property "injured" by the original and enlarged canals, some upstaters now faced new disruptions with the state's financial cutbacks. In 1838, for example, the owner of a grist mill near the Champlain Canal had expended $3,000 on repairs. In the early 1840s, when the canal commissioners removed the dam that fed his mill, he complained that he "was under the impression supported by the opinion of all [my] neighbors, that the big dam would never be abandoned . . ." According to the miller, the state had the obligation to keep the dam in repair to protect his investment as well as those of his neighbors. When millers depending on water from the Fort Miller Dam heard that the state intended to discontinue its use, they argued that "mills would not have been erected . . . if the owners had supposed that the Feeder would have Ever Closed up, by the State . . ." When they made material investments based on the artificial reshaping of the landscape, when they did what the state encouraged them to do by building the Canal, many New Yorkers thought they had struck a bargain with the state.[46]

William Adams had literally done so. Instead of demanding damages for his farmland that the state appropriated for the enlargement project, Adams agreed to give the state the property in exchange for certain improvements to his remaining land. The state had consented to dig a ditch for him and to clean out the canal bed near his property. Rather than living up to his end of the deal, Adams charged, the state engineer intentionally neglected his duties and used the state's weak financial circumstances as an excuse for "this evasive break of . . . agreement on the part of the State [that] has destroyed my property and turned it into a nuisance." The state, Adams continued, "was wrong, rich or poor, so to use my release [of property rights] and I want this corrected. It is my right that it should be." He then argued that the state, as much as any individual, had an obligation to live up to its agreements, regardless of its financial strains.[47]

Like the well-dressed young man who did not follow through on his agreement to buy Alexander Coventry's horse, the state, too, had turned out to be something other than what it first appeared. When property owners initially embraced the artificial changes in the landscape, they thought those changes would themselves be immutable. Instead, from their point of view, the state had continued its triumph over the landscape, now destroying productive agrarian property in favor of mercantile ventures. They began to distrust the state because, in a world of competing interests, the state seemed more often an adversary than an ally.

5

The Politics of Business

MANY RESIDENTS of the Canal corridor, including some of the same people disappointed by the handling of their claims for property damage, turned to the state as a powerful advocate in their quest for individual commercial opportunity. The Canal Board decided far more than whether to compensate its citizens for appropriated and damaged land. As a result, New Yorkers expended a great deal of energy attempting to persuade state officials that the Canal should run through *their* town, that the toll collector's office should be located in the building next to *their* tavern, or that the toll should be lowered on the type of broom handles *they* sent to market. Intent on winning government sponsorship of policies that served their personal ends, businessmen argued that their commercial success bore an intimate connection to the state's well-being.

A wide range of people made their living from commerce. The wives of canal diggers, for example, peddled cakes to workers, while children jumped from canal boat to canal boat selling apples or pears. Farmers, many of whom did not share the Lansings' qualms, set up grog shops along the Canal. Others relied on commercial transactions to sell their crops in distant markets. But the term "businessmen" will be applied here to a more select group of people, those whose prime economic activity involved providing goods that they had neither grown nor made themselves in exchange for money (or for credit calculated in monetary terms). Still, a variety of people (almost exclusively males) fit this designation. The owner of a small grocery store found himself in quite different circumstances from a forwarding merchant, who took care of storing, shipping, and reselling goods. Some of these commercial merchants controlled tremendous amounts of capital. They also employed clerks and agents, who made their living from commerce but who did not directly control any capital—should these men be viewed as businessmen or workers? Complicating matters further, it was not unusual for the same person to hold several commercial occupations during his lifetime, starting as a clerk, buying a share in a small grocery, and moving on to become a large commercial merchant.[1]

Whatever the particulars of their circumstances, most of the upstate businessmen who addressed the Canal Board articulated their arguments in ways that were consistent with Whig ideology. While we only occasionally know their actual political affiliations, we can draw generalizations about the language they chose to use. Although upstate Democrats and Whigs alike tended to support economic progress through government intervention, they nonetheless imagined a different sort of social order. Instead of joining the Democrats in seeing society as divided into the "many" and the "few"—the powerless and the powerful—the Whigs tended to see a harmony among society's different interests. They envisioned a political economy that would produce an "aristocracy of nature"—a group of talented and virtuous men whose economic success and moral rectitude made them well positioned to make decisions for those below them on the social ladder. Whig entrepreneurs, like Democratic farmers, tended to make claims based on the sanctity of established practices (their "vested rights"), and they, too, emphasized that their personal interests were consistent with the common good. But what emerged over time were distinct notions of what the "common good" actually meant.[2]

From the very beginning, state officials faced the persistent challenge of allocating canal resources fairly. Before DeWitt Clinton poured his barrel of Lake Erie water into New York Harbor in 1825, New York State businessmen had joined farmers in making clear that they expected the state to fulfill its promises that the artificial waterway would spread opportunity and prosperity throughout the entire state. While the Canal's promoters acknowledged that the waterway would bestow its benefits primarily on people living within twenty miles of the Canal, upstate residents suspected that benefits would be distributed more narrowly. They knew that canal towns would attract business away from those located off the waterway, and that one town's good fortune might be another's misfortune. These businessmen expressed strong support for the Canal project, but they jostled for equal opportunities to profit from the remapped landscape.[3]

Unhappy with the way the Canal had changed the geography of the upstate region, the towns of Rome and Schenectady tried to counter the "universal jubilation" of the Grand Celebration of 1825. As the celebratory flotilla made its way from Buffalo to New York City, it was to dock at thirty towns, where local celebrations were to honor it. After months of planning, the celebration got off to a prompt start and for three days met with exuberant receptions. When the celebratory flotilla reached Rome on the fourth day, though, the celebration took a twist the Canal sponsors could hardly have anticipated. Mocking the planned "wedding of the waters" ceremony, the residents of Rome staged a funeral instead. Citizens dressed in military uniforms (a symbol of their patriotism) headed the procession, while the town's other residents followed behind. At the banks of the Erie Canal, they poured out water from a barrel painted black —a color more appropriate for commemorating a death than a marriage. Yet after completing this solemn ceremony, according to the Grand Celebration's official diarist, the residents of Rome "in quick time . . . put aside their ill humor, and joined with heart and hand" in celebrating the Canal's completion. The celebratory flotilla then continued on its way, meeting enthusiastic crowds everywhere but in Schenectady, where its reception was "grave."[4]

No one knew better than the citizens of Rome and Schenec-

tady what the "exertions of art" could achieve. In the years leading up to the construction of the Erie Canal, both towns owed
much of their prosperity to improvements in the natural landscape. Rome was located on a two-mile canal built in the 1790s
by the Western Inland Lock Navigation Company. The black
barrel emptied by the citizens of Rome contained water from
that old canal. By staging their mock funeral (a traditional symbolic gesture of loyal opposition in England), the people of Rome
protested that the artificial river, rather than passing directly
through their town's center, passed half a mile away. Rome's
advantageous location on the older canal no longer counted for
much, as the town stood to lose much of its commercial activity
to neighboring towns directly on the new Canal. Schenectady
faced a similar problem, having been the eastern terminus of the
navigable portion of the Mohawk River. The town had long been
a commercial hub and boat-building center, but the Erie Canal
produced economic rivals to its east and west. Schenectady would
lose its status as a transportation center to Albany, while for-
feiting much of its boat-building business to western towns
closer to sources of cheap lumber. For residents of Rome and
Schenectady, the Canal seemed to close more opportunities than
it opened.[5]

While Rome and Schenectady turned to symbolic protest,
other towns made their discontent known through more official
channels. Seeing how the Canal promised to help certain locations at the expense of their own, New Yorkers appealed to the
government for water connections to the main Canal. The village
of Manlius, for example, was located four miles south of the Erie
Canal, and its residents petitioned for permission to build a connecting canal with money they would raise themselves. As a
resident explained in 1825,

> The inhabitants of our village are wide awake for making
> a side cut from the main Canal to this place . . . which if
> done I think will be the making of this village, it is getting
> to be rather dull times with us here in consequence of our

situation with respect to the canal, neither on it nor far enough from it not to feel that those immediately upon its banks have a decided superiority over us in the transactions of most kinds of mercantile speculations—but if we succeed in getting our side cut we think that we shall still be able to cope with our neighboring villages on the canal.

The citizens of Danube argued in that same year that the state should build them a connector to the Canal because "our want of participation in the benefits, not to mention our silent sufferings on account of the Erie Canal, furnish us with strong and unquestionable claims upon the attention and munificence of the state." Although the Erie Canal caused the residents of Manlius and Danube to "suffer," their solutions were to demand from the state another canal; they did not shun progress but rather wanted to have equal access to the "mercantile speculations" it promised. For the first decade of the canal era, towns across the state made similar appeals to state officials and met with mixed success.[6]

They continued to push the government for new canals because they knew that such waterways would bring prosperity. The banks of the Canal and its tributaries, as the state's appraisers pointed out, made ideal locations for small businesses— groceries, taverns, supply stores—serving boat workers and passengers. Meanwhile, settlers turned to canalside merchants for the basic tools and supplies needed to clear their land. Finding that other merchants in Rochester could not keep up with farmers' demands for axes, Horace Wheeler began importing axes from New Hampshire in 1825. And just as a New Hampshire ax maker needed a merchant like Wheeler to sell his tools in western settlements, western farmers needed merchants to sell their produce in distant markets. After chopping down their trees and planting wheat among the stumps, farmers shipped their surplus grain eastward to where it could be sold to industrial laborers who did not have the land or time to grow their own food. But how could a farmer near Rochester sell his wheat to industrial laborers in Lowell, Massachusetts, or even Manchester, England? The wheat had to pass through many hands. It had to be purchased, stored, milled, perhaps stored again, shipped, and sold once it reached port—all of which involved businessmen, including local merchants, millowners, commercial merchants, and forwarders. Warehouses and storefronts soon lined the Canal; in many towns the artificial river replaced the main street as the principal thoroughfare. The façades of new buildings overlooked the Canal rather than the streets that ran beside it.[7]

To established and aspiring merchants, the possibilities opened by the Canal might have seemed endless. Each week's newspaper brought a new report of the immense quantities of produce being shipped on the Canal, even before the entire waterway had been completed. Nathaniel Rochester rejoiced over the "stupendious canal" with its "immense quantity of produce." The young merchant Henry Cole reported in 1821, "Utica is now very busy—Navigation on the 'Big Ditch' is the order of the day." Some even gloated that canal towns had taken on the

Syracuse, like many other upstate communities, grew up along the Erie Canal, which served as its main thoroughfare

(John W. Barber and Henry Howe, *Historical Collections of the State of New York*, 1841, Columbia County Historical Society, Kinderhook, New York)

appearance of seaports, with their abundance of shipping and mercantile establishments.[8]

Upstate businessmen rushed to take advantage of these new opportunities. They displayed an almost frantic enthusiasm for beating out others to secure prime real estate along the Canal. In 1822, Lyman Spalding, a twenty-two-year-old merchant, resolved to seek his fortune along the new waterway. Spalding and his partner had run a successful grocery store in Canandaigua for two years. Located at the northern tip of Canandaigua Lake (one of New York's Finger Lakes), the town by the same name was home to a Seneca Indian village until the Revolutionary Army destroyed it in 1779. Resurrected shortly thereafter as the administrative center of the 8,600,000-acre Phelps and Gorham land purchase, in 1789 Canandaigua became the seat of Ontario County. The construction of a turnpike through town in 1804 clinched Canandaigua's reputation as a promising site for business, attracting young men like Spalding to try their luck in the flourishing town. But then the state officials decided that the Erie Canal should pass about thirteen miles to the north, and the town's citizens desperately appealed to the government for a canal to connect them to the main waterway. If the state would not pay for the proposed canal, then the people living along its route would finance it. They assured legislators that although they did not have much money, they could muster plenty of labor and food to support the undertaking. The legislature rejected their offer. Lyman Spalding and his partner soon found that more and more goods sat unsold on their shelves.[9]

Spalding lost no time proposing to an acquaintance that they join forces to set up a forwarding business in Rochester. That town, he thought, "will stand superior to any other place west of Albany." Spalding urged his friend to decide quickly, since "in case of making an establishment it is important that a scite should be secured—this can now be done to advantage." Spalding inserted the word "now" apparently as an afterthought, as if he realized that he should make explicit the need for a speedy decision. When his plans in Rochester did not pan out, Spalding hurried to scout out more modest possibilities in the new village of Lockport. He loaded two wagons with goods, left his partner to tend the store in Canandaigua, and set out for the Canal's banks. After brisk early sales there fulfilled his expectations, Spalding and his partner packed up their remaining goods, boarded up their Canandaigua store, and resettled in Lockport. Although Spalding's capital was limited, he soon discovered what other young merchants would learn as well: those who did not have much capital could often find other people who were more eager to invest money than time. Once Spalding's business began to flourish in Lockport, a cousin of his wrote to him observing that "Lockport must be at present a verry money making place . . ." Keen to take advantage of the growth in the new town, the cousin mused that if he "could make an arrangement with you to employ a considerable sum so as to realize as much as about 20 percent it would suit my pocket very well."[10]

Lockport, as the name suggests, was a creation of the canal era. As late as the summer of 1821, only three families lived in the area that would become the town. Six months later, 337 families had moved permanently to the new village. (The census takers excluded canal laborers from that total.) Lockport grew at a tremendous rate, with a settled population of 3,007 by 1825. A visitor in that same year saw

> the canal—the locks—stone and frame houses—log-buildings—handsome farms—warehouses—grist-mills—waterfalls—barbers' shops—bustle and activity—waggons, with ox-teams and horse teams—hotels—thousands of tree stumps, and people burning and destroying them—carding machines—tanneries—cloth works—tinplate factories—taverns—churches.

This scene led him to exclaim, "What a change in four short years from a state of wilderness." Lockport would soon grow into one of the largest upstate cities. But when Lyman Spalding moved there in the fall of 1822, he was among the first to risk opening a business in a town that had been created by, and that depended for its prosperity on, the Erie Canal. The young merchant's friends applauded his decision. Upon hearing of Spalding's relocation, for example, A. W. Howe declared, "I must my Dear Friend congratulate you on leaving old Canandaigua for I think for us young folks we shall find a little better pickings on the confines of the great ditch!"[11]

When one merchant raised his glass at a Canal celebration to toast the "artificial rivers of wealth, which flow, but never ebb," he touched the core of merchants' jubilant expectations for the canal era. But while many aspiring merchants shared this enthusiasm, they did not always fare as well as Lyman Spalding. The increasing use of commission agents, or middlemen, could make life difficult for shopkeepers, local merchants who traded directly with small-scale producers. These agents collected produce from several local merchants at a time, and would generally store it in warehouses until they had collected enough to fill an entire boat. Shopkeepers often disagreed with them over the terms of storage; they worried that perishable items would sit in the warehouses for too long and that their quality would decline before reaching New York City. As the owners of the produce, they would suffer if the goods rotted before reaching market. They depended on middlemen, a relationship they frequently lamented.[12]

Business could be difficult for commercial merchants, too. A commercial merchant's prosperity rested greatly on speculation, which favored merchants with considerable amounts of capital. Commercial merchants purchased goods outright and then rushed to get them to market before their market value dropped. With the vagaries of international markets, the fluctuation in market prices could earn—or cost—merchants huge sums of money. Jamie Archbald's speculations on wheat and then lumber had both failed by 1824, so he turned his attention to the more modest enterprise of opening up an "ice house" along the Canal, where he sold eggs, milk, and ice cream to passersby. A. W.

Howe, for his part, did not join his friend Lyman Spalding in his frantic endeavor to find canalside property. "I can assure you," he noted in 1823, "it is hard for a young man to establish himself in business at the present time without a pretty large capital, and that I cannot command at present, and I must remain in the capacity of a clerk untill my fund is sufficiently increased to ennable me to commence business on a decent scale." Yet despite their inability to take full advantage of business opportunities created by the Canal, neither Archbald nor Howe gave up the idea that the waterway nurtured business opportunities from which they would be able to profit. Archbald switched from middleman to local merchant, while Howe bided his time until he, too, could take up business along the artificial river.[13]

Just as merchants believed that greater economic opportunities existed in communities along the Canal, they assumed that certain businesses benefited from proximity to canal-related structures such as collectors' offices (tollhouses), locks, basins, and city bridges. Merchants coveted land next to such structures. While the toll collector and his assistants examined a boat and its cargo, the boat's crew and passengers visited neighboring stores and taverns. "At almost every lock and water place through the whole rout," noted one traveler in 1843, "there are from 3 to 6 groggeries, and all these for the benefit of the travelling public . . . 'Rum, Gin, Brandy, Wine, Beer, Cider, Bread, Milk, and Groceries,' meet the eye every few miles . . ." While other local residents complained about the rowdy crowds that gathered at the locks, store owners eagerly awaited the arrival of boats. Freight boats carrying passengers were an especially welcome sight, since the emigrants on board had to supply their own food and often replenished it along the way. Tavern keepers served hot meals as well as drinks to passengers and boat workers. These customers did not want to stray far when they went ashore, eager to keep an eye on their boats for fear of having their belongings stolen or of being left behind.[14]

The government further influenced merchants' prosperity

when it collected tolls on produce, goods, and passengers. The state did not intend for the Erie Canal to be a revenue-raising venture, but nevertheless assessed tolls to pay off the waterway's construction debt, to support its operation and maintenance, and to pay for lateral canals to satisfy the demands of communities that had been bypassed by the waterway. State officials as well as merchants recognized that tolls—much like national tariffs—affected the marketability of goods as well as the development of manufacturing. Higher tolls led to higher—and therefore less competitive—market prices, which influenced the demand for a particular raw material or manufactured item. An increase in the toll on flour, for example, might encourage merchants in New York City to buy from Pennsylvania millers instead. Local producers, however, might benefit from increased tolls on manufactured goods. If the toll on axes went up, then a Rochester ax maker could raise his prices and still undersell a New Hampshire manufacturer, which made the ax-making business a more desirable enterprise.

That the state chose to levy different tolls on different freight—rather than simply applying a universal toll based on weight—reflected its interest in promoting the development of certain crops and industries. To see a telling example, New Yorkers had only to look at the state's efforts to protect its investments in the salt manufactories near Syracuse. Many upstaters, in fact, complained about the market implications of the high tolls on foreign, but not domestic, salt. As a result, western farmers—who used large quantities of salt for meat-packing and who generally preferred the coarseness of foreign salt—purchased far greater amounts of domestic salt because of the state's tinkering with market forces.[15]

Few businessmen objected in principle to the state's regulation of the market. These men had ardently supported the Canal from the beginning, and could only have welcomed DeWitt Clinton's reminder in 1828 that the Canal's purpose was "to augment the general opulence, to animate all the springs of industry and exertion, and to bring home to every man's door an easy and ec-

onomical means of access to the most advantageous places of sale
and purchase." Yet they also saw how proximity to the Canal
brought boom and distance brought bust, how low toll rates
meant market advantage and high toll rates, market disadvan-
tage. Thousands of New Yorkers tried to hold the state to its
pledge to distribute the Canal's prosperity as equitably as possible. Like the citizens of Danube, they did not think they should
have to suffer while others profited from the Canal. One group
of petitioners interested in the lumber trade along the Champlain
Canal, for example, complained in 1828 about the state's decision to put a higher toll in effect on their canal two months
earlier than on the Erie. The petitioners "perceive[d] no good
reason for this discrimination."[16]

Businessmen, like farmers, expected the state to adhere to
their view of its moral obligations to its citizens. Some argued
that these obligations should mirror the obligations of individuals to one another. Complaining about the state's method of
calculating the weight of boats' cargoes, representatives from several forwarding companies argued that "transactions between the
public and individuals should be conducted in the same fair and
equitable principles that like transactions between individuals
would be." Especially as the Canal economy grew more complicated after 1835 with the enlargement project, businessmen began articulating a more precise set of moral imperatives, one that
tied them ever more closely to the state.[17]

The enlargement project brought a rash of petitions appealing
to the state's moral obligation to protect as well as promote its
citizens' commercial investments. While designed primarily to
widen and deepen the waterway, the enlargement also involved
minor rerouting of the Canal to improve navigation. Especially
since bigger boats would make their way along the broadened
waterway, sections of the Canal's original route were too winding
or otherwise treacherous. Even with the best intentions, the state
would have been unable to protect all the private investments

that had been made along the Canal's original route. Still, though, thousands of New Yorkers petitioned the Canal Board to live up to its citizens' "faith in the stability of the public works." They tried to persuade the state to retain the original route of the Canal where it bordered on their property, or at a minimum to compensate property owners along abandoned portions of the older route. Even New Yorkers who wanted a change in the route—so that it would run through their bypassed towns—acknowledged that the state had an obligation to try, whenever possible, to protect investments already made.[18]

To reroute the Canal away from a town was a serious affair, which state officials recognized. In the 1835 law authorizing the enlargement of the waterway, legislators had included a clause stipulating that "nothing in this section shall authorise the [canal] board to abandon the present canal through cities or villages" even when it did not seem advisable to enlarge the Canal along its original route. Instead, the board should maintain the old route as an "independent canal"—or a small section of canal separate from, but linked to, the enlarged Canal. The canal commissioners' annual report to the legislature in 1836, the first year of the enlargement project, describes two decisions reached by the board regarding the Canal's route. In the first case, the board decided that it had compelling reasons to alter the Canal's course over a distance of four miles: the new route required three fewer locks, which would greatly increase the speed of navigation while reducing the cost of lock-tending. These changes, in other words, served the larger public interest. But in the other case, the board decided not to abandon an old canal route because

the idea . . . of abandoning about thirteen miles of the present canal, where the damages to private property had been assessed and paid, where farms were arranged, buildings erected, private investments made, and business establishments created in reference to the canal, was calculated to make strong impressions against so material a change.

Citizens had made their investments based on the assumption that the Canal route would be permanent, an idea that made a "strong impression" indeed on state officials.[19]

In situations when it had to choose between providing equal opportunities to towns off the Canal and maintaining its implied contract with towns on the Canal, the government's stated policy was to honor its contracts. When a legislative committee investigated the request by a group from Schoharie and Greene counties to reroute the enlargement through their towns, for example, the committee found the petitioners' arguments persuasive. But the committee felt that its quasi-legal obligations pulled them in another direction. The government, the members wrote, had

> no wish or desire to disturb the present settled policy of the State regarding the Erie canal, or its present location, the contemplated alteration of the same by the Canal Commissioners in its enlargement, nor with the numerous public and private interests connected therewith. These propositions they consider as established; as sacred; and in conformity with the good faith of the State to all parties concerned.

When the state decided on a canal route, it made a "sacred"— almost a religious or moral—promise to its citizens, if not necessarily a legal one. The obligation benefited "all parties concerned." Even though the citizens of Schoharie and Greene counties would be denied their equal opportunities to benefit from the Canal, the assemblymen reasoned, they, too, should want to be governed by a state that takes seriously its commitments to its citizens.[20]

Sometimes, though, the desire to facilitate "progress" trumped the state's commitment to protect vested rights. Because the Canal Board did decide in some cases that it had compelling reasons to change a canal route, citizens such as George Folts suffered severe business losses as a result of state policy. Folts owned three acres of land along the north side of the old Erie

Canal next to the lock at Frankfort. He had constructed several buildings next to the lock, including a grocery store to service boat workers. His grocery had an ideal location: while their boats lined up to wait their turn at the locks, boat workers could gossip over mugs of beer in his shop. Even if the line to pass up the lock was short, workers could run into his store, buy refreshments, and jump back on the boat—all within a matter of minutes.

But when the state constructed the enlarged Erie Canal, it moved the locks slightly: they were still on Folts's three-acre plot, but not near his grocery. Folts would have to move his shop. Although he did not explain why, his reasons seem clear. Unless the grocery was within easy sight of the locks, workers might hesitate to linger in his store (with the temptation of buying more), afraid that they would miss spotting their boat's turn to pass through the locks. And boaters in a rush would not have time to stock up on essentials; they would wait until another lock, where the grocery stood closer to the canal banks. As a storekeeper in another town explained when the Canal Board considered moving the collector's office away from his storefront, he would be "used up as to business . . ."[21]

Folts petitioned the Canal Board in 1845 to compensate him for moving his grocery across his property so that it would stand adjacent to the new locks. The appraisers who investigated Folts's case did not believe that the state had a legal responsibility to compensate people for damage done by the abandonment of the Canal's original route. But the same state officials experienced "no surprise that such claims should be presented and urged by the Claimants, with a conviction of their justice . . ." Prevailing ideas about the state's moral obligations suggested that, out of fairness if not legal imperative, the state had either to maintain the route of public works or to compensate its citizens when it failed to do so. Unable to follow through on their own sense of justice, the appraisers encouraged Folts to petition the legislature for a private bill to settle his case. After several unsuccessful attempts, the state senate passed a bill awarding Folts monetary compensation in 1856—twelve years after his initial appeal to the Canal Board.[22]

Throughout the state, citizens with commercial interests tried to make the government live up to its stated policy of maintaining the Canal route. Faced with the threat of losing the Canal, even the businessmen of Schenectady had to admit that the Canal brought them a great deal of advantage. "Our knowledge of the power of the canal to do good," they announced in 1836, "leads us to dread more sensibly the desolation that would follow its removal." Once again, they based their appeals on the state's obligation to spread prosperity evenly. Incensed that the Common Council of Albany proposed rerouting the Canal away from Schenectady, the citizens of that town argued, "Our canals were made to . . . make the peculiar advantages of one section of country, as much as possible, common to all." Were the Canal's route changed, it would "destroy" their business prospects.[23]

Although most upstate businessmen would acknowledge that the state could change the Canal route for "good and substantial reasons," petitioners invariably failed to recognize the presence of such good reasons in cases where their business investments depended on the waterway's original route. When the board proposed changing the Canal route between Oriskany and Frankfort in 1836, the citizens of Frankfort resolved that "any material change in the location of the Erie Canal through this place would be destructive of its rights, interests, growth and prosperity injurious to the interest of the State and a violation of its plighted faith to its citizens." Some towns had raised money to maintain a piece of independent canal that might otherwise have been abandoned as a consequence of the enlargement, and they felt that by accepting their money, the state had agreed to keep the Canal open. When the canal commissioners announced their intention to abandon the Little Falls aqueduct even though townspeople had donated $10,000 as well as land to keep it in operation, residents of the town expressed their "convictions that the good faith of the state is virtually pledged to the preservation

of these works . . ." "Good faith" should guide state policy, even
when the obligation was moral, not legal.[24]

Businessmen argued that the state's implied obligation to
maintain established policies extended beyond issues related to
the Canal's route. In 1847, manufacturers of salt in Syracuse
objected to a proposed toll on fuel required for the salt works.
Their main grievance was that the toll would impose "a burthen
from which we have allways heretofore been exempt." Although
few others argued that their freight should be exempted from
tolls outright, some complained that the state violated their trust
when it raised tolls without adequate notice. By doing so, it
interfered with their established business practices. Forwarders
of merchandise competed to transport goods over the course of
the upcoming season. They based their fees, in part, on the tolls
that would be assessed on the goods to be transported. If the
Canal Board raised the toll after the forwarders had already drawn
up contracts, then the forwarders would not reap their expected
profits, since they could no longer pass along the costs. They
had a legal contract with their customers, and they felt as though
the state had almost as binding a one with them. When several
merchants contracted during the Canal's closed season to transport or purchase pine lumber, one petition noted, they had acted
"if not upon the implied faith, at least in the most confident
expectation, that the tolls would not be raised, until reasonable
notice was given." The state was perhaps within its legal rights
when it raised tolls, the petitioners maintained, but it had an
ethical obligation to avoid policies that added yet another risk
to commercial investment. It was difficult enough for businessmen to try to predict the caprices of the international market;
they did not think they should also be subjected to the vagaries
of state policies.[25]

Businessmen argued as well that the state could and should
guard them against other undesirable aspects of an extended market economy. When the Erie Canal connected the hinterlands of
New York to the Atlantic market, it transformed commercial
relations among upstate residents. As market transactions bur-

geoned and credit relations increased in complexity, the national economy experienced booms and busts, business enterprises appeared and disappeared overnight, and individuals weathered mercurial shifts in their financial well-being. Although this market instability affected the entire population, it had its most direct impact on the merchants and agents who facilitated market exchanges. A national shortage of cash, for example, limited the universal means of exchange for everyone, but it could devastate men whose livelihood depended on the flow of commerce. A rapid expansion of commercial activity, on the other hand, could bring quick wealth. Because the Erie Canal was the literal conduit of commercial exchange, New York State's businessmen argued that the state should use the Canal to enhance market growth while limiting the potential for busts. If the Canal Board had no control over the flux of international business cycles, it did have the power to make other decisions that could significantly alter an individual's or a community's commercial prospects.[26]

By acting in good faith, according to Canal Board petitioners, the state could help insulate its citizens from financial ruin. The economic mobility accompanying the market revolution worked in two directions, up and down. From his humble beginnings as one of the first small-time merchants in Lockport, for example, Lyman Spalding rose to become one of the city's wealthiest and most prominent citizens. In 1825, a few years after opening his shop along the Canal's banks, Spalding bought land along the Lockport basin, where he established a flour mill propelled by the Canal's surplus waters. When the state ruled a few years later that those waters legally belonged to his neighbors, Spalding tried to link his personal fortune (he valued his mill at $60,000 by 1830) to that of the greater good: financial ruin threatened not just a businessman and his family but also the workers he employed. By stopping the water flow to Spalding's mill, he argued, the state had made his investments "unproductive, and more than fifty persons [were] out of employment some of whom had families depending on support for their daily wages." Moreover, farmers within a ten-mile radius, he claimed, relied on his mill for their grinding. The Canal Board did not find his appeal persuasive, but Spalding took the losses in stride, sold his property, and bought another piece of land along the Lockport basin, where he set up a new mill.[27]

By 1841, Spalding's milling business was thriving once again when a devastating fire at his mill led him to declare bankruptcy. Although Spalding's accounts of his life make no reference to what followed immediately afterward, other records indicate that he violated the terms of his bankruptcy and ended up spending several months in the Niagara County jail. But by September 1842, he was able to purchase his old mill and note, "Commenced my own work again—after passing through the fiery ordeal of Bankruptcy." He had lost seventeen years of earnings, the huge sum of $100,000. Yet he shrugged off these ordeals in his diary: "No matter—I can try it again. My health & spirits are good as new." Showing a remarkable faith in upward mobility, and the continued prosperity of the Canal, Spalding decided to continue in the milling business. During these years, Spalding also became an active member of the Whig Party, clearly drawn to its rhetoric of mobility and its ardent support of government-sponsored economic development.[28]

For the next twenty years, Spalding's milling business had its ups and, mostly, its downs—and Spalding finally blamed the state for failing to protect him from ruin. In 1860 and 1861, he claimed to the Canal Board that the wintertime diversion of water from his mill during the twenty-two-year enlargement project near Lockport left him on the brink of poverty. Although he did move his family to a smaller house in 1858, Spalding appears to have lived the rest of his life in comfort, if not his earlier opulence. The Canal's surplus waters (which he had misappropriated on several occasions) had led to his rapid financial success, and their diversion had led to his gradual decline. Spalding's attempt to hold the state responsible for his losses is somewhat curious. He had made the decision to repurchase his mill in 1842, four years after the enlargement project had stopped the wintertime flow of water, yet he blamed the state, not himself, for his impending financial ruin. Once the Canal Board had supplied his mill site with water, Spalding implied, the state was obliged either to continue the flow of water or to offer material compensation for its failure to do so. In at least two important ways, Spalding typified antebellum entrepreneurs: his fortune was unsteady, and he thought it would be reasonable, or at least worth a try, to hold the state responsible for allocating its resources in ways that would have helped prevent his financial decline.[29]

Businessmen frequently cried "ruin" when they wanted to persuade the government to maintain the public works to protect their private investments. They wrote to state officials to say that changes in canal policy would result in their "utter ruin," "loss of their all," or the "destruction of their property." Arguing in 1836 that the state should keep a lock where it was, residents of Lyons claimed that removing the lock would "prove highly injurious and almost ruinous to those enterprising Citizens who have erected permanent, convenient and expensive buildings for business in the vicinity of the Lock." On the back of the petition, a member of the Canal Board marked, "Not removed." When inhabitants of the village of Geddes, near Syracuse, complained in 1838 that "there are sixteen salt manufactories erected on the canal in this village which will be rendered nearly valueless if the canal be lowered five feet in the enlargement thereof," the Canal Board granted their request to pursue the enlargement in a different manner.[30]

That such laments were so frequent—and that state officials found some of these appeals persuasive (though not Lyman Spalding's)—suggests that prevailing wisdom held that the government should consider businessmen's financial fortunes when determining its canal policy, even if it would cost the state additional money. A petition against changing the route of the Canal away from Kirkville asserted that "in our opinion the wealthy State of NYork are better able to Suffer a Small Loss which they will not feel than a few worthy citizens to loose their

all and leave them pennyless and without support . . ." From
the project's outset, the claimants remembered, state officials had
made clear that their primary aim was to spur economic development and spread economic prosperity—and not to maximize
the state's financial return on its investment. Businessmen
thought the government could afford canal policies that shielded
its "enterprising" citizens from certain effects of unrestrained
capitalism. When the state became involved in economic development, its citizens believed, it also took on the responsibility
of attempting to ensure that their financial mobility would only
be upward. That was their idea of progress.[31]

Businessmen, with very few exceptions, were unembarrassed by
their desire to pursue wealth beyond the minimum needed for a
comfortable existence. When they pushed for a canal route or
toll schedule, they boldly admitted their financial interest in
seeing a certain course of action adopted. Yet they also realized
that in a system based on the pursuit of profit, the public purse
was at constant risk of being sacrificed to individual gain. Businessmen therefore tried to convince state authorities that policies
which benefited them would also promote the common good,
though their understanding of the common good bore the influence of Whig rather than Democratic ideology. In exchange for
the state's efforts to maintain their economic stability, businessmen assumed—rhetorically, if not necessarily in practice—their
own moral responsibilities.

   Diversity within the business classes, of course, meant that
financial aspirations varied widely. Some pointed to how the construction of a particular canal route would preserve their "large
investments" or otherwise maintain the value of their real estate
speculations. In 1845, for example, a group of merchants and
forwarders in Albany petitioned against the proposed change of
location of the collector's office in that city. The current location
was more central, and "time is money & it will be a serious tax
upon the business community to be obliged to send to a remote

part of the City to enter & clear boats and pay tolls." Yet while some businessmen talked of preserving their sizable investments, small-time merchants often had more modest aspirations. When the state did not properly maintain a city bridge across the Canal in Rochester, one man who owned and rented out business plots in the vicinity informed the canal authorities that he was "dependent upon my Rents to support a large family." For many small businessmen, their canalside property was the foundation of their livelihood; their groceries or warehouses provided them with cash incomes to reduce their debts and feed their families.[32]

While all businessmen were eager to profit, many professed a belief in certain moral limitations on their pursuit of wealth: they should not ask the state to harm anyone else's economic prospects. To bolster their claims to the Canal Board, businessmen therefore regularly accused one another of doing just that, of trying to profit at someone else's expense or trying to create a "monopoly." They condemned one another for being "interested and designing" or operating out of "the blind spirit of avarice." They told canal officials, in other words, that their adversaries had violated the moral limits on enterprise. State officials generally agreed that such accusations were serious. A legislative committee investigating a dispute over the location of a Rochester basin in 1839 dismissed one of the parties involved for trying to "subserve some selfish ends . . ." It was not the desire to profit that was selfish; it was the desire to profit at another's expense. As an observer of a controversy over the Brockport collector's office noted, although some of the people involved made a proposal based on selfish interests, "it is a selfishness that is not calculated to injure any one else in the slightest degree . . ."[33]

The pursuit of profit became even more justifiable when it contributed to the general welfare. Even as they admitted their financial interests, businessmen emphasized the broader worthiness of their preferred canal policies. They attempted to identify their private gain with the communal good. When the citizens of Rochester pushed state officials to speed up the enlargement construction through their town, which meant allocating additional public resources to ensure their prosperity, they reminded their audience, "If there ever was a public work diffusive in the benefits it confers—in which an entire state was deeply interested, it is the ERIE CANAL. The benefits of other public works may be partial and local; no such objection can be proferred against this." What was good for the business interests of Rochester, in other words, was good for New York State. Nearly every petition to the Canal Board, in fact, suggested that the interest of the state, the "public," or the "community" would be served by the adoption of the petitioners' requests.[34]

Upstate businessmen understood the state's interest as resting on two related issues: revenue-raising, and protecting New York's internal improvement projects from the competition of private railroads and the public works of other states. Goods diverted from the Erie Canal to competing transportation meant revenue lost to New York State. Although canal officials repeatedly avowed that revenue-raising was not an end in itself, the state did need to pay off its debts and meet its expenses. Those obligations, moreover, grew ever more urgent during the financial difficulties of the late 1830s and early 1840s, which were brought on partly by the state's investment in side canals whose costs invariably exceeded the direct revenue they generated.

Businessmen's interest in the state's well-being stemmed in part from a recognition that what was good for the state was also good for them. The government's economic health very much influenced their prospects. In an immediate sense, should the state's financial difficulties cause the Canal to slip into disrepair, businessmen would suffer from the ensuing delays in navigation. Businessmen argued that by following merchants' suggestions to lower the tolls on the produce they shipped, the Canal Board would also enrich the state coffers. A standard argument for lowering tolls suggested that by reducing tolls, the state would actually increase its income through increased volume. By raising the market price of an item, businessmen explained, high tolls lessened demand, which in turn reduced the toll revenue.

High toll rates also led forwarding merchants to ship produce and goods by alternative routes—either canals in other states or railroads—which meant a loss of toll revenue altogether. A prominent Rochester merchant told the Canal Board in 1860 that he had 20,000 bushels of potatoes and apples in a storehouse and that he had planned to ship them to New York City by canal. But then he added, "Of course at present rates of Toll [I] Shall Ship by Rail Road." Because high toll rates encouraged merchants to ship by alternative transportation, agreed citizens from Orleans County, "the canals will derive little, if any benefit" from the large fruit and potato crop in western New York. Just as businessmen recognized that their well-being was linked to the state's economy, they reminded the state that its welfare depended on the support of businessmen.[35]

When arguing for a particular canal route, businessmen made similar arguments about benefits to the state's financial welfare. By constructing the Canal along a route that favored their commercial activity, businessmen explained, the state would increase the traffic of goods subject to toll collection. Other petitioners claimed that the route they proposed for the Canal would cost less to construct than the alternatives: it was shorter, or ran through easier terrain, or was less likely to injure private property and subject the state to a flurry of damage claims. Even if New Yorkers expected their government to lose a few pennies to save their private investments, they still recognized that the state's purse was not bottomless.

In addition to their appeals to the state's financial interest, Canal corridor businessmen made continual reference to the government's moral duties and its commitment to promoting the common good. In its broadest sense, entrepreneurs defined the common good as "the greatest good for the greatest numbers" or the "accommodation and good of all." They argued that by adopting policies that suited their private interests, the state could promote the common good. Because changes in the Canal route put the financial fortunes of proprietors like George Folts in jeopardy, other businessmen found it difficult to justify morally their desire to have the Canal rerouted through their towns or property. The state had made clear that its obligation to the established route should be considered "sacred"—unless truly compelling circumstances suggested otherwise.[36]

Nonetheless, towns located off the original waterway eagerly took advantage of any small opportunity that provided compelling reasons to change the waterway's route, any opportunity that would allow them to justify rerouting the Canal away from another location for their own benefit. They argued that by rerouting the Canal through their town, the state would make navigation safer and easier. Or if the state moved the collector's office to a different building, its policy would "not only be more conducive to the general interests of the Village, but would add greatly to the convenience as well as facilitate the business of the boating community." By advocating policies that would promote the broader good, businessmen hoped they had found a moral justification for pushing their commercial benefit at someone else's expense.[37]

The common good also had a further nuance for businessmen, one that illustrates how they differed from the freeholders who identified their personal good with the common weal. Farmers had argued that a bridge across their property would benefit their neighbors as well as themselves; their own good was part of the common good, and the common good embraced the interests of all property-owning farmers. But while businessmen paid rhetorical homage to the common good, they tended to emphasize that proposed changes to the Canal would promote the "industrious classes." Some businessmen asserted that if the state built a bridge near their shops, it would also help "Mechanics, machenists and labourers" to get to the mills where they worked; the absence of the bridge was a "daily & repeated hardship and injury." It may not have been coincidence that their logic in these claims very closely paralleled the decision in the *Charles River Bridge* case, which the U.S. Supreme Court finally decided one year into the enlargement project. While the circumstances of that case did not directly match the issues that arose in the Canal corridor, upstate businessmen knew that identifying the promotion of venture capital with the interests of mechanics would resonate within the prevailing legal and political climate.[38]

Some businessmen suggested that what benefited them would help not just the industrious classes but also the least-fortunate members of society, the very poor. Thus one petitioner urged a lowering in the toll rate on firewood "if for no other reason, certainly for its bearings on the poor." Business would benefit from increase sales, but—more important—the poor would have access to fuel for warmth against the bitter upstate winters. One group of businessmen even argued that the state should build a dock near their places of business solely so that "the unimployed laborers in this vicinity may be relieved of some of the miserable hardships to which the[y] are Exposed. . . ." Lower toll rates, claimed others, would spur production and provide employment to hundreds or even "tens of thousands." By serving the needs of business, in short, the state would help the merchant classes to meet their obligations to the broader public.[39]

Businessmen, like farmers, noted that the public welfare rested on more than economic opportunities. As one group of citizens arguing against moving the route of the Canal from their towns reminded the government, "The public health is as closely allied with the welfare of the State as its commerce . . ." Businessmen drew especially on issues of public morality to push the worthiness of their causes. In 1842, for example, one group of citizens in Schenectady who owned and rented property in an area called the Battle Ground petitioned the Canal Board to move the collector's office to that part of town. But another group of businessmen argued against relocating the office. They phrased their argument in terms of the state's obligation to safeguard the character of the notoriously wayward boat workers. The Battle Ground, they argued, was "decide[d]ly the most loathsome and filthy place in our city," a crime-ridden area that was "almost entirely occupied for Rum Shops, gambling & baudy houses, according to public fame." By favoring their location, they argued by implication, the state could serve the "boating community" by steering it away from a location known as a haven for filth, licentiousness, and intemperance. Drawing on a similar association of alcohol with immorality, other businessmen suggested that lower toll rates on certain grains would encourage farmers to produce foodstuffs rather than liquor. Rochester's civic leaders petitioned for a bridge near business properties, noting that the bridge would also provide a convenient route to churches. By arguing that those policies which would fill their pocketbooks would also serve public morality, businessmen implied that there were altruistic components to their requests.[40]

The business classes identified themselves more with the government than with the general public. Businessmen offered to form a partnership with the state; in exchange for policies promoting their economic growth, they would advise the state on how to fill its treasury and provide economic opportunities to the laboring classes. Theirs was a paternalistic view: together, the state and business would govern the political economy in a way that would offer citizens economic opportunities and moral guidance; in return, these leaders expected hard work and deference. Such a partnership between the state and business, as we have seen, is just what many farmers suspected—and feared. Farmers with modest landholdings criticized the state for failing to live up to what they saw as its obligation to protect their property's agricultural value, failing—in a sense—to live up to its role as paternal protector. In response to what they saw as the state's failings, they withdrew their deference, attacked the state's morality, and criticized it for abusing constitutional principles of governance.

In the market morality that entrepreneurs espoused —but did not always practice—their individual interest was supposed to be in harmony with the public good and the interests of other classes, such as farmers and laborers. The public welfare became a moral obligation, something that businessmen—as claimants to greater vision if not always greater wealth—owed. Their rhetoric, in this sense, echoed that of the Whig Party. They saw themselves as the "aristocracy of nature," talented and virtuous men who had risen to the top of a social order nurtured, ironically, not by nature but by the artificial river. In their view of the political economy, it became their duty to help to uplift the less "worthy" people below them on the social ladder. Progress, in their view, did not mean an egalitarian society but rather one in which anyone would have the opportunity to improve in all senses: economic, political, social, religious. Any native-born white man could prove himself worthy of the role of paternal overseer of public virtue. With this same sense of obligation to promote public morality, some businessmen—along with their wives, daughters, and sons—would support a full-scale assault on what they saw as the vice and depravity of the boating community.

6

The Perils of Progress

W HEN MERCHANTS pointed fervently to the social value of
their endeavors, they were responding to growing worries
that upstate New York teetered on the brink of moral break-
down. Despite the promises of the waterway's sponsors, it had
become clear that the United States could not develop its commerce without serious human costs. From a middle-class perspective, the Canal had become a haven for vice and immorality;
the towpaths attracted workers who drank, swore, whored, and
gambled. And unlike canal diggers, who moved on, boat workers
remained. These canallers provided a daily reminder of what fluid
market relations—and progress—could bring.

Most disturbing of all to the middle classes, children (mostly
boys) made up more than a quarter of the workforce. In an era
when Northern communities placed increasing emphasis on
schooling as a supplement to moral education in the home, these
boys—sometimes as young as six, though on average eleven or
twelve years old—found themselves separated from their homes
and without access to formal education. Most of them worked
as drivers, handling the horses that pulled the boats. Even those
who worked as boat hands, scrubbing decks or keeping towing
ropes untangled, learned few skills that they could later apply
to a trade. What sort of men—and citizens—would these boys
grow up to be? And what sort of mothers would cabin girls
grow up to be, given that, by reputation at least, they were often
maids or cooks during the day and prostitutes at night? How

could such girls be expected to instill virtue in the following generation? Middle-class reformers began accusing merchants of undermining the country's moral future for immediate monetary gain. "With you it rest to say," one group of reformers reminded the merchants of Rochester, "let these waters be pure; let the canal be a proud monument to the passing stranger, as well as of our public virtues as of our commercial enterprize, or let it prove to all that we recklessly sacrifice our country's good and the very souls of these youth to our views of personal advantage." Inspired by the evangelical revivalism of the Second Great Awakening, upstate reformers not only tried to save the souls of canal workers; they also pressured merchants to live up to their promise to be the moral guardians of a political economy based on market expansion and progress.[1]

By the 1840s, thirty thousand men, women, and children labored day and night to keep the artificial river in operation. Within a decade or two, this throng of workers had helped to transform upstate New York into a bustling commercial corridor, where the main economic activity was moving goods and people. To move a single keg of oysters from Albany to Buffalo required scores of strong bodies and able clerks. When the oysters landed at Albany, having passed up the Hudson from the Atlantic, an "along-shore-man" (a "longshoreman") unloaded them from a river-going vessel and reloaded them onto a wagon. The cartman hauled the keg to the Canal's banks, where another longshoreman hoisted it onto a freight boat. The forwarding agent responsible for transferring the keg from its previous owner to its new purchaser had already informed the boat's captain of the cargo's destination and had made arrangements for payment. After receiving the keg and recording its contents on his bill of lading, the captain hollered to his two crew mates to prepare to shove off. Hearing the captain's order, a foreman from a towing company dispatched two drivers to harness their horses to the boat's towrope.[2]

Workers near the entrance of the Erie Canal into the Hudson
(John Hill, 1830s, Collection of the New-York Historical Society)

Within minutes of casting off, the steersman directed the boat into the Albany weigh lock, where state workers cradled the boat onto a hydraulic scale while a clerk prepared a paper showing the boat's current weight as well as its weight when it had been weighed empty or "light" at the beginning of the season, and then calculated the weight of the freight it carried. A boat inspector next verified the captain's bill of lading by inspecting the cargo. After leaving the weigh station, the boat passed through twenty-seven locks in the first thirty miles; by the end of its journey to Buffalo it would pass through a total of eighty-three. Each lock employed one or two lock tenders to open and close the gates that sent water rushing into or out of the locks, thus lifting or lowering the boat and carrying it to a level even with the next stretch of Canal. At the seventeen toll offices along the route, clerks made certain that the captain carried the Albany toll collector's clearance, the paper recording the amount of toll paid and the weight and contents of the boat. In Buffalo, a longshoreman unloaded the keg of oysters and handed it over to a cartman, who waited for an agent of the merchant forwarding company to give him instructions on where to haul it.[3]

The men, women, and children who worked to keep New York's 3,400 canal boats in motion represented virtually all segments of society. The jobs of repair superintendent and toll collector were doled out by political patronage and went to well-connected citizens. Those boat captains who owned their vessels, hired their own crews, and contracted with their own customers also found themselves toward the upper end of the social hierarchy; these entrepreneurs (almost exclusively male) generally came from rural areas of the upstate region or New England. Other captains worked for monthly wages and came from the ranks of displaced farmers, aspiring businessmen, and ambitious boat hands. One contemporary observed that "the masters of the boats are often taken from the ploughs . . ." These captains drew their crews—the lower rung of the Canal's social ladder—from the large pool of available laborers. Recent immigrants swelled the ranks of canal laborers in the 1840s. Throughout the antebellum period, though, boat hands were both native-born and foreign, rural and urban, white and black, adult and minor, male and female (though overwhelmingly male).[4]

Some canal employees received their wages from the state, others from private employers. The state hired lock tenders, toll collectors, and repair workers. Boat owners, either companies or individuals, engaged crews. Boat companies also paid men to work in their offices, recruit passengers, and solicit shipping customers. Towing companies paid boys (and at least a few girls disguised as boys) to lead the horses that pulled the boats. Simply put, the state built, maintained, and operated the waterway, while merchants and their workers transported freight and passengers.[5]

Many others contributed to the Canal's operation, even though they did not directly handle either boats or freight. Farmers grew oats to feed the canal horses or tended the animals between towing trips and over the winter months. Rural women boarded and fed some of the boys who led the horses. Blacksmiths made shoes for the horses' feet. Craftsmen joined farmhands in providing emergency labor to repair the frequent breaches in the Canal's banks. But when contemporaries referred to "boatmen," "watermen," or "canallers," they meant those people whose physical labor directly contributed to the movement of goods and people along the artificial river: the boat crews, animal drivers, long-shoremen, and lock tenders.[6]

These workers, according to widespread belief, posed a threat to civilized society. Middle-class observers portrayed them as profane, lewd, and violent. Most middle-class New Yorkers would probably have agreed with Daniel Wandell, a resident of Watervliet, who told the Canal Board in 1839 that "the Boys who Drive the horses I think I may safely say that they these boys are the most profain beings that now exist on the face of this hole erth without exception." So prevalent was the negative reputation of canal workers that some transportation companies felt compelled to advertise that *their* workers were nothing but responsible and polite. The narrator of *Marco Paul's Travels on the Erie Canal,* a children's instructional novel published in 1843, noted that "the man who had charge of the lock looked very rough and ill-natured, as was very often the case, in respect to the workmen along the canal." Because the man was just a "common laborer," the story continued, he probably performed his tasks without understanding how the locks worked. Common labor dulled a man's senses, and middle-class boys like Marco Paul should study hard so that their "formation of character" would allow them to pursue more intellectual endeavors than the degrading work of opening and closing locks. Not only did the middle classes scorn canal workers; they tried to instill in their children a fear of becoming one of these rough, profane workers. Middle-class boys, in other words, should work hard to make themselves cultured and intelligent, lest they, too, join the masses of uncivilized and disdained boys working on the Canal.[7]

The Canal's reputation as a magnet for delinquents was, like many stereotypes, partially grounded in reality. Contemporary newspapers carried numerous reports of assaults, robberies, rapes, and murders on the Canal or its towpath. More routinely, police arrested canal workers for intoxication, fighting, creating nuisances, vandalism, and soliciting sex. In 1837, according to a state report, about one-quarter of the inmates in the Auburn State Prison had "followed the canals." Even the Canal Board acknowledged that boatmen did not always respect the property of others. When Pardon Thompson appealed to the board for compensation because, he argued, the Canal had diverted water that he might have used to run a mill, the board denied his claim mostly on the ground that neither he nor any previous tenants had ever constructed a mill on the property. But in their general assessment of the value of Thompson's land—which was near but not adjacent to the Canal—the appraisers added that his property value had in part been sustained by its "lying at such a distance from the Canal, as to prevent it from those depridations, which are not infrequently committed by Boatmen, on land lying contiguous to the Canals . . ." David Hughes, a farmer who did own land directly along the Canal, complained in his diary that boat drivers stole eggs and fruit—perhaps the sort of depredations that the Canal Board had in mind. Hughes did not regret that the Canal had been built in front of his property, for he derived much of his income from growing oats to sell to towing companies. But he made it clear that he wanted nothing to do with the boatmen. After keeping a group of boat drivers in his home overnight, Hughes did not specify what offenses they had committed, but he did exclaim, "I hope that we never will be oblige to log aney more of the drivars!!!"[8]

Some contemporary observers took care to recognize that not all canal workers deserved condemnation. During a trip on the Canal in 1835, Clarissa Burroughs implicitly compared the crew of one boat to workers she had previously encountered. "The hour of rest is announced by the appearance of a steward & a cabin maid, which every one dreads, but this boat was clean, and the attendants obliging and attentive, which rendered it more tolerable . . ." Harriet Loring, who traveled on the Canal a decade later, noted that a cabin maid was a "very fine girl" but that "the depravity of the drivers is dreadful." Travelers' complimentary remarks about certain workers lend credibility to their descriptions of other workers whose behavior violated middle-class notions of propriety.[9]

If the middle classes, from farmers to merchants, were joined together in their quest to maintain social order, they did not agree on strategies for doing so. When, for example, the New York State Legislature received thirty-three petitions in 1825 asking for a law prohibiting Sunday travel on the Canal, some citizens replied in a counterpetition that less harm would come from violating the Sabbath than from having boatmen congregate onshore during an idle day. The legislature ultimately agreed. Members of the committee investigating the issue argued that the Canal should remain open on Sundays, in part because

> the boats on the canals are numerous, and should the locks be closed on the Sabbath, vast numbers would throng the canal above and below, and many persons from on board would resort to the taverns, grog shops and houses of ill fame, that would soon abound in the vicinity of the locks, and most of the vices which degrade and debase mankind would no doubt be encreased to a much greater extent than if the boats were permitted to pass.

Throughout the antebellum period, pious New Yorkers continued to debate whether greater moral harm would result from allowing depraved workers to come ashore than from requiring them to work on the Lord's day.[10]

Some canal workers, it seems, intentionally cultivated images of themselves as morally and physically dangerous. Herman Melville, who had traveled on the Canal and who may have briefly worked on it in the 1840s, described boat workers through the voice of one of his characters in *Moby-Dick*: "the brigandish guise which the Canaller so proudly sports; his slouched and gaily-ribboned hat between his grand features. A terror to the smiling innocence of the villages through which he floats; his swarthy visage and bold swagger are not unshunned in cities." As Melville suggests, some boat workers proudly adhered to their canaller ways. Drinking, swearing, and fighting were part of their culture, a way of life they had no desire to shed. Many boys came to the Canal in search of wages, adventure, and freedom from family restraints; they did not invest their work with any larger social aspirations. Rather than signing on as apprentices learning a trade, these boys took up jobs that offered them few skills and little fatherly oversight from their bosses. When these boat workers hurled curses at "ladies" on passing boats or tore down fences on surrounding farms, they flouted middle-class notions of propriety and respect for property.[11]

If a quest for adventure and independence drove some boys and young men to take jobs on the Canal, others came out of desperation. Many canal drivers, in particular, found themselves in dire circumstances. These boys usually had few occupational skills and came from poor families. Reformers estimated, moreover, that half the drivers were orphans. Although some boys might have falsely claimed to be orphans to win pity or to prevent reformers from sending them home, it nonetheless seems that a high percentage of the children working on the Canal were parentless. Recording a conversation with a fourteen-year-old driver, one reformer noted how the boy had been an orphan for the past three years. A poor but generous man had looked after him, finally telling him "that he was big enough, he must earn his own living; he had come to the canal for that purpose."[12]

These boys often met with poor treatment on the Canal. Many boat captains, reformers agreed, abused their drivers. Sufficient numbers tried to cheat their drivers out of their wages that reformers proposed that the state set up a registry of all drivers under twenty so that officials could make sure that captains honored their contracts with them. They also proposed monitoring

the boys' places of work and rest, since so many of their employers exposed them to dangerous and unhealthy conditions.
Boat drivers, for example, often went shoeless and dressed in
meager cotton garments that provided little protection from the
cold or rain. After traveling on the Canal through a heavy rain-
storm, one boat passenger commented, "The poor driver I guess
is nearly as wet as if he had been swimming in the Canal." When
one boat captain discovered that one of his workers had cholera,
a reformer reported, he pushed the youngster off the boat and
left him to die on the towpath.[13]

Most of the boat drivers slept on the floors of barns or in the
cargo holds of boats, and ate few regular meals. They went for
long periods without an uninterrupted night's sleep. Bugles
sounded in the middle of the night to alert them to the arrival
of a boat needing a change of horses. Moses Holden and his team,
for example, pulled the boat *William Tell* up to a station barn
at eleven-fifteen one evening. After cleaning and feeding Jake
and Farmer (the horses), eating a quick supper of crackers, and
bantering with the other boys at the barn, Moses would not have
slept very long before being awakened to pull out the boat *Wodworth* at five-twenty in the morning. After pulling the *Wodworth*
for ten to twelve miles, or between six and seven hours, Holden
would have arrived at another station barn around noon. He
would have rested for a few hours before starting on another ten-
to-twelve-mile shift. Although he sometimes rested in a barn for
as long as eight or nine hours, at other times his rest, which
included tending to the horses in his charge, was as short as two
or three hours. If he dozed off while riding his horse, he risked
enraging the boat captain, whose goal was to make as quick time
as possible so that he could deposit one cargo and pick up another. By responding to unreasonable treatment with insolence,
workers could maintain some sense of self-esteem. One young
horse driver told a missionary, "We can't help but swear when
the Captain comes off, and swearing at us, jerks us off the horse
and kicks us because we did not pass some boat, or do something
else just to his liking."[14]

Fatigue, especially when combined with alcohol, led to accidents. And alcohol was plentiful on the Canal. According to detailed reports kept by reformers, more than fifteen hundred grog shops lined the Erie's banks in 1835. That figure converted to a staggering average of one tavern or grocery (an alcohol-selling concern) every quarter mile. One traveler reported seeing thirteen "broad and blazing signs" for groceries from a single canalside vantage point. While waiting for their boats to pass through locks, workers visited these establishments, where they did not drink in moderation—making it difficult for them to perform their work. Snared towropes pulled drivers into the Canal, and missteps plunged boat workers and longshoremen into the water. In an era when many people never learned how to swim, a tumble into the seven-foot-deep enlarged Canal could prove fatal. According to reformers, the combination of employers' disregard for their employees' well-being and the boat workers' own intemperate habits contibuted to the canallers' short life expectancy, which did "not on average exceed twelve years after they embark[ed] in the watermen's employment."[15]

During the winter, when the Canal closed down for four or five months, these boys' lives became tougher, as their employers left them to forage for themselves. The boys lost not only their incomes but their sources of shelter—their boats and barns. Wintertime brought seasonal unemployment for many occupations, not just boat workers, so finding another job during the frigid, blizzardy months was virtually impossible. In December 1843, a Syracuse newspaper reported that " a number of young boys, whose business on the canals is now ended for the season, are loafing about the city, without a place to sleep, or money to purchase food or clothing." Desperate for a warm place to sleep and daily meals, some canal workers tried, successfully, to get themselves locked up as vagrants.[16]

Most captains assumed no paternal responsibilities for their young workers. Since many, in fact, treated their employees more like animals than like sons, it is not surprising that these children felt little respect for the middle classes. Having no paternal bonds with family or bosses, many of these workers saw no need to behave deferentially. They would respond to disrespect with disrespect for middle-class mores. That canal workers were quite capable of temporarily shedding their profanity in deference to missionaries who showed concern for them suggests that at least some intentionally adopted vulgar and profane demeanors in other situations. Unlike their critics, not all canallers agreed that middle-class manners set the standard for which they should necessarily strive.

Boat workers formed a distinct class; and in doing so, they provided a fearsome reminder that the Canal might not, after all, be a tribute to republicanism. "This rapid growth of ours into a great commercial nation," noted one group of concerned citizens, "has been attended by all those evils that have always heretofore accompanied an extended commerce." The expansion of commerce had created a degraded class of workers who seemed unfit for republican citizenship. By middle-class standards, they were non-productive and shiftless. A writer whose sympathies lay with the workers protested that "boating is in reality as necessary, as honest and as honorable an occupation as any other, but still it is almost universally cried down, and Boatmen are regarded as a low class in society." Those boatmen who swore, drank, and fought (the most common complaints against them) violated Christian definitions of respectable behavior and, in the words of one reformer, "seem[ed] to be regarded as outcasts." While middle-class boys might have engaged in such behavior to create a "social space of their own," these decidedly working-class canal boys and men did not simply assume the role of social outcasts; they *were* outcasts.[17]

Canal workers were not the only Americans who lived in filthy and diseased surroundings, who drank excessively, or who rejected middle-class mores. With the revolutions in manufacturing and marketing—revolutions set off in large part by the expansion of internal improvements—more and more Americans found themselves working for wages and subject to the whims of bosses with whom they shared no personal connections. Cultural independence provided them with some consolation for their precarious economic conditions. While canallers sported their "gaily-ribboned" hats, boys and girls in New York City's Bowery jolted the middle classes with their own flamboyant clothing. Such independence frightened the middle classes, especially as politics became more democratic. If these rowdy workers would not defer to middle-class social customs, they also could not be counted on to defer at the polls. These were not the sort of citizens whom DeWitt Clinton envisioned when he outlined his plan for progress.[18]

Had canallers been utterly unlike other antebellum workers, they might have caused less concern. Instead, they seemed to represent the future of commercial society, and that was an aspect of progress that many middle-class upstaters had hoped they could avoid. One might expect to find thugs and prostitutes in crowded port cities, but the country's interior—its middle landscape—was supposed to be more pure. Whatever boatmen's aspirations, the middle classes—broadly defined—tended to see them as dangerous, ungodly, even subhuman. If such workers represented the way of the future, then how would the United States ever achieve its special destiny?

The first few decades of the canal era coincided with the Second Great Awakening. Rural women and men by the thousands attended camp meetings, where they slept out for days at a time to hear the fiery sermons of revivalist preachers. Their urban counterparts, meanwhile, attended daily church services and prayer meetings, sometimes for months on end. Whether delivered under a tent in the forest or from a church pulpit, the revivalist preachers' exhortations resulted in thousands upon thousands of loud and sometimes physically dramatic conversions. These men and women believed that by perfecting their own wayward behavior—and by helping to convert their sinning brothers and sisters—they could hasten the onset of the millennium, a period of one thousand years of peace on earth preceding the Second Coming of Christ.

Although the Awakening's revival surfaced nationwide during

the late eighteenth and early nineteenth centuries, evangelicalism peaked in western New York in the late 1820s, just a few years after New Yorkers had applied an almost equal fervor to their celebrations of the Erie's completion. The Canal ran down the center of the "Burned-Over District," the region south of Lake Ontario through which evangelical fires were raging. When Charles Finney, one of the era's most prominent revivalist preachers, christened the region the Burned-Over District, he spoke from firsthand knowledge: the greatest successes of his circuit took place in towns along the Erie Canal, particularly in the city of Rochester.[19]

While a variety of social and economic changes wrought by the Canal helped to make the region ripe for religious revival, not least among them was the presence of such an enormous and unruly assemblage of wage workers. When Josiah Bissell, a Rochester merchant and land speculator, invited Finney to preach in that new city in 1829, he pressed the urgency of his case by focusing on the canal workers' depravity. Bissell wrote to Finney of a canal line which, in one season, "dismissed nine women from their boats in a stage of pregnancy." According to the report of one boat captain, a driver "might as well be sent to the state prison as to the Canal. That at 12 years old they are sometimes diseased by their unlawful lives—these are only specimens of a large budget of evil rolling thro our land & among us." To Bissell and others, pregnant girls and diseased boys provided vivid examples of the extensive moral decay accompanying the expansion of transportation and commerce. The boats that transported luxuries to the country's interior also carried moral degradation with them.[20]

Canal workers, simply by their daily presence, threatened both Jacksonian and Whig visions of progress. Reformers warned that the consequences of neglecting the spiritual welfare of boatmen would be far-reaching. These workers not only spread vice over space and into the country's interior; they also threatened to spread it over time as well. As one reformer fretted, "It is high time something efficient should be done upon the lines of our canals, particularly the great Western Canal [i.e., the Erie]; otherwise the vices of its population will soon become too firmly rooted to be eradicated, except by the destruction and perdition of one whole generation." In a millennial age, when many Christians thought they could usher in God's kingdom on earth by converting fellow sinners, the possibility of losing a whole generation to depravity was of great consequence. Moreover, reformers warned that without "moral improvement," boat workers would undermine economic expansion. Unless conditions on the Canal improved, they argued, "steady, honest, and respectable persons, of both sexes, will refuse to be employed on the canal. You will be reduced to the necessity of entrusting your business to the dregs of the community . . . " Reformers reminded the middle classes that the streams of religious, social, and commercial progress could not be separated.[21]

The revivals of the 1820s ignited a concerted effort to reform wayward boat workers, a reform movement that crossed denominational lines and enlisted the help of paid missionaries as well as lay people. Caught up in the evangelical fervor inspired by Finney and others, some middle-class New Yorkers donated money and time to help bring depraved and degraded canal workers into God's fold. They joined together in associations that offered material relief to workers while trying to change the boatmen's ungodly habits. Through reform, they thought it possible "for a canal driver to make a man"—to become a "respectable," God-fearing citizen.[22]

Reformers interested in boatmen came together in several organizations, all of which eventually fell under the auspices of the American Seamen's Friend Society. These organizations waged wars against intemperance and Sabbath-breaking, issues that inflamed the passions of many middle-class people across the North. Founded in 1828, the society was concerned with American sailors around the globe. In upstate New York, it initially supported two auxiliary organizations that paid particular attention to men and, to a much lesser extent, women navigating the nation's inland waters: the Boatmen's Friend Society, founded in

1830 and committed exclusively to upstate canal workers, and the Western Seamen's Friend Society, concerned more broadly with workers on western waterways. These organizations established Bethel churches—churches founded especially for boatmen—in Troy, Albany, Utica, Rochester, and Buffalo. They also hired missionaries—some well seasoned and others straight out of seminary—to carry out most of the day-to-day activities of the organizations. These paid theologians preached to canal workers and distributed tracts and Bibles in places where workers spent their precious leisure time: in the horse barns where drivers awaited their next assignments, in the grog shops where they sought refreshment and company, and on the boats where they worked.[23]

But in the mid-1830s, a significant shift occurred in the efforts to reform boat workers. These years, as we have seen, were a period of transition in the Canal corridor. Work began on the enlargement project; financial panic struck; and a variety of middle-class people changed their views of the waterway. The Canal began to disappoint settlers' expectations that it would reduce distance and time; modest property owners began losing faith in the government; merchants began to see their interests as more fully connected to those of the state. And in 1836, the American Bethel Society, with offices in Buffalo, expanded efforts to reach out to the astonishingly large numbers of workers on the nation's western inland waters, numbers that they knew would only further increase when the enlargement project was completed. A decade later, the American Bethel Society would also affiliate with the American Seamen's Friend Society, uniting all the principal movements to improve conditions along America's inland waters.

Two years after the American Bethel Society's founding, in 1838, its officers redirected the older strategy of establishing independent Bethel churches along the route of the Canal. They adopted instead a policy of enlisting "existing agencies"—that is, established churches—to provide boatmen with preachers and pew space. When necessary, the society reimbursed local

churches for the additional expenses they incurred in accom-
modating the boatmen. The society signed on churches at intervals of thirty-five miles, so that no point on the Canal was
beyond a day's ride to a place of worship, and worked toward
decreasing the distance between Bethel-affiliated churches to fifteen miles. While the churches held special Sabbath worship for
canal workers, they also encouraged workers to attend regular
services. At the same time, the society began sending lay volunteers to distribute tracts in five languages to workers and passengers on canal boats; in fact, it took credit for being the first
organization of any kind in the United States to make use of lay
persons as missionaries. Without abandoning its reliance on paid
missionaries, the society began a concerted effort to involve a
broader range of middle-class citizens in its efforts to redeem the
commercial highway.[24]

While the changes instituted by the Bethel Society also cut
costs and expanded services, they reveal an important shift in
the underlying philosophy of the movement to reform boatmen.
Well aware that middle-class New Yorkers viewed the canallers
as a self-contained community, as outcasts from civilized society,
the Bethel Society attempted to integrate these workers into the
wider Christian community. No longer would boatmen worship
separately from members of the middle classes. The moral health
of society depended on these workers' reintegration in the godly
community. In its second annual report, the society reminded
interested upstaters that the canal workers' influence

must be great, for good, or for evil. During the season of
navigation they come in contact constantly, night and day,
with their fellow-men, and exert an influence over tens and
hundreds of thousands. And when navigation closes, this
neglected and consequently, as a general thing, abandoned
multitude, are scattered all through our communities and
counties, remote from our canals and commercial places; *and
spread abroad moral desolation* . . .

From this point on, reformers would emphasize that canallers could not be contained within their own community—that they threatened to spread their moral infections to the broader society. Just as canal boats carried cholera into New York's interior, they could carry moral decay as well.[25]

Missionaries argued that boat workers inevitably came in contact with the more stable elements of society and lured additional innocent boys—even middle-class boys—into the den of iniquity. As one reformer explained: "A boy comes from a distance; he drives one summer, returns home in the fall and shows the seventy dollars he has earned on the Canal. He tells the boys that he is rich, that the canal is the place to get rich, and perhaps the next year he will take half a dozen other boys with him." Whether they liked it or not, members of the middle classes could no longer isolate themselves from canal workers. Since they could no longer shield themselves—or their children—from moral infection, they should join in trying to combat it. This meant welcoming boatmen into their churches. The Bethel Society's new face emphasized community. Everyone's salvation depended on it.[26]

The various Bethel associations tried to reach out to boatmen and the middle classes by publishing their observations, accomplishments, and ideas on a regular basis. *Sailor's Magazine*, which the American Seamen's Friend Society began publishing monthly in 1828 and which the Bethel Society took over in 1846, brought together reports from missionaries and organizations scattered around the world. Distributed primarily on canal boats, on seagoing vessels, and in ports, the *Magazine* displays the rhetoric that reformers used in trying to persuade both boatmen and their employers to adopt Bethel reform. The annual reports of the American Seamen's Friend Society and the American Bethel Society, for their part, show reformers' attempts to reach out to actual and potential middle-class reformers and benefactors. By looking at Bethel reformers' activities and rhetoric, we are offered an unusual view of an otherwise elusive subject: the ways in which boatmen and their employers responded, in the years after

1830, to the transportation revolution's creation of a degraded class of workers.

By the Bethel reformers' own accounts, their efforts to improve the moral conditions of boatmen met with uneven success. Some workers showed considerable interest, while others were outright hostile. Missionaries faced taunts and curses, and occasionally a fist or even a knife. While some years brought noticeable improvement in Canal morality, subsequent years brought backsliding. In the Bethel Society's annual report for 1843, for example, a missionary declared that "the cause of temperance has greatly prospered of late among all employed upon the water." But four years later, the society reported, "*Temperance.* —On this topic we have nothing favorable to say." The ebb and flow reflected, in part, general fluctuations in the appeal of moral and religious revival. The year after the society reported the success of temperance campaigns, Abigail Marks exclaimed, "You know we are an exciting community here, last winter it had the appearance of a religious zeal, and this season it seems much the reverse, such extremes I can hardly comprehend." As employers' concern for temperance waned, they may have put less pressure on their workers to reform themselves.[27]

Moreover, the economic hardships of the early 1840s—resulting in the 1842 "Stop and Tax" law—had slowed commerce while also prompting the state to stop construction on the Erie's enlargement, sending construction workers scampering for jobs as boatmen. In 1843, with more people fighting for fewer jobs, workers had incentives to keep themselves sober and reliable. As the crisis eased by the late 1840s, the demand for workers once again taxed the supply.

Reformers added another explanation for shifting patterns in alcohol consumption: once converted to Christian ways, boatmen left the evil waterway, only to be replaced by a new crop of sinners. Although most missionaries agreed that the general moral state of the Canal improved vastly by the end of the antebellum period, they also admitted that a great deal of sin continued to thrive on the waterway. A. H. Mather, a Bethel missionary at West Troy in 1854, sighed, "I am in doubts if with all the exertions of Missionaries and other Christian influences brought to bear, there is any actual progress made; that is, if there are more brought to Christ than led away from him."[28]

The frankness with which Bethel reformers acknowledged that they faced resistance from some boatmen suggests that their reports of workers' improvements and, sometimes, conversions may well have been accurate. Reformers insisted that many canal workers greeted their efforts with a degree of interest and respect. Even though boatmen did not always modify their behavior to suit the Bethel reformers, most of them refrained from cursing or threatening the preachers who considered them the most dissolute group in all America. Assuming that many otherwise profane canal workers did indeed welcome Bethel reformers with courtesy, how do we explain these workers' willingness to lend an ear to the very men who constantly proclaimed their wickedness?

The reformers offered a few explanations. While they would have liked to believe that boatmen were eager to discover Christ, missionaries realized that boatmen had other reasons for listening to preachers. Having expected to encounter more hostility from canallers, one missionary remarked with cynicism, "As it is in our army, so on our canals—the scarcity of reading make the irreligious even eager to get tracts." Others noted how missionaries won over canallers by approaching them with sympathy rather than exhortations. Deacon M. Eaton, a popular missionary, remembered how some ministers "have told the boatmen that they were the worst class of men in the world, and ought to go to the State prison. This, perhaps was too true." Yet it was not a good strategy for reform, prompting Eaton to add, "But the truth is not to be spoken at all times." The Bethel Society tried to select compassionate missionaries. At least one, the Reverend Lyman Judson, had been a canal driver. His experience, the Society's officials believed, allowed him to win the confidence of his listeners and to provide them with a model for their redemption.[29]

Canal workers had various reasons for welcoming the missionaries. However, since so few workers left written records, we can only speculate from reformers' reports what inspired certain canallers to welcome the missionaries or, even, the evangelical message they spread. A few possibilities emerge from these and other sources: some workers genuinely sought a more devout life; others saw piety as a vehicle for social mobility, for realizing middleclass respectability; and still others appreciated the reformers' attention to their physical and emotional needs.

Many workers showed apparently genuine interest in evangelical teachings, and at least some underwent full-fledged conversions. Often workers reported to the missionaries that they had grown up in pious homes. Separation from their families and communities discouraged workers from acting righteously (or so missionaries thought), but they did not require much encouragement to reawaken their religious selves. And some workers came to the Canal as converted Christians and never lost their religious devotion despite the depraved conditions in which they found themselves.

Sabbath attendance at most Bethel churches varied significantly from week to week, from a dozen to several hundred. Canallers who bothered to attend church at all probably genuinely sought salvation. Church attendance, of course, does not reflect religiosity: in Rochester, according to historian Paul Johnson, "the most powerful source of the workingman's revival was the simple, coercive fact that many wage earners worked for men who insisted on seeing them in church." But external pressures made it less likely, not more, that boatmen would enter a house of worship. Most canallers had to work on the Sabbath and attended church at the peril of losing their jobs. While a small number worked for Sabbath-observing lines, even their employers could not easily compel them to attend church, since—unlike manufacturers in Rochester—the proprietors of boat companies could not easily keep track of their crews' whereabouts. Crews spent the Sabbath wherever their boats happened to tie up on Saturday nights—and not necessarily in the same city as the boats' owners. Pious captains might enforce church attendance, but otherwise boatmen would have felt little compulsion to worship on Sundays.[30]

If few boatmen felt coerced to go to church, some might have gone in the hopes of elevating their status in a fluid class system. Just as middle-class parents worried that their children might slip into the ranks of canal drivers, some canal workers hoped to uplift themselves into the middle classes. They did not all take pride in being associated permanently with a group seen as vulgar and violent. Missionaries frequently commented that converted boatmen felt compelled to leave the waterway because of its evil influences. But it seems just as likely that these boatmen adopted pious ways, however consciously or unconsciously, precisely so that they could leave the Canal and join middle-class life onshore.

Some workers clearly thought that the waterway might lead to enhanced social and economic opportunities. Eleazor Conkey provides a stark illustration of these aspirations. "Discontented" with his work on the family farm in Livingston County, New York, nineteen-year-old Eleazor set out in 1825 for the booming town of Rochester. Having left with only his "father's blessing," a three-pound note, and a change of clothes, the young Conkey's discontent probably stemmed from bleak economic prospects on the farm. His father had already shared ownership of the family farm with Eleazor's brother and did not have the means to provide his younger son with land. That the elder Conkey supported his son's departure yet did not give him more than his three-pound note also suggests that the family did not have the material means to set Conkey up in a business other than farming. Thus, Conkey reported, "My father [gave] me leave to go and seek my fortune."[31]

Within hours of arriving in Rochester, Conkey met a canal boat captain in need of a bowsman—the hand riding in the front of the boat who alerted the rest of the crew to upcoming obstacles in navigation, kept towlines untangled, and helped cast off and land the boat. Conkey immediately signed on at eight pounds per month. For the next four years, he held a variety of positions on boat crews. Conkey then left the Canal in 1829 to take a job in the town of Livonia as a store clerk—a job that provided a low-level entry into the new business classes. In 1831, at the age of twenty-five, he sought to improve his economic prospects further and returned to Rochester "in pursuit of business." There he took employment as a canal boat captain. Although some boat captains failed to win the respect of their middle-class acquaintances onshore, those who comported themselves in accord with middle-class norms usually did. Captains who supervised passenger boats, in particular, commanded both crews and authority. When, in 1836, Conkey was made captain of a forty-passenger packet boat, he noted that his appointment to that coveted position came "to the great disappointment to my brethren in business." His good fortune meant a lost opportunity to other ambitious captains.

Conkey continued to work as a boat captain until 1839, when economic prospects on the Canal began to look discouraging in the wake of the Panic of 1837 and the expansion of railroad lines. With his expectations depressed, at the end of the 1839 season Conkey "laid my boat up and settled off with my crew and wound up my boating business for the season and I hope forever." After that, he joined a partnership running a distilling and grocery business. He had come to the Canal in search of economic opportunity, and he had found it. His work on the waterway earned him cash, which ultimately allowed him to buy into a business. Conkey's business prospered, he bought a larger share of it and a bigger house, and in 1843 his fellow citizens affirmed his social status by electing him a Rochester alderman.[32]

Conkey was not alone in dreaming of finding his "fortune" through canal work. One of his steersmen left him to become a captain of a prestigious lake boat. Michael Moran, an Irish immigrant, worked as a driver in the early 1850s, was promoted to steersman, saved his money, bought his own boat, and by

1860 owned and operated a fleet of canal and river boats. President James Garfield got his start as a driver on the Ohio canals, prompting Horatio Alger to write a biography of him. While these men were exceptional, their aspirations might not have been so unusual. In an 1833 advertisement for accommodations on his packet boat, a boat owner rhymed:

> Our Boats are fine, them none surpass,
> Our captains polite, if only ask'd
> And Stewards wide awake, you'll see—
> For captains—they expect to be.

Just as this doggerel suggests that boat passengers anticipated finding impolite and lazy crew members on canal boats, it also suggests they would not find it implausible that canallers dreamed of upward mobility.[33]

While we know little about Conkey's religious beliefs and practices, we do know that he admired the same qualities in workers as did the Bethel reformers. Not only did he dismiss one worker for being unsteady and another for fighting, but—at least after he became a shop owner—he encouraged temperance. Although he owned a distillery, Conkey, ironically, jotted down in his diary that indolence and intemperance could break a man. When a brother-in-law fell prey to these vices, Conkey gave him shelter and a job and resolved to give him wages "whether he deserves them or not." Since his brother-in-law had once been "one of the smartest appearing young men of the town," Conkey's doubts about his ability to truly earn his wages shows that Conkey believed that intemperance reduced productivity and social advancement. While we do not know whether Conkey welcomed Bethel missionaries on his boat, he clearly agreed with them that an even and sober temperament was a prerequisite to upward mobility—and he, like many others, sought such mobility along the Canal.

Whether socially ambitious or not, whether genuinely pious or not, some boatmen greeted Bethel missionaries warmly because of the material aid they offered. Even those workers who had no intention of ever giving up their drinking or swearing were often relieved to see the preachers who worked to improve their living and working conditions. One missionary reported that workers "seem to feel the missionary and the chaplain are their peculiar friends, and often even those who are not professing Christians, have tried to say something to encourage their hearts and manifest their respect for them." Missionaries cared for the sick, found Christian families to provide canallers with warm meals and occasionally a bed, supplied workers with clothing, intervened to protect them from abusive employers, and buried the "friendless dead." This helps explain why even some dedicated Catholics welcomed the Protestant missionaries.[34]

For similarly practical reasons, the Bethel Society's crusade for the suspension of canal business from sundown Saturday to sundown Sunday must have met with near-universal approval among overworked canal workers. If some truly desired a day devoted to worship, all canal workers—from drivers to toll collectors—faced long hours at the job, since the Canal operated twenty-four hours a day, seven days a week. Missionaries claimed that boatmen who worked seven days a week earned the same monthly wages as their counterparts employed by boat lines that observed the Sabbath—the so-called six-day lines or pioneers (named after the original Sabbatarian boat company, the Pioneer Line). They also observed, "We believe, from personal conversations with boatmen and others, that those employed feel dissatisfied with this state of things, and want a day of rest. Though not Christians, they feel that God has given them a right to one day in seven." William Liddle and John Homan, clerks in the Rochester collector's office, made an appeal to the Canal Board along exactly those lines. They complained in 1851 that "they are required to work nights as day times: and average each not less than fifteen hours constant & arduous labor in every twenty four. That they have no days of rest from the commencement to the end of their service—no Sabbaths & no opportunities for relaxation." Middle-class New Yorkers who opposed Sabbatarian laws, as we have seen, claimed that canallers would use the Sabbath to drink, gamble, and visit houses of ill fame. If this were indeed the case—and it is consistent with many contemporary observations—then ungodly canallers certainly would have welcomed the missionaries' efforts to secure them a day of rest (and diversion) on Sunday.[35]

Perhaps it is not so surprising after all that non-Christian canal workers welcomed missionaries "who sympathize[d] with them in all their troubles, advise[d] them in circumstances of difficulty and perplexity, and urge[d] upon them the claims of the Gospel for present attention." Canal workers faced no shortage of troubles, and while on rare occasions they came together to strike for higher wages, usually these young men protested their work conditions by quitting. But that was not always an option for the more desperate among them. So some welcomed missionaries, from whom they could receive material help even when they did not offer their souls in return. Moreover, unlike many other members of the middle classes, missionaries were willing to relate to these workers on a human level, as people fully capable of salvation—and worthy of improved living and working conditions. So it was that unhealthy conditions and long hours made many of these boys unusually willing to attach themselves to the reformers who described them as "young in years, but old in sin, very giants of wickedness." And perhaps they had one final reason for seeing the missionaries as their allies: reformers placed much of the responsibility for the workers' depravity on the shoulders of the commercial classes.[36]

While Bethel missionaries held boatmen responsible for their own wickedness—the Second Great Awakening was, after all, based on a belief in moral free agency—they placed even more blame on the businessmen who created the conditions that tempted canal workers into vice. Merchants and forwarders, according to the society's official publications, helped to bring ruin upon the boatmen by excluding them from Christian society, separating them from the moral influence of their homes and families, neglecting their physical welfare, setting a bad example by consuming large quantities of alcohol themselves, and—most egregiously—denying them the Sabbath as a day of rest and prayer. The society declared, "it is *unjust*, as well as unchristian, thus to subject a class of men, who toil and suffer to our benefit, to such evils—such loss of morals and of happiness." Employers had the responsibility to create a working environment that would allow lost boys to develop into virtuous men.[37]

The Bethel Society made clear that it did not see the degradation of canal workers as the inevitable consequence of the market revolution. Rather, responsibility for the canallers' moral ruin rested squarely with their employers' conscious decisions to worship Mammon more than God. Reformers sought to remind businessmen that, despite protestations to the contrary, they did indeed profit at someone else's expense. When merchants required their workers to labor on God's day, reformers argued, they opened the door for other sins to follow. Deprived of a day to honor God and to hear His teachings, canallers were forced to sink deeper and deeper into iniquity.

Nothing outraged Bethel reformers more than the desecration of the Sabbath. "The greatest obstacle in the way of improvement and salvation of this class of men [boatmen] is, *the unjust and wicked conduct of their employers, in* DEPRIVING THEM OF THE PRIVILEGES AND BENEFITS OF THE SABBATH . . . ," declared the society's first annual report. Commercial men who themselves attended church with their families expected their employees to work on the Sabbath. New York did have a Sabbatarian law on the books, and attempts to enforce the law dated back to the earliest years of the Canal. But debates in the legislature consistently failed to bring the laws back to life. Some legislators argued against the laws on practical grounds: they would entail a loss of revenue, increase competition from alternative transportation routes, and encourage the congregation of immoral workers onshore. Some people, particularly Jacksonians (who often voted against the laws while supporting their aims), were ideologically opposed to the state's involvement in the issue because of constitutional guarantees related to the separation of church and state. Such arguments did not convince the Bethel reformers, who thought that the state was itself in need of reform, since it demanded that its canal employees work on the Lord's day. C. T. Beach, a Bethel missionary at Syracuse, protested that "at every lock, men are employed and paid by the officers of this State for violating the Sabbath. If the opening of these Locks on the Sabbath was a private and unauthorized desecration of the Lord's Day it would be comparatively harmless and innocent, but it receives the *high and solemn* sanction of the *People, of the State of New York.*"

What caused this hypocrisy among the business classes as well as state officials? Why were otherwise pious men tempted to act in such "unjust and wicked ways"? And why did the state exempt the Canal from Sabbatarian laws? *"The love of money,"* *Sailor's Magazine* responded, "is the cause of most of the Sabbath breaking in the land."[38]

The same concern for money, however, led other pious merchants to support the enforcement of the state's Sabbatarian law. Without the legally mandated closing of the locks, they worried that their observation of the Sabbath would make them lose out to less pious competitors. By turning to the state for moral regulation of the economy, these businessmen apparently hoped (like many of those who petitioned the Canal Board about routes and tolls) that the state would make sure that no businessman would profit at another's direct expense. In 1845, one "Harlow" wrote to the *Rochester Daily Democrat* that he could not understand why the Democratic-controlled legislature did not pass a law shutting down the locks on Sunday, since "all (or nearly all) of the forwarders petitioned for this the last spring . . . As one, whose business is almost entirely on the canal," Harlow continued, "I should be glad to see this law pass, not only for our own rest and comfort, but for the well being of those who are engaged as captains and hands on the boats." Yet nothing would have prohibited Harlow from joining the other businessmen who voluntarily closed on the Sabbath—nothing but fear of loss of business to competitors. Only if his competitors rested could Harlow—and his workers—rest. The Bethel Society's missionary at Rochester recalled that "in conversations with proprietors and agents, a general desire was expressed for a reformation in regard to running the boats on the Sabbath, accompanied however with the apprehension that others would get their patronage, should they attempt." To try to allay such fears, the society published accounts illustrating how proprietors of six-day lines had actually fared better financially than their counterparts who conducted business on the Sabbath. By linking material and moral prosperity, the society hoped to sway business owners.[39]

While the Bethel Society lambasted businessmen for desecrating the Sabbath and corrupting their employees, the society turned to these same men—and their wives, sisters, and children—for financial help. And despite the harsh criticisms levied against them as a group, merchants and their families did indeed donate substantial amounts of money to the Bethel cause. During the financial panic of 1837, however, donations to the Bethel Society waned. The society's officers explained that "commercial men have heretofore (the acknowledgement is but just) been the most liberal supporters of the Bethel cause, and much reliance was placed upon this source for funds to sustain our efforts. Hence the commercial embarrassment has disappointed our expectations, and greatly diminished the receipts in our Treasury." When a cholera epidemic struck New York State in 1849, the society once again reported that its finances were very much tied to those of the entrepreneurial classes: "Those desolations, as a general rule, followed the channels of inland navigation, greatly crippling the business of commercial men, and consequently diminishing our pecuniary expectations from them." Women's auxiliaries and youth associations raised money for the society as well, even though the participants frequently came from families headed by a man who made his money from commercial activities.[40]

Why would individuals contribute money, and occasionally

time, to an organization that held them responsible for the degradation of canal workers, a degradation that supposedly threatened the moral fabric of American society? Why would these
men and women support reform societies whose agents claimed
that business practices not only perpetuated vice and wickedness
but also threatened the very destiny of the nation? Silas Marks,
the Lockport merchant, volunteered one answer: the middle
classes defined themselves in part by involvement in reform and
benevolent causes. He wrote to relatives in Connecticut that "the
Ladies here are also engaged in the same kind of benevolent
Matters as those of down East   I mean the Great objects of the
day such as pioneering and supporting societies such as aboli-
tionism, Moral Reform &c and what not and its heresy not to
wink at their proceedings and give liberly constantly." By supporting reform movements—whether or not they genuinely believed in their causes—women and men confirmed their standing
as upright citizens. In a time when economic mobility could be
downward as well as upward, members of the commercial classes
in particular were eager to define their class status in terms of
culture rather than simply economics. Although an economic
collapse could deprive them of their money, it could not take
away their piety and social concern. Benevolence, moreover,
served as a reminder to the community—and voters—that others depended on the businessmen's goodwill. It allowed businessmen to feel as though they were fulfilling their paternal role
in society.[41]

Like other regions that experienced widespread evangelical
conversions during the Second Great Awakening, the Burned-
Over District hosted dozens of reform movements throughout
the antebellum period. Some New Yorkers did their best to
bring on the millennium by perfecting themselves and others
through movements that tried to remedy a legion of evils in
society. Although the Bethel Society represented just one in a
long list of antebellum reform organizations, its efforts to reform
canal workers tapped a particularly emotional chord among the
region's entrepreneurs. Each morning when merchants went to

their offices and warehouses along the canal banks, the sights, sounds, and smells of the Erie Canal greeted them. They saw sleepy young boys, dressed in ragged cotton trousers, repeatedly kicking their gaunt and sluggish horses; they heard boatmen shouting obscenities, in a variety of accents, at "respectable" passengers on other boats; they saw young women leaving their houses of "ill fame"; and they smelled the alcohol and filth on men stumbling out of grog houses to catch up with their boats waiting in lines to clear the locks. But they also saw freight boats, loaded with sacks of grain, with a man at the tiller, his wife in the cabin, and the children on deck reading. The first sensual bombardment represented a social nightmare—a reminder that the commercial success depended on the labor of tens of thousands of wage earners, many of whom never even had a chance at "respectable citizenship" because of their accents, skin color, sex, or age. The second represented the dream of the market revolution: the creation of unlimited possibilities for commercial expansion within the older context of a family-centered, socially stable community. Finding themselves embroiled in an economic and social revolution, a revolution that promised them immense prosperity if it also brought the risk of serious failure, some commercial men may have supported canal reform in an attempt to direct the market revolution away from the nightmare and toward the dream. Within the context of widespread religious and reformist fervor, then, some commercial men and women probably genuinely shared the Bethel Society's goals of bringing Christianity and civility to the artificial river.[42]

But by holding employers responsible for the workers' circumstances, the Bethel Society reminded businessmen that the market revolution that had made them prosperous had also debased workers. The harmony of class interests, reformers implied, depended as much on employers as on the employed. Those commercial men who kept their businesses open on Sunday, as most did, imperiled their workers' moral and physical health. "But who are these men, who make such wicked exactions on their fellow beings?" asked the American Bethel Society in preparing to offer its own response. "They are generally men who hold a respectable rank in the community, and who claim to have high regard for morals. Many of them, too, are the professed *followers of Christ, and are perhaps at the house of God,* or sitting around the communion table, while these men are toiling in their service and for their profit." Closing their businesses on the Sabbath, while a good start, would not be enough to compensate for the accumulated harm that businessmen had inflicted on their workers. Writing in 1851 about canal drivers, the Bethel missionary Sereno Bishop pushed employers to take greater responsibility for their workers' well-being. Canal drivers, he pleaded, "are susceptible enough of good influence, though many of them are grossly wicked. Their neglected condition is greatly to be pitied. It is time that all the care that is shewn them should not be from the missionary alone." For merchants to give money to support Bethel missionaries was not enough. Instead, the boys' "employers should feel the responsibility which attaches to that relation, and exercise careful attention toward their moral and physical welfare." Businessmen, in other words, had paternal responsibilities.[43]

When they chose to support Bethel reforms, some businessmen thought that their pocketbooks would ultimately benefit. Employers throughout industrial America supported temperance campaigns because heavy drinking among workers tended to decrease productivity, encourage irregular hours, and lead to accidents. Thaddeus Joy, who was by occupation a forwarding agent and by avocation the president of the Canal Temperance Society, illustrated another manner in which an employer's self-interest could coincide with reformers' attempts to elevate workers' circumstances. Joy described the practices of the Albany and Troy Towing Company, which hired 450 boys to drive horses along the Canal. During the first year of the company's operation, the boys spent their evenings and free time at the horse barns along the towpath. The boys "contracted habits of intemperance, and became otherwise dissolute and vicious." The following year, in order to combat the drivers' drunkenness, the company placed its drivers on the boats with the crews. "The drivers are now members of the captain's family, are kindly treated, and are entirely under his control and government," Joy happily noted. Boys ruled the station barns; adults supervised boats.[44]

By bringing the drivers under the close supervision of adults, the towing company gained some control over its employees. Paul Johnson, in his study of the Rochester revivals, has suggested that some shopkeepers embraced evangelical revivalism because it replaced some of the social control they had lost over their workers with the advent of industrialization. When masters and journeymen lived under the same roof, employers could exert tight controls over their workers' habits. But once factories replaced shops, and journeymen moved into their own neighborhoods, employers lost control over their workers' leisure-time habits and morals. Similarly, when some businessmen supported the Bethel cause, they reacted in part to the missionaries' emphasis on placing workers under tighter supervision. (Although the Bethel Society often argued that boat captains provided dubious moral examples, it—and its commercial supporters—perhaps reasoned that the boys would at least do less damage if fewer of them congregated in one place.) Bethel missionaries recognized that some commercial men supported their reforms for self-interested reasons. "Many of the boatmen and capitalists who are not religious persons, and some even who are skeptics," wrote one missionary, "are much interested in the work of the canal missionary; because say they, 'It tends to reform and elevate the class of men we employ.' "[45]

In addition to enhancing employers' control over their workers, tighter supervision of workers—businessmen could rationalize to themselves—served the nation's common good. Some commercial men remarked that by supporting the boatmen's improvement, and encouraging social order, they would help to keep the country on course toward its manifest destiny. When several hundred businessmen signed petitions in 1838 and 1839 asking forwarders to obey the Sabbath, they appealed to their fellow men of commerce to do so for the Republic. They wrote that "the welfare of country" requires the observance of the Sabbath. "A despotic government can exist where people are degraded, but free institutions will be sustained only by an intelligent and moral people—Make then this people ignorant and immoral, and you will destroy our prosperity, peace, and republic." The Bethel Society also played on both religious and secular fears in order to plead the canallers' cause; the two, in fact, were inseparable. "Any business arrangement that necessarily involves a constant desecration of the Sabbath is not only contrary to the express commandment of God, but *also* derogatory to the nature and undeniable rights of our citizens," resolved members present at the third annual meeting. The Bethel Society constantly warned commercial men against relegating their workers to a shunned and lowly class and thereby threatening the moral, economic, and political future of God's chosen nation.[46]

The society reminded the commercial classes that prosperity and progress had their costs. They could choose to pay now, by giving up business activity on the Sabbath and assuming paternal responsibility for their workers. Or they could pay later—at a compounded rate—by creating an unsteady workforce, undermining the Republic, and delaying the onset of the millennium. Some businessmen found themselves in a bind: they felt persuaded by calls for reform, yet they felt equally pulled by the "love of money." The Bethel missionaries would not let them forget that commercial prosperity and moral virtue did not always go together—that they were in fact sometimes at odds. Some businessmen expressed ambivalence over the moral expenses of the commercial revolution from which they profited. They acknowledged that "justice to the laboring classes, with a proper sense of the wrongs they are made to endure, by being compelled to violate the 'Laws of the State,' and break the 'Holy Sabbath,' or lose the situations they occupy connected with the business of the Canals, demands that all engaged should enjoy their inalienable rights, and be freed from oppression . . ."[47]

Businessmen continued to draw on Revolutionary rhetoric when they spoke of inalienable rights and oppression, but their more general views of progress and society had evolved a great deal since Judge Richardson's 1817 ceremony. Looking around them, businessmen could see that progress was driven by what was fast becoming a distinct class of workers, a class defined as much by employers' "oppression" as by its own culture of violence and profanity. They tried to solve these problems by turning to churches and families to re-create social stability and, perhaps, a modicum of deference. With very few exceptions, though, not even reformers considered slowing the commercial revolution and sending canallers back to farms to earn honest livings off the land. Progress had taken on a life of its own, one they could no longer stop but could hope only to guide by improving the moral and physical conditions of canal workers within the commercial context. They worked to close the locks on Sunday, to discourage the sale and consumption of alcohol, and to lodge canal drivers on boats rather than in barns. By doing so, they could remove the "wickedness" from the commercial revolution—and possibly increase their profits at the same time. Together, they and their workers could hasten the earthly perfection that would usher in the millennium. For in God's Kingdom, they knew, commercial progress and moral virtue could surely coexist.

Becoming Second Nature

I N 1858, the New York State Legislature once again debated the Sabbath closing of the Erie Canal locks. This time, though, two of the bill's opponents, George Jeremiah and Dwight Bacheller, raised a novel issue. The state, they said, could not stop canal traffic on Sunday for a simple reason: it did not have the authority to do so. The Canal and its tributaries had ceased to be wards of the state; these waterways could no longer be "regarded as common channels of conveyance, in the nature, that is, of public roads . . ." The Canal now shared more in common with lakes and seas. And just as "no one" would call for a halt to oceangoing navigation on Sunday, so it was unthinkable to close the Erie. The emphasis in the term "artificial river" had shifted from "artificial" to "river," from man-made to natural.[1]

For all its technological brilliance, the Erie Canal had created a landscape that people took for granted. As its sponsors had promised nearly a half century earlier, the Canal—and the commercial revolution—had quickly transformed the upstate "wilderness" into "civilization." Hundreds of thousands of people now called the Canal corridor home. Farmers and merchants alike made property investments based on what they assumed were permanent alterations to the region's topography, and some vigorously protested changes to that already artificial landscape. Without a second thought, farmers kept an anxious eye on the price of wheat in England and dressed their children in ready-made shirts and shoes. Syracuse, Utica, and Albany—among other inland cities—took on the bustle of seaports. Meanwhile, New York became the nation's preeminent port; and Niagara Falls, a leading destination for honeymooners. But by helping to make possible this busy commercial setting, the Erie Canal had guaranteed its own obsolescence. Railroads, not canals, would ultimately meet the middle classes' raised expectations.

The iron horse came to the Empire State in 1831, when amid much fanfare a train called the *DeWitt Clinton* took its maiden voyage between Albany and Schenectady. The irony in naming the state's first train after the Canal's chief supporter, who had died three years earlier, did not strike observers at the time. They initially envisioned trains that would complement, not compete with, canals. By avoiding the twenty-seven locks between Albany and Schenectady, the *DeWitt Clinton* saved Canal passengers a day's travel. Public officials worked hard to protect the state's substantial investments in artificial waterways. The state's initial railroad charters prohibited freight trains along routes that competed with the Erie (except during the months when the waterway was frozen). In 1847, the legislature began permitting railroads to haul freight all year long in exchange for paying canal tolls during the season of navigation, and then in 1851, after years of pressure from merchants, the state repealed the tolls altogether. Two years later, Erastus Corning brought the state's existing short railroad lines under the control of the New York Central Railroad, thus foreshadowing the Canal's demise. Although the waterway continued to carry more freight than the consolidated railroad until the 1880s, by the 1850s the New York Central was steadily draining the Canal of business. Railroads did not close down in winter, and steam locomotives traveled in all weather at speeds unimaginable to those who first marvelled at the swiftness of canal passages. If the Erie Canal compressed distance and time, the railroads annihilated them, or so it appeared to the amazed observer in the mid-nineteenth century.[2]

When Governor William Seward delivered his first annual message to the New York State Legislature in 1839, he echoed words that DeWitt Clinton had first spoken more than twenty years before. "Nature, never jealous of our co-operation, supplies us with resources and facilities, but presents few of her works finished for our immediate use . . . The policy of our state is so legibly written upon its surface that to err in reading that policy, or to be slothful in pursuing it, is equally unpardonable." Seward, like Clinton, believed that economic and moral progress bore an intimate connection to each other, and that internal improvements would lead New York and the nation toward their manifest destiny. But Seward spoke of railroads as well as canals.[3]

The governor of 1839 also addressed a different audience, one that gave different meanings to these familiar-sounding words. Born in 1801 and more than thirty years Clinton's junior, Seward had grown up in a "nation of traders" and became one of the country's leading Whigs. Unlike the Canal's original sponsors, Seward recognized the role of wage labor, even immigrant labor, in sustaining economic progress. When other Whigs vilified immigrants as threats to American stability and prosperity, Seward rejected such nativist rhetoric. He knew only too well that immigrant workers played a crucial role in building and operating the state's internal improvements. Still, Seward did not celebrate diversity; instead, he accepted it as a temporary evil that could be overcome. At a ceremony marking the completion of the Boston–Albany railroad in 1842, he noted that "we of New York are not . . . a homogeneous people. It is one of our cares, by the agency of benign and equal institutions, to assimilate all these various masses and reduce them to one great, harmonious, united, and happy people." Like the Bethel reformers, Seward believed that no matter how depraved the "masses," they were capable of citizenship and upward mobility. Moreover, the nation's very future depended on this seemingly simple belief—a belief that came to be called free labor.[4]

In the following decades, free-labor ideology would prove a rallying cry not just for middle-class New Yorkers but for a wide range of Northerners. Belief in upward mobility became central to their idea of progress; "it is possible," as the Bethel reformers had reminded their listeners, "for a canal driver to make a man." Otherwise, how could the middle classes celebrate the commercial revolution? How else could they justify working conditions that did not befit "republican free men"? How else could they allay their fears about class conflict? Slavery was antithetical to their vision of a fluid society. Not only did it deny slaves the possibility of upward mobility; more important, it degraded poor whites, who at best deferred to aristocratic slave owners and who at worst worked side by side with slaves. If slavery took hold in the western territories, what would the prospects be like for canal drivers and their counterparts in factories and garret sweatshops? It was not coincidental that some Bethel reformers joined the antislavery movement—or that in 1854 Seward became one of the founders of the Republican Party, whose diverse membership coalesced around a shared opposition to the westward expansion of slavery.

In October 1858, Seward—who had served in the U.S. Senate since 1849—made a chilling observation that continues to influence our understanding of the years leading up to the Civil War. While campaigning in Rochester, he compared the South's slave labor to the North's free labor. These two systems would collide, he predicted, as Americans in search of economic opportunity relentlessly flooded the western territories, a process that he—along with many others—deemed crucial to the nation's progress. "It is an irrepressible conflict," he warned, "between opposing and enduring forces, and it means that the United States must and will, sooner or later, become either entirely a slaveholding nation, or entirely a free-labor nation." Whether he fully believed the alarm he sounded, Seward clearly hoped to win votes for his Republican Party. On the most obvious level, he tried to unite Rochesterians by invoking the specter of Southern slavery—the common enemy that threatened the North from without. But when he pointed to the virtues of the free-labor system, Seward also appealed to Northerners worried about the growing divisions within Northern society.[5]

Free-labor rhetoric could calm the nerves of a variety of voters. To those already securely in power, Seward offered the comforting message that while progress fostered class *competition*, the free-labor system, with its promise of upward mobility, could actually help to quell class *conflict*; "the unchecked and equal rivalry of all classes of men, at once secures universal contentment, and brings into the highest possible activity all the physical, moral and social energies of the whole state." To those at the lower end of the ladder, Seward held out the promise of upward mobility. Any free-labor state, he promised, "inevitably becomes, sooner or later, a republic or a democracy." By effectively redefining American democracy as founded on the premise of free labor, Seward and his fellow Republicans led their party to a dominant position in the North, sending waves of fear throughout the white South.[6]

DeWitt Clinton, too, would have cringed at an association of "the Republic" and the "common people." What had happened to deference? Seward accepted the notion of democracy, perhaps because he, unlike his predecessor, realized that social divisions and disorder could occupy even the "middle landscape" of the Canal corridor. Seward championed uplifting the masses into a "united" political community—to use his term—precisely because he recognized that the antebellum North was far from harmonious. Seward, along with many other Republicans, adapted his understanding of progress to the contentious demands of the commercial era. For if protest and reform represented a growing dissatisfaction with affairs as they were, protest and reform also suggested that ordinary men and women still thought the world was theirs to shape.

But the secession of the Southern states tested the imagination of the optimists, even while the railroad's iron tracks were leading Northerners to a vastly different future from the one projected by Clinton and the early visionaries of internal improvements. That future would also diverge substantially from the initial expectations of the men and women whose quotidian existence centered on the Canal and its tributary enterprises. Yet even before an 1862 act of the legislature blandly declared the completion of the Erie Canal Enlargement—an event that occasioned scant public comment, and no celebration whatsoever —few middle-class Northerners dwelled on the ironies wrought by America's revolution in transport. By the outbreak of the Civil War, their equation of progress and American destiny, like the Erie Canal itself, had become second nature.

NOTES

INTRODUCTION:
FRESH OYSTERS AND SOUR DEALS

1. *Republican Advocate*, November 5, 1825.
2. For examples of comments on oysters, see *Report, on the Subject of a Communication between Canandaigua Lake and the Erie Canal* (1821), 13; *Ontario Freeman*, April 15, 1823; *Rochester Telegraph*, October 21, 1823; *Niagara Sentinel*, December 5, 1823, in *Bottoming Out* 17 (1960); *Ontario Freeman*, January 5, 1825; *Republican Advocate*, February 4, 1825; *Buffalo Journal* in *Bellows Falls Intelligencer*, November 28, 1825; scattered entries, Lyman Spalding Journals #3, 4, 5, Syracuse University; Silas Marks to Silas Curtis family, December 21, 1842, Curtis Family Papers, University of Rochester. While an express stage could have made the trip to Batavia more quickly, freight wagons did not regularly follow this route. Because transporting freight between these two cities was so expensive, New York oysters may well have never made it to Batavia before the Canal's construction. Caroline E. MacGill estimates that the cost of transporting commodities by wagon from Buffalo to Albany could be five or six times the value of the commodities themselves: *History of Transportation in the United States before 1860* (1917), 168. DeWitt Clinton, "His Private Journal— 1810," in William W. Campbell, *The Life and Writings of DeWitt Clinton* (1849), 143.
3. Entry dated January 11, 1825, *Memoirs of an Emigrant: The Journal of Alexander Coventry . . .* , Vol. II (typescript prepared by the

Albany Institute of History and Art and the New York State Library, 1978), 2054.

4. For a discussion of the scholarship on the era's technological, political, and economic histories, see Sources.

5. This definition of "progress," which will be fleshed out throughout the book, modifies Raymond Williams's definition in *Keywords: A Vocabulary of Culture and Society*, rev. ed. (1983), 243–45. For a grand account of the meanings of progress in American history and culture, see Christopher Lasch, *The True and Only Heaven: Progress and Its Critics* (1991).

6. For the most eloquent explanation of the role of "progress" in helping define Northern sectional identity, see James M. McPherson, "Antebellum Southern Exceptionalism: A New Look at an Old Question," *Civil War History* (September 1983), 230–44. McPherson is responding, in part, to arguments by Edward Pessen that perhaps the antebellum North and South had more in common than historians have generally assumed; Pessen, "How Different from Each Other Were the Antebellum North and South?," *American Historical Review* (December 1980), 1119–66. Pessen proposed that what set the two sides at odds was their "perceived" interests rather than their tangible social, political, and economic differences, including their transportation systems. McPherson suggests that maybe it was the rest of America, not the South, that was exceptional because of its commitment to progress—and that the founders of the Confederacy saw this exceptionalism as dangerously revolutionary, an assessment that helped propel them toward secession. I have drawn here on both of their arguments: although this book does not enter the debate on how different the two regions were in measurable terms, it explores the ways in which Northerners perceived their region as committed to the notion of progress. McPherson elaborates on his ideas in *Battle Cry of Freedom: The Civil War Era* (1988), which is also a wonderful one-volume introduction to the most important themes of the period. For insightful overviews of the antebellum era's rapid social, political, cultural, and economic changes, see Robert H. Wiebe, *The Opening of American Society: From the Adoption of the Constitution to the Eve of Disunion* (1984), and Charles Sellers, *The Market Revolution: Jacksonian America, 1815–1860* (1991).

7. George Rogers Taylor, in the classic work on the transportation

revolution, estimates that freight wagons averaged twenty miles in a day; *The Transportation Revolution, 1815–1860* (1951), 138. An 1825 newspaper also estimated that the benefits of the Erie Canal extended to the area that fell within twenty miles of the waterway; *People's Friend*, February 16, 1825. On economic development in antebellum America, see Douglass C. North, *The Economic Growth of the United States, 1790–1860* (1961); Thomas C. Cochran, *Frontiers of Change: Early Industrialism in America* (1981); Stuart Bruchy, *Enterprise: The Dynamic Economy of a Free People* (1990). On agriculture, see Paul W. Gates, *The Farmers' Age: Agriculture, 1815–1860* (1962); Clarence H. Danhof, *Change in Agriculture: The Northern United States, 1820–1870* (1969); Percy Wells Bidwell and John I. Falconer, *History of Agriculture in the Northern United States, 1620–1860* (1925); Hal S. Barron, *Those Who Stayed Behind: Rural Society in Nineteenth-Century New England* (1984). On agriculture in New York, see Ulysses Prentiss Hedrick, *A History of Agriculture in the State of New York* (1933 and 1966); Neil Adams McNall, *An Agricultural History of the Genesee Valley, 1790–1860* (1952); David Maldwyn Ellis, *Landlords and Farmers in the Hudson-Mohawk Region, 1790–1850* (1946); William Wyckoff, *The Developer's Frontier: The Making of the Western New York Landscape* (1988); William Chazanof, *Joseph Ellicott and the Holland Land Company: The Opening of Western New York* (1970).

8. The Canal Board Papers are catalogued as Series A1140, New York State Archives; the records covering the period up to 1862 include more than twenty-four cubic feet of material.

9. John Kasson offers an excellent general account of the relationship between technological change and republican values in *Civilizing the Machine: Technology and Republican Values in America, 1776–1900* (1976). Leo Marx's thesis in *The Machine in the Garden: Technology and the Pastoral Ideal in America* (1964) is dealt with in chapter 3. For two excellent local studies of responses to progress, see Robert A. Gross, " 'The Most Estimable Place in All the World': A Debate on Progress in Nineteenth-Century Concord," *Studies in the American Renaissance* (1978), and Carl Siracusa, *A Mechanical People: Perceptions of the Industrial Order in Massachusetts, 1815–1880* (1979). *The Artificial River* focuses on the perceptions of the white middle classes, since virtually no surviving sources reveal the ways in which either African Americans or Native

Americans perceived the Canal. By the time of the Canal's construction, much of the Iroquois population of the region had left for Canada after the American Revolution or, more recently, for Wisconsin and other western points; however, several small communities of Iroquois remained on reservations.

1: VISIONS OF PROGRESS

1. *Utica Gazette*, July 15, 1817, in *Our County and Its People: A Descriptive Work on Oneida County, New York*, ed. Daniel E. Wager (1896), 180. In later years, disputes arose over who had actually dug the first spadeful of soil. Some said that it was not Richardson but either Joshua Hathaway or DeWitt Clinton. Ibid., 179–80; see also statement in Joshua Hathaway Papers, Oneida County Historical Society.

2. For an extremely readable account of the region's geologic origins, see John McPhee, *In Suspect Terrain* (1983).

3. For an explicit attempt to apply modernization theory to antebellum history, see Richard Brown, *Modernization: The Transformation of American Life, 1600–1865* (1976).

4. Scholars have hotly debated the timing of the market revolution in American history. For insightful overviews of the vast historical literature on the transition from a moral economy to a market economy, see Gordon S. Wood, "Inventing American Capitalism," *The New York Review of Books*, June 9, 1994; Christopher Clark, *The Roots of Rural Capitalism: Western Massachusetts, 1780–1860* (1990), 3–17; Allan Kulikoff, "The Transition to Capitalism in Rural America," *William and Mary Quarterly* (January 1989), 120–44. The introduction to Steven Hahn and Jonathan Prude, eds., *The Countryside in the Age of Capitalist Transformation: Essays in the Social History of Rural America* (1985), offers a concise look at the issues confronting scholars participating in this lively historical debate. Among those scholars who argue that the moral economy extended into the nineteenth century are Clark; Allan Kulikoff, *The Agrarian Origins of American Capitalism* (1992); Michael Merrill, "Cash Is Good to Eat: Self-Sufficiency and Exchange in the Rural Economy of the United States," *Radical History Review* (1977), 42–71; James Henretta, *The Origins of American Capitalism* (1991); Charles Sellers, *The Market Revolution: Jacksonian America, 1815–1860* (1991); and John Mack Faragher, *Sugar Creek: Life on*

the Illinois Prairie (1986). Among these scholars' critics—those who argue that capitalism emerged along with the ideology of the American Revolution—are Joyce Appleby, *Liberalism and Republicanism in the Historical Imagination* (1992); Gordon S. Wood, *The Radicalism of the American Revolution* (1992); Winifred Barr Rothenberg, *From Market-Places to a Market Economy: The Transformation of Rural Massachusetts, 1750–1850* (1992). For an earlier argument along these same lines, see Louis Hartz, *Economic Policy and Democratic Thought: Pennsylvania, 1776–1860* (1948). Contemporaries did not confuse bartering with a lack of profit orientation. Two English immigrants living near Rochester, for example, wrote home in 1833, "here's a deal of battering [bartering] done for the Americans will part with any thing rather than Money . . ." J[oseph] and A[nn] Webb Letter, October 26, 1833, "Letters—Local—1820–1890s," Rochester Museum and Science Center.

5. Much like Christopher Clark in his study of the Connecticut River valley, I have found that most inhabitants of the Erie Canal region embraced market opportunities with a mixture of impulses; they were neither wholly precapitalist nor wholly capitalist in outlook. Whether they settled along the banks of the Mohawk River before 1817 or along the Erie Canal after that date, most residents of what would become the Canal corridor eagerly turned to market exchange in order to make their daily lives more comfortable and to provide economic opportunities for their children. Yet, as I will suggest in chapters 4 and 5, many farmers and even a number of merchants publicly criticized the notion of allowing individuals to profit at someone else's expense. In that sense, they liked to believe that they could pursue profits within the confines of a moral economy; in the eyes of people like the horse dealer Alexander Coventry, profiting at someone else's expense violated the ethos of a market-based moral economy. On the development of the upstate region, see William Wyckoff, *The Developer's Frontier: The Making of the Western New York Landscape* (1988); George Rogers Taylor, *The Transportation Revolution, 1815–1860* (1951); William Chazanof, *Joseph Ellicott and the Holland Land Company: The Opening of Western New York* (1970); Neil Adams McNall, *An Agricultural History of the Genesee Valley, 1790–1860* (1952). On the Western Inland Lock Navigation Company, see Ronald E. Shaw, *Erie Water West: A History of the Erie Canal, 1792–1854* (1966), 15–21.

6. Mary Ann (Wodrow) Archbald Papers, Sophia Smith Collection,

Smith College. All quotations from this manuscript collection (hereafter, "Archbald Papers") are based on a typescript copy of Mary Ann Archbald's letter book. For citations here, see the following letters: Mary Ann Archbald to "Mr. G.," March 1810; Archbald to Margaret Wodrow, August 7, 1818; Archbald to Margaret Wodrow, October 10, 1828. Since Archbald's husband left no written records, his outlook is unclear.

7. Archbald to "Mr. Summerville," 1808, Archbald Papers. On the War of 1812, see Harry L. Coles, *The War of 1812* (1965).

8. Archbald to Margaret [Wodrow], December 31, 1824, Archbald Papers.

9. Archbald to Margaret Wodrow, December 31, 1822, Archbald Papers. "Republicanism," its meanings, and its influence have been the source of much scholarly controversy. For a recent critical overview of the scholarship on republicanism, see Daniel T. Rodgers, "Republicanism: the Career of a Concept," *The Journal of American History* (June 1992), 11–38. The most useful discussion of the concept in relation to the early national period is Drew R. McCoy, *The Elusive Republic: Political Economy in Jeffersonian America* (1980). Some of the most influential works on republicanism include Robert E. Shalhope, "Toward a Republican Synthesis: The Emergence of an Understanding of Republicanism in American Historiography," *William and Mary Quarterly* (January 1972), 49–80; Shalhope, "Republicanism and Early American Historiography," *William and Mary Quarterly* (April 1982), 334–56; J.G.A. Pocock, "Virtue and Commerce in the Eighteenth Century," *Journal of Interdisciplinary History* (Summer 1972), 119–34; Pocock, *The Machiavellian Moment: Florentine Political Thought and the Atlantic Republican Tradition* (1975); Lance Banning, *The Jeffersonian Persuasion: Evolution of a Party Ideology* (1978); Banning, "Jeffersonian Ideology Revisited: Liberal and Classical Ideas in the New American Republic," *William and Mary Quarterly* (January 1986), 3–19; Robert Kelley, *The Cultural Pattern in American Politics: The First Century* (1979).

10. McCoy, *Elusive Republic*, 76–104; G. Edward White, *The Marshall Court & Cultural Change, 1815–1835*, abridged ed. (1988, 1991), 69–73; Stanley Elkins and Eric McKitrick, *The Age of Federalism: The Early Republic, 1788–1800* (1993), 257–302.

11. Taylor, *Transportation Revolution*, 132–33; he cites an 1816 U.S.

Senate Committee Report in *American State Papers: Miscellaneous*, II (1834), 287.

12. The best overviews of Jacksonian economic policy are Peter Temin, *The Jacksonian Economy* (1969), and Robert V. Remini, *Andrew Jackson and the Bank War: A Study in the Growth of Presidential Power* (1967).

13. Taylor, *Transportation Revolution*, 15–32.

14. Wyckoff, *Developer's Frontier*, 94–102. On reaching Albany, some shippers would have used boats along the improved Mohawk River as far as Utica before transferring to wagons. Thomas Brotts and Philip Kelley, eds., *Richard Barrett's Journal, New York and Canada, 1816* . . . (1983), 35.

15. Wyckoff, *Developer's Frontier*, 98–100.

16. Shaw, *Erie Water West*, 24–29.

17. Hawley quoted in ibid., 27. Each route involved making use of the Mohawk River for its eastern portion. Ibid., 29–35.

18. Shaw explores the political history behind the Canal in ibid., chapters 3 and 4.

19. See, for example, The New York *Evening Post*, March 29, 1817, cited in ibid., 68.

20. Ibid., chapter 4.

21. Ibid., 71–80; Cadwallader D. Colden, *Memoir, Prepared at the Request of a Committee of the Common Council of the City of New York, and Presented to the Mayor of the City, at the Celebration of the Completion of the New York Canals* (1825), 48–49. In 1819, the land tax was suspended; *Laws of the State of New York, in relation to the Erie and Champlain Canals* . . . , Vol. I (1825), 434.

22. Those eight lateral canals were the Genesee Valley, Crooked Lake, Oswego, Black River, Chenango, Chemung, Cayuga and Seneca, and Oneida Lake. Like nineteenth-century New Yorkers, I have concluded that people's experiences varied in large part according to their physical location in relation to the Erie Canal *or* one of its tributaries. What mattered was how far people found themselves from *some* part of the canal network—and not *which* part. To simplify the narrative, *The Artificial River* will tell the institutional story of just one canal, the one that vividly stood as a symbol of progress: the main Erie Canal.

23. Two excellent overviews of this period are Robert H. Wiebe, *The Opening of American Society: From the Adoption of the Constitution to*

the Eve of Disunion (1984), and George Dangerfield, *The Era of Good Feelings* (1952).

24. Steven E. Siry uses the phrase "practical republicanism"; see his *DeWitt Clinton and the American Political Economy: Sectionalism, Politics, and Republican Ideology, 1787–1828* (1990), 5. The classic biography of Clinton is Dorothie Bobbé, *DeWitt Clinton* (1933). On the imperatives of Clinton's generation to make its mark through economic development, see Siry, *DeWitt Clinton*, 4–17; Roger Evan Carp, "The Erie Canal and the Liberal Challenge to Classical Republicanism, 1785–1850" (Ph.D. diss., University of North Carolina at Chapel Hill, 1986), 250–67.

25. Williams, *Keywords: A Vocabulary of Culture and Society*, rev. ed. (1983), 160–61; 243–45. As Edward Balleisen astutely pointed out after reading this book in manuscript form, the rhetoric used by Northern promoters of internal improvements bears a striking resemblance to that used by proponents of Indian removal in the South. See, for example, Andrew Jackson, Second Annual Message, First Term, December 1830, in David Brion Davis, *Antebellum American Culture: An Interpretive Anthology* (1979), 240–43. This parallel in the 1820s and 1830s only makes more stark the growth of Northern distinctiveness over the years leading up to the Civil War. In both regions, political rhetoric advocated replacing savagery with civilization, but the understandings of "civilization" increasingly diverged. As we will see, by the 1840s, at least for Northern Whigs, economic progress generally meant the promotion of commercial development in the continent's interior, while Southern Democrats interpreted God's plan as involving the expansion of their existing system of slave-based staple agriculture. Adopting different interpretations of the nation's manifest destiny, leaders in the two regions, along with the majority of their respective constituents, embraced very different—and ultimately conflicting—paths of development.

26. The concept of the "middle landscape" is discussed in Leo Marx, *The Machine in the Garden: Technology and the Pastoral Ideal in America* (1964). In Marx's interpretation, contemporaries identified "civilization" with the present rather than the future.

27. For a discussion of the role of newspapers in reporting celebrations, in particular, see David Waldstreicher, "Rites of Rebellion, Rites of Assent: Celebrations, Print Culture, and the Origins

of American Nationalism," *Journal of American History* (June 1995), 37–61.

2: THE TRIUMPH OF ART OVER NATURE

1. "Ode for the Canal Celebration, written at the request of the Printers of New-York," 1825, Broadsides Collection, American Antiquarian Society; Ronald E. Shaw, *Erie Water West: A History of the Erie Canal, 1792–1854* (1966), 36.

2. For example, the nine members of the 1823 celebration committee in Albany included four or five merchants, two lawyers, and a postmaster. One of the merchants was also the last-remaining patroon. *Albany Argus*, October 3, 1823; *Klink's Albany Directory for the year 1823* (1823), in *American Directories through 1860: A Collection on Microfiche* . . . (1969). The directory did not list an occupation for the ninth member of the committee. Generalizations about the sentiments voiced at canal celebrations are based mostly on the events' extensive newspaper coverage and the commemorative pamphlets published for some of the larger ceremonies. On the 1819 celebration, see the *Utica Observer*, October 26, 1819, in *Our County and Its People: A Descriptive Work on Oneida County, New York*, ed. Daniel E. Wager (1896), 185–88; *Geneva Gazette*, November 3, 1819; and *Plough Boy*, November 6, 1819. On the 1823 celebration in Albany, see *Albany Argus*, September 23 and 30 and October 10, 1823; and *New York American*, reprinted in *Albany Argus*, October 14 and 24, 1823. The 1825 Grand Celebration was covered extensively in the press throughout the country, but for the most complete account see Cadwallader D. Colden, *Memoir, Prepared at the Request of a Committee of the Common Council of the City of New York* . . . *at the Celebration of the Completion of the New York Canals* (1825). Another major celebration was held in Lockport in July 1825; see *Cherry-Valley Gazette*, May 31 and July 12, 1825; *Albany Argus*, July 8 and 29, 1825; *Rochester Telegraph*, June 28, 1825; and F. H. Cuming, *An Address, Delivered at the Laying of the Cap-Stone, of the Ten Combined Locks at Lockport, on the Anniversary of St. John the Baptist, June 24, 1825* (1825). I am very grateful to Steve Bullock for alerting me to the Cuming pamphlet. Scattered reports survive for some of the smaller celebrations; for specific citations, see the author's doctoral dissertation (Yale,

1993). Although the evening events required participants to purchase tickets, the proceeds did not always meet the expenses, requiring members of the organizational committees to make up the difference from their own pockets; *Memoirs of an Emigrant: The Journal of Alexander Coventry* . . . , Vol. II (typescript prepared by the Albany Institute of History and Art and the New York State Library, 1978), 2181.

3. Archbald to Margaret Wodrow, September 29, 1821, Mary Ann (Wodrow) Archbald Papers, Smith College (hereafter, "Archbald Papers"); entry dated May 22, 1820, Coventry, *Memoirs of an Emigrant*, Vol. II, 1755.

4. Steamboats did not regularly travel the Hudson River until 1815; George Rogers Taylor, *The Transportation Revolution, 1815–1860* (1951), 57. Constance McL.Green, *Eli Whitney and the Birth of American Technology* (1956), 61.

5. The scholarly literature on early industrialization as a social process is rich. Some of the more accessible works include Alan Dawley, *Class and Community: The Industrial Revolution in Lynn* (1976); Thomas Dublin, *Women at Work: The Transformation of Work and Community in Lowell, Massachusetts, 1826–1860* (1979); Paul G. Faler, *Mechanics and Manufacturers in the Early Industrial Revolution: Lynn, Massachusetts, 1780–1860* (1981); Joan Jensen, *Loosening the Bonds: Mid-Atlantic Farm Women, 1750–1850* (1986); Paul E. Johnson, *A Shopkeeper's Millennium: Society and Revivals in Rochester, New York, 1815–1837* (1978); Bruce G. Laurie, *Artisans into Workers: Labor in Nineteenth-Century America* (1989); Christine Stansell, *City of Women: Sex and Class in New York, 1789–1860* (1986); Anthony F. C. Wallace, *Rockdale: The Growth of an American Village in the Early Industrial Revolution* (1978); Sean Wilentz, *Chants Democratic: New York City and the Rise of the American Working Class, 1788–1850* (1984).

6. Noble E. Whitford, *History of the Canal System of the State of New York, Together with Brief Histories of the Canals of the United States and Canada* (1906), 1030, 1107, 798; Shaw, *Erie Water West*, 87. Taylor's *Transportation Revolution* offers excellent background on technology during the period. See also Brook Hindle, *Technology in Early America* (1966); Hindle, ed., *America's Wooden Age: Aspects of Its Early Technology* (1975); Dirk J. Struik, *Yankee Science in the Making* (1948).

7. Webb Harwood to Daniel T. Terry, November 25, 1825 (typescript), Valentown Museum; Ira Blossom to H. J. Huidekoper, October 31, 1825, Ira A. Blossom Papers, Buffalo and Erie County Historical Society Library; Caroline Gilman, *The Poetry of Travelling in the United States* (1838), 103.

8. Henry Tudor, *Narrative of a Tour in North America* . . . , Vol. I (1834), 233–34.

9. Cuming, *Address, Delivered at the Laying of the Cap-Stone*, 8; S[amuel] Woodworth, *The Meeting of the Waters of Hudson & Erie* (1825), Sheet Music Collection, American Antiquarian Society.

10. Raymond Williams, *Keywords: A Vocabulary of Culture and Society*, rev. ed. (1983), 219; Barbara Novak, *Nature and Culture: American Landscape and Painting, 1825–1875* (1980), 3.

11. William Leete Stone, *Narrative of the Festivities Observed in Honor of the Completion of the Grand Erie Canal* (1825), 296; *Niles' Weekly Register*, November 12, 1825.

12. The theme of the Canal and republicanism is explored in Roger Evan Carp, "The Erie Canal and the Liberal Challenge to Classical Republicanism, 1785–1850" (Ph.D. diss., University of North Carolina at Chapel Hill, 1986); Shaw, *Erie Water West* and *Canals for a Nation: The Canal Era in the United States, 1790–1860* (1990); John Seelye, " 'Rational Exultation': The Erie Canal Celebration," *Proceedings of the American Antiquarian Society* 94:2 (1985), and *Beautiful Machines: Rivers and the Republican Plan, 1755–1825* (1991). *Albany Argus*, July 29, 1825. Carp, "Erie Canal and the Liberal Challenge," 263–65.

13. Whitford, *History of the Canal System*, 797, 1163; Daniel Hovey Calhoun, *The American Civil Engineer: Origins and Conflict* (1960), 24–34; Shaw, *Erie Water West*, 88–89.

14. *Laws of the State of New York, in relation to the Erie and Champlain Canals, together with the Annual Reports of the Canal Commissioners, and other Documents* . . . (1825), Vol. I, 403. On immigration during the antebellum period, see Maldwyn Allen Jones, *American Immigration*, 2nd ed. (1992), and Marcus Lee Hansen, *The Atlantic Migration, 1607–1860: A History of the Continuing Settlement of the United States* (1940). On Irish immigration, see Kerby Miller, *Emigrants and Exiles: Ireland and the Irish Exodus to North America* (1985). On Irish immigrants to the upstate region, see Daniel J. Casey and F. Daniel Larkin, "From Dromore to the Middle Sprite:

Irish Rural Settlement in the Mohawk Valley," *Journal of the Clogher Historical Society* 12:2 (1986), 181–91. Neither federal nor state censuses during this period called for information on places of birth. Calculations based on the 1820 federal census show that the number of "foreigners not naturalized" represented less than 1 percent of the populations of both New York in particular and the Northeast in general. When contemporary observers made reference to immigrants working on the Canal, they seem to have been referring to recent arrivals, who would be included in the "non-naturalized" category. In any case, it seems certain that the percentage of immigrants—naturalized and unnaturalized—in the broader population and the workforce was significantly less than 25 percent. Shaw, *Canals for a Nation*, 38; Peter Way, *Common Labour: Workers and the Digging of North American Canals, 1780– 1860* (1993), 97. Shaw, *Canals for a Nation*, 168.

15. Stephen and Elizabeth Watson to "Father and Mother," October 5, 1823, in *Twenty-Four Letters from Labourers in America to their Friends in England* (1829), 14. Laura S. Haviland, *A Woman's Life-Work: Labors and Experiences* (1889), 20; Archbald to M[argaret] Wodrow, January 1, 1821, Archbald Papers. Cathy Brekus provided me with the Haviland quotation.

16. David M. Ellis et al., *A History of New York State* (1957, 1967), 146–49; Dixon Ryan Fox, *The Decline of Aristocracy in the Politics of New York*, ed. Robert V. Remini (1965; orig. ed. 1919), 273– 74.

17. Drew R. McCoy, *The Elusive Republic: Political Economy in Jeffersonian America* (1980), 37–38, 66, and 149; Way, *Common Labour*, passim.

18. David S. Bates to Commissioners of the Erie and Hudson Canals. In *Laws of the State of New York, in relation to the Erie and Champlain Canals*, Vol. II, 501. Bates is referring to the route of the Oswego Canal around Oswego Falls. I am grateful to Don Wilson for drawing this passage to my attention.

19. Stephen and Elizabeth Watson to "Father and Mother," October 5, 1823, in *Twenty-Four Letters from Labourers*. Way, *Common Labour*, 193–94; see also Taylor, *Transportation Revolution*, 290. Archbald to Gov[ernor] Clinton, October [1821], Archbald Papers. Archbald wrote on behalf of an Irish worker who she felt had been too harshly sentenced for assaulting a constable and starting a riot.

Archbald admitted that her "early prejudices were all against the Irish," but that she had changed her mind after having had some of them board with her. According to Archbald's own notes, Clinton responded to her letter, promising to investigate the matter; the man was released from jail in 1822.

20. Taylor, *Transportation Revolution*, 292. In 1817, the New York State Legislature passed a law allowing for the employment of convicts on the Erie Canal. In what was viewed as an experiment, the contractor on the Rochester aqueduct employed 150 convicts. *Laws of the State of New York, in relation to the Erie and Champlain Canals*, Vol. I, 365; *Rochester Telegraph*, July 31, August 7, September 25, October 30, and March 26, 1821; *Schoharie Observer*, August 1, 1821; *Plough Boy*, October 20, 1821, and January 26, 1822. In 1834, a "Mechanics' Convention" in Utica denounced convict labor as "degrading" to the mechanics. *Niles' Weekly Register*, September 20, 1834.

21. Way writes: "Although it is impossible to determine exactly, it is not too far-fetched to say that the overwhelming majority arrived as labourers and remained so for some time." Way would disagree with my view that immigrants were drawn to the United States by the opportunities the new nation presented; he writes: "To characterize emigration, then, as a rational decision made in light of prevailing social and economic conditions is to miss the fact that conditions for two centuries and more had been increasingly stacked against those involved and imposed an ultimatum more than a free choice"; Way, *Common Labour*, 96, 93. *Dublin Journal*, September 9 and October 21, 1817; June 12, 1818. During the Erie's construction period, this newspaper published almost no negative accounts of life in the United States. One article did recount the contents of an article in *The Exile*, an Irish paper in New York City, that painted a grim picture of life in North America; *Dublin Journal*, August 14, 1817.

22. Pádraig Phiarais Cúndún to Partolan Suipéal, December 17, 1834, in *Pádraig Phiarais Cúndún, 1776–1856*, ed. Risteárd Ó Foghludha (1932), 24–30. Translation by Bruce D. Boling (typescript and correspondence with author). Bruce Boling and Kerby Miller very generously shared with me this material from their forthcoming work.

23. *The Exile*, August 2, 1817. William Thomas to his father, mother,

brothers, and sisters, August 17, 1818, in Alan Conway, ed., *The Welsh in America: Letters from the Immigrants* (1961), 61. In the second quotation, Thomas is referring to all carpenters, not just foreign-born ones.

24. Way, *Common Labour*, 112–15. For a study of wage rates among the Canal's repair workers (usually recruited locally on an ad hoc basis), see Walter B. Smith, "Wage Rates on the Erie Canal, 1828–1881," *Journal of Economic History* (September 1963), 298–311.

25. David Richard to his brother, December 11, 1818, in Conway, ed., *Welsh in America*, 62. *Rochester Telegraph*, October 16, 1821; *Bellows Falls Intelligencer*, August 5, 1822. The *Intelligencer* says that the demand for laborers in Lockport was 1,900, which was apparently a misprint. Two other sources, which provide no information about wages, reported the figure as a round 1,000; *Plough Boy*, August 6, 1822; F. A. Fenn to Samuel Dakin, July 29, 1822, Samuel Dakin Papers, New York State Historical Association. *Laws of the State of New York, in relation to the Erie and Champlain Canals*, Vol. II, 7. Donald R. Adams, Jr., "Wage Rates in the Early National Period: Philadelphia, 1785–1830," *Journal of Economic History* (September 1968), 406.

26. William Thomas to his father, mother, brothers, and sisters, August 17, 1818, in Conway, ed., *Welsh in America*, 61; Hugh Jones to his parents, September 7, 1818, in ibid., 61–62.

27. New York Canal Commissioners, *Annual Report* (1820), 17. Failing Twitchell & Co., Canal Board Papers, Box 1, "1828, Box 1, Folder 2," and J. E. Smith & Company, ibid., Box 1, "1828, Box 1, Folder 2."

28. Although newspaper editors and other residents reported canal accidents as they happened, the state did not systematically keep statistics on accidents; we therefore do not know exactly how many workers were killed or maimed while working on the Canal. For examples of references to accidents, see the clippings on accidents in the vertical files at the Onondaga Historical Association in Syracuse. Examples of the sorts of accidents mentioned here can be seen in *Plough Boy*, February 2, 1822; *Bellows Falls Intelligencer*, December 16, 1822; *Albany Argus*, June 13, 1823; *Rochester Telegraph*, September 30, 1823; Lyman A. Spalding, *Recollections of the War of 1812 and Early Life in Western New York* (1949), 17. Some

people also drowned in the four-foot-deep original Canal; it seems that many of them were intoxicated at the time of their accidents. *Lockport Observatory*, October 29, 1825.

29. Ulysses Prentiss Hedrick, *A History of Agriculture in the State of New York* (1933 and 1966), 350–51; Hal S. Barron, *Those Who Stayed Behind: Rural Society in Nineteenth-Century New England* (1984), 8–9.

30. Speech of Lieutenant-Governor James Tallmadge reprinted in *Albany Argus and City Gazette*, November 8, 1825; toast of "Mr. Sherwood of Delhi" at the opening of the Rochester aqueduct, reported in *Rochester Telegraph*, October 14, 1823. Paul Johnson, " 'Art' and the Language of Progress in Early Industrial Paterson: Sam Patch at Clinton Bridge," *American Quarterly* (1988), 440–43.

31. Cuming, *Address, Delivered at the Laying of the Cap-Stone*, 8. Later in his address, Cuming does seem on the surface to refer to the contribution of laborers: "Let us remember also that those who have served only as *entered apprentices*, especially those who *here* have stretched the line and handled the other *implements* of their art, richly deserved to be *passed* and *raised*, to higher degrees, and to be received and acknowledged as *Most Excellent Masters*." Ibid., 9–10. Even here, though, Cuming seems to ignore common laborers. His reference to stretching the line probably refers to surveying, a very different sort of labor from that performed by the majority of canal workers. Given that the ceremony at which Cuming officiated was run by the Masons, his references to apprentices and masters may also relate to Masonic ritual and have little to do with literal apprentices. For another ambiguous reference to laborers, see the toast offered by Nathaniel Rochester, reported in *Rochester Telegraph*, October 14, 1823.

32. *Albany Argus and City Gazette*, November 8, 1825.

33. Lyrics reprinted in the *Geneva Gazette and General Advertiser*, November 9, 1825. Stone, *Narrative of the Festivities*; *Albany Argus*, September 23 and 30 and October 10, 1823; *New York American*, reprinted in *Albany Argus*, October 14 and 24, 1823. For more on the celebration of craftsmen in New York City, see Wilentz, *Chants Democratic*, 87–90, and Seelye, " 'Rational Exultation': The Erie Canal Celebration."

34. On cartmen, see Graham Russell Hodges, *New York City Cartmen,* *1667–1850* (1986).
35. Way, *Common Labour,* 173. *Utica Observer,* October 26, 1819, in *Our County,* ed. Wager.
36. Hutchinson to Lyman Spalding, November 16, 1822, Lyman Spalding Papers, Cornell University.
37. Colden, *Memoir,* 70. *Albany Argus and City Gazette,* November 8, 1825. The colonel referred to is probably William Leete Stone.
38. Webb Harwood to Daniel T. Terry, November 25, 1821 (typescript), Valentown Museum.
39. *Messages from the Governors* [*of New York*], ed. Charles Z. Lincoln (1909), Vol. II, 966–67.

3: REDUCING DISTANCE AND TIME

1. Nathan Miller, *The Enterprise of a Free People: Aspects of Economic Development in New York State during the Canal Period, 1792–1838* (1962), 115. Tolls raised more than $500,000 in 1825 alone; the total debt on the construction exceeded $7,000,000; Noble E. Whitford, *History of the Canal System of New York Together with Brief Histories of the Canals of the United States and Canada* (1906), 958. In addition to the works cited in Sources, see Ronald W. Filante, "A Note on the Economic Viability of the Erie Canal, 1825–1860," *Business History Review* (Spring 1974), 95–102; Carter Goodrich, "The Revulsion Against Internal Improvements," *The Journal of Economic History* (November 1950), 145–69; Albert W. Niemi, Jr., "A Further Look at Interregional Canals and Economic Specialization: 1820–1840," *Explorations in Economic History* (Summer 1970), 499–520; Roger L. Ransom, "A Closer Look at Canals and Western Manufacturing," *Explorations in Economic History* (Summer 1971), 501–8; Julius Rubin, "Canal or Railroad?: Imitation or Innovation in the Response to the Erie Canal in Philadelphia, Baltimore, and Boston," *Transactions of the American Philosophical Society* (November 1961), 5–106.
2. Elisha Loomis, "Diary of Trip Rochester to Mackinac Island," ed. Philip P. Mason, *Michigan History* 38 (1853), 30; Ephraim Arnold to his parents, July 20, [1820?], Erie Canal Museum, 73:58; Sabrina Y. White, "The Erie Canal's Role in the Underground Railroad," in *Homefront: The Erie Canal in the Civil War* (1987), 21–

23; Evamaria Hardin, *Syracuse and the Underground Railroad* (1989); Cadwallader D. Colden, *Memoir, Prepared at the Request of a Committee of the Common Council of the City of New York, and Presented to the Mayor of the City, at the Celebration of the Completion of the New York Canals* (1825), 88; *People's Friend*, June 23 and 30, 1824; June 25, 1829; *Wayne Sentinel*, June 9 and 23, 1824. George Combe, *Notes on the United States of America . . .* (1841), Vol. II, in Clayton Mau, *The Development of Central and Western New York . . .* (1944), 358; *New York Advertiser* in *Hampden Journal*, July 28, 1824. Paul Johnson shared with me the citations from the *Wayne Sentinel*.

3. Charles Lanman, *Recollections of Curious Characters and Pleasant Places* (1881), 15.

4. By law, boats were restricted to moving at four miles an hour in order to limit the wake they produced, and thus protect the canal's banks. But captains of passenger boats often risked the ten-dollar fine for exceeding the speed limit; passengers preferred the faster boats, so—in a competitive market—captains found it worth their while to incur an occasional fine. The extra fares helped make up for the fines. A stagecoach usually traveled at nine miles an hour on a New York plank road; a freight wagon, at two miles an hour. George Rogers Taylor, *The Transportation Revolution, 1815–1860* (1951), 142 and 138. Caroline E. MacGill, *History of Transportation in the United States before 1860* (1917), 168.

5. William Dunlap, *A Trip to Niagara, or Travellers in America, A Farce* (1830), 42. For an interesting discussion of the actual experiences of women traveling on the Erie Canal, see Patricia Cline Cohen, "Safety and Danger: Women on American Public Transport, 1750–1850," in *Gendered Domains: Rethinking Public and Private Women's History*, ed. Dorothy O. Helly and Susan M. Reverby (1992).

6. Leo Marx, *The Machine in the Garden: Technology and the Pastoral Ideal in America* (1964).

7. Nathaniel Hawthorne, "The Canal Boat," *Mosses from an Old Manse* (1887), 484–94. See Marx, *Machine in the Garden*, on Hawthorne's views of railroads.

8. Elizabeth McKinsey, *Niagara Falls: Icon of the American Sublime* (1985). On tourism in the region in general, see McKinsey; Hans Huth, *Nature and the American: Three Centuries of Changing Attitudes*

(1957); Patricia Anderson, *The Course of Empire: The Erie Canal and the New York Landscape, 1825–1875* (1984); Patrick McGreevy, *Imagining Niagara: The Meaning and Making of Niagara Falls* (1994); Seymour Dunbar, *A History of Travel in America* (1937). Stewart Scott Diary, 1826, Manuscripts Collection #13145, New York State Library, 63.

9. For examples of uses of this phrase, see *Plough Boy*, July 15, 1820; "Third Annual Report of the Albany Marine Bible Society," excerpted in *Albany Argus*, February 11, 1823; Toast to "Canals" printed in *Rochester Telegraph*, October 14, 1823; *Geneva Gazette*, October 29, 1823; Colden, *Memoir*, 90; E[verard] Peck to Samuel Porter, April 22, 1828, Porter Family Papers, University of Rochester.

10. *A Canalboat Primer on the Canals of New York State* (1981), 8. One traveler reported that 130 passengers crowded her boat; Frances Buell to Mariann, August 19, [1822], Ward (Joseph Buell) Family Papers, Box 1, "Correspondence, 1817–1826," University of Rochester. Patrick Shirreff, *A Tour through North America . . .* (1835), 308. In 1823, Mary Ann Archbald described the accommodations on packet boats and then wrote: "[M]any go intirely for pleasure who have neither business nor friends to visit." Archbald to Wodrow, December 31, 1823, Mary Ann (Wodrow) Archbald Papers, Smith College (hereafter, "Archbald Papers").

11. Basil Hall, *Travels in North America in the Years 1827 and 1828* (1829), 75. During this part of his journey, he traveled through the Canal corridor by stage. "Account of Journey of Sibyl Tatum with her Parents from N. Jersey to Ohio in 1830" (typescript), New York State Historical Association, [9]. (Hereafter cited as "Sibyl Tatum Diary.") An extensive scholarly literature exists on the meanings of nature. Among those works that helped shape my thoughts here are William Cronon, *Nature's Metropolis: Chicago and the Great West* (1991); Simon Schama, *Landscape and Memory* (1995); Barbara Novak, *Nature and Culture: American Landscape and Painting, 1825–1875* (1980); Henry Nash Smith, *Virgin Land: The American West as Myth and Symbol* (1950); Roderick Nash, *Wilderness and the American Mind*, 3rd ed. (1982); Perry Miller, "The Romantic Dilemma in American Nationalism and the Concept of Nature," *Harvard Theological Review* (October 1955), 239–53; Neil Everndon, *The Social Creation of Nature* (1992); Angela Miller, *The*

Empire of the Eye: Landscape Representation and American Cultural Politics (1993); Marx, *Machine in the Garden*; John R. Stilgoe, *Common Landscape of America, 1580 to 1845* (1982); Cecelia Tichi, *New World, New Earth: Environmental Reform in American Literature from the Puritans through Whitman* (1979); Anderson, *Course of Empire*. For a concise exploration of the meanings of wilderness, see Cronon, "The Trouble with Wilderness," *The New York Times Magazine*, August 13, 1995.

12. Clarissa Burroughs Travel Diary, 1835 (typescript), Cornell University Library, 21; Freegift Wells, "Minutes of a Journey to Lyons, Wayne County and back to Watervliet," Microfilm roll 47/C/317, Western Reserve Historical Collection; typescript in "Canals— NY—Erie Canal—Eyewitness Accounts," Erie Canal Museum; Sibyl Tatum Diary, [7].

13. *Atkinson's Casket*, 1833, 21. [Theodore Dwight, Jr.], *Things as They Are: or, Notes of a Traveller* . . . (1834), 231–32. I am grateful to Edward Balleisen for providing me with the *Atkinson's Casket* citation.

14. Clarissa Burroughs Travel Diary, 19.

15. For an excellent introduction to scholarly discussions over the role of consumption, see *Consumption and the World of Goods*, ed. John Brewer and Roy Porter (1993); virtually all the leading scholars of consumption contributed to this volume. The articles by T. H. Breen and Joyce Appelby were particularly influential on my account here. *Rochester Telegraph*, October 21, 1823.

16. Some of the cases brought to the Canal Board involve toll collectors' charging boat captains with fraudulently claiming that their freight belonged to emigrants.

17. Everard Peck to Samuel Porter, April 22, 1828, Porter Family Papers, University of Rochester; *Buffalo Journal* in *Bellows Falls Intelligencer*, November 28, 1825; Archbald to Wodrow, November 13, 1838, Archbald Papers. For a discussion of the Canal's influence on cultural exchange, see Ronald J. Zboray, "The Transportation Revolution and Antebellum Book Distribution Reconsidered," *American Quarterly* (Spring 1986), 53–71. Although he does not deal with the Erie Canal specifically, Richard Brown's look at the transmission of news in the antebellum period is relevant and thought-provoking; Brown, *Knowledge Is Power: The Diffusion of Information in Early America, 1700–1865* (1989).

18. "New York Canal Lands on Sale," October 1823, Broadsides Collection, American Antiquarian Society.

19. J[oseph] and A[nn] Webb letter, October 26, 1833, Rochester Museum and Science Center; entry dated April 1, 1838, William B. Harris Farm Journal (typescript), Cornell University.

20. For example, 70 percent of the people listed in Rochester's 1827 city directory had left by 1834. Blake McKelvey, *Rochester: The Water-Power City, 1812–1854* (1945), 165; entry dated March 7, 1837, Eleazor Conkey Diary (typescript), Erie Canal Museum; Samuel Porter to his grandfather [April 1828], letter appended to Everard Peck to Samuel Porter, April 22, 1828, Porter Family Papers. See Thomas Bender, *Community and Social Change in America* (1978), for a concise and provocative treatment of the role of community in American culture.

21. *Connecticut Herald* in *Schoharie Observer*, August 22, 1821; Archbald to M[argaret Wodrow], January 1, 1821, Archbald Papers.

22. Archbald to Wodrow, September 1836, Archbald Papers.

23. Entry dated February 23, 1838, William B. Harris Farm Journal; Abigail Marks to her sisters, June 18, 1840, Box 1, Curtis Family Papers, University of Rochester.

24. [James Lumsden], *American Memoranda, by A Mercantile Man, during a Short Tour in the Summer of 1843* (1844), 28.

25. Thomas McKenney, who traveled on the Canal in 1826, wrote: "[T]he bridges appear to me to average at least one for every quarter of a mile from Schenectady to where I now am, which is some twenty miles from Utica." McKenney, *Sketches of a Tour to the Lakes* (1827), excerpted in Mau, *Development of Central and Western New York*, 264. DeWitt Clinton, Annual Message, 1826, *Messages from the Governors [of New York]*, ed. Charles Z. Lincoln (1909), Vol. III, 120.

26. William H. Seward, Annual Message, 1842, ibid., 957.

27. Archbald to Wodrow, June 12, 1828, Archbald Papers. The section of Canal between Albany and Schenectady contained twenty-seven locks and was twice as long as the land route. When contemporary observers compared the two routes, they usually pointed to the Canal's locks as being the impediment to quick travel. There is a rich scholarly literature on gender and the landscape. See, for example, Angela Miller. *The Empire of the Eye*; Carolyn Merchant, *The Death of Nature: Women, Ecology, and the*

Scientific Revolution (1980); Carol P. MacCormack and Marilyn Strathern, eds., *Nature, Culture and Gender* (1980); Michelle Zimbalist Rosaldo, "Woman, Culture, and Society: A Theoretical Overview," in *Woman, Culture and Society*, ed. Michelle Zimbalist Rosaldo and Louise Lamphere (1974); Annette Kolodny, *The Lay of the Land: Metaphor as Experience and History in American Life and Letters* (1975).

28. Entry dated June 9, 1847, Lyman Spalding Journal #3, Spalding Family Papers, Syracuse University; Clarissa Burroughs Travel Diary, 21; New York Canal Commissioners, *Annual Report* (1851), 68; *Rochester Republican*, May 21, 1839.

29. "To the Honorable the Legislature of the State of New York" (printed petition), #78.24.1, 78.24.2, 78.24.5, "Canal-related Material," Box 6, Erie Canal Museum. The residents of Rochester made a similar plea to the legislature, saying that a delay in navigation at a basin near that town "causes delays in the navigation of the canal, and is the occasion of quarrels and riots in consequence of the accumulation of boats and business at that point"; Report of the Committee on Canals and Internal Improvements, on the Petition of the Proprietors of the Canal Basin at Rochester, known as "Child's Slip," Assembly Doc. 120, January 28, 1839, 5; *Rochester Republican*, July 4, 1837; American Bethel Society, *Eleventh Annual Report* (1847), 20.

30. Horace Wheeler to Robert Rand, December 6, 1825, Horace Wheeler Papers, Rochester Historical Society; Silas Marks to Silas Curtis Family, December 21, 1842, Curtis Family Papers.

31. Entry dated April 16, 1832, Asa Eastwood Diary #1, Asa Eastwood Papers, Syracuse University.

32. J[oseph] and A[nn] Webb letter, October 26, 1833, Rochester Museum and Science Center.

33. Archbald to Wodrow, December 31, 1832, Archbald Papers; Abigail Marks to Silas Curtis family, December 25, 1840, Curtis Family Papers.

34. *Rochester Daily Democrat*, November 24, 1842; *The New York Times* in *Onondaga Standard*, December 9, 1835, "Tr[ansportation]—Canals—Erie and Oswego, 1830–39," Vertical File, Onondaga Historical Association.

4: THE POLITICS OF LAND AND WATER

1. *A View of the Grand Canal, from Lake Erie to the Hudson River* . . . (1825), 14.
2. This same basic ambivalence was recognized almost four decades ago by the historian Marvin Meyers; *The Jacksonian Persuasion: Politics and Belief* (1957), 11–12. While *The Artificial River* concentrates on popular attitudes toward the role of the state in regulating internal improvements, scholars have produced excellent studies focusing on legislative debates and actions. On New York in particular, see Nathan Miller, *The Enterprise of a Free People: Aspects of Economic Development in New York State during the Canal Period, 1792–1838* (1962); L. Ray Gunn, *The Decline of Authority: Public Economic Policy and Political Development in New York State, 1800–1860* (1988); Ronald E. Shaw, *Erie Water West: A History of the Erie Canal, 1792–1854* (1966). On government sponsorship of canals generally, see Harry N. Scheiber, *Ohio Canal Era: A Case Study of Government and the Economy, 1820–1861* (1969); Carter Goodrich, *Government Promotion of American Canals and Railroads, 1800–1890* (1960); Goodrich, "The Revulsion Against Internal Improvements," *The Journal of Economic History* (November 1950), 145–69; Ronald E. Shaw, *Canals for a Nation: The Canal Era in the United States, 1790–1860* (1990). On the role of the state in economic development more generally, see Richard L. McCormick, *The Party Period and Public Policy: American Politics from the Age of Jackson to the Progressive Era* (1986), chapter 5; Harry N. Scheiber, "Government and the Economy: Studies of the 'Commonwealth' Policy in Nineteenth-Century America," *Journal of Interdisciplinary History* (Summer 1972), 135–51; Morton Horwitz, *The Transformation of American Law, 1780–1860* (1977); Oscar Handlin and Mary Flug Handlin, *Commonwealth: A Study of the Government in the American Economy: Massachusetts, 1774–1861* (1947 and 1969); Louis Hartz, *Economic Policy and Democratic Thought: Pennsylvania, 1776–1860* (1948).
3. Horwitz, *Transformation of American Law*, 31–62; G. Edward White, *The Marshall Court & Cultural Change, 1815–1835*, abridged ed. (1988, 1991), 59–61, 595–602.
4. The officials included the lieutenant-governor, comptroller, attorney general, surveyor general, secretary of state, and treasurer. Af-

ter the adoption of the new state constitution in 1846, the Canal
Board also included a State Engineer and Surveyor. Shaw, *Erie
Water West*, 241–42; Noble E. Whitford, *History of the Canal System of the State of New York, Together with Brief Histories of the Canals
of the United States and Canada* (1906), 1130–32.

5. On juries and property awards, see Horwitz, *Transformation of
American Law*, 28–29.

6. On the legislature, see Gunn, *Decline of Authority*, 82. A precise
analysis of who petitioned that body with canal-related claims is
not possible, since most of the relevant manuscript petitions were
damaged in a fire at the turn of the twentieth century and have
not yet been made available for public use.

7. A rough calculation based on an official digest of Canal Board
claims published in 1858 yields a total of about six thousand
claimants. Yet many, if not most, of the manuscript claims I examined are not recorded in this digest, which suggests the numbers were much higher. Moreover, this digest records only
property damage claims and not the many other issues which citizens brought to the board. S. P. Allen, *Digest of Claims, and the
Action Thereon by the Legislature and the Canal Board, . . . from 1818
to 1858* (1858).

8. Archbald receipt, Series A1125, Canal Contracts, New York State
Archives; Mary Ann (Wodrow) Archbald Papers, Smith College,
passim; Daniel Hovey Calhoun, *The American Civil Engineer: Origins
and Conflict* (1960), 210.

9. Daniel Walker Howe, *The Political Culture of the American Whigs*
(1979), 27. See also Gary Wills, *Lincoln at Gettysburg: The Words
That Remade America* (1992).

10. This calculation includes the redigging of the Erie Canal during
the enlargement project.

11. *Laws of the State of New York, in relation to the Erie and Champlain
Canals, together with the Annual Reports of the Canal Commissioners,
and other Documents . . .* (1825), Vol. I, 332–33. Most of the land
ceded directly to the state was undeveloped property in the western
part of the state. The Canal Commissioners reported in 1817 that
90 percent of the people asked to cede land in that section of the
state had agreed to do so. Since the value of such lands stood to
appreciate considerably with the building of the Canal, it is not
surprising that western landowners—including a large number of

speculators—would be willing to contribute land to launch the canal project. The law regarding compensation read: "And it shall be the duty of the said appraisers, or a majority of them, to make a just and equitable estimate and appraisal of the loss and damage, if any, over and above the benefit and advantage to the respective owners and proprietors or parties interested in the premises so required" for the Canal. *Laws of the State of New York, in relation to the Erie and Champlain Canals*, Vol. I, 360–61.

12. For vivid accounts of damages caused by workers, see Sarah Beaston to Simon Dexter, February 20, 1828, "Correspondence— Business . . . 80.53.1," Box 3, Canal-related Material, Erie Canal Museum; John Hollister, Canal Board Papers, Box 23, "1861, Box 1, Folder 3," New York State Archives; John G. Wheelock Deposition, March 28, 1851, Manuscript #14315, New York State Library. Since chapters 4 and 5 rely so heavily on the Canal Board Papers, future citations for the Canal Board Papers will be abbreviated to "CBP."

13. Richard Davis, CBP, Box 1, "1831, Box 1, Folder 1." Davis was writing about water damage to his land.

14. After cutting down the trees' branches, farmers burned them, producing potash, a potassium compound that was sold for use in both manufacturing and agriculture. Many farmers made their first land payments in the form of potash, which the agents of the land companies then transported to New York City on canal boats.

15. Sarah Beaston to Simon Dexter, February 20, 1828, Erie Canal Museum. Beaston states explicitly that her objection does not arise from the fact that the canal runs through her land but from other losses.

16. Cadwallader D. Colden, *Memoir, Prepared at the Request of a Committee of the Common Council of the City of New York, and Presented to the Mayor of the City, at the Celebration of the Completion of the New York Canals* (1825), 86.

17. Petition of Inhabitants of Territory between Genesee River and Oak Orchard Creek, CBP, Box 1, "1828, Box 2, Folder 1." On surplus water generally, see John Xavier McConkey, "Development of the Surplus Water Leasing Policy on the Erie Canal System, 1817–1903" (Ph.D. diss., Syracuse University, 1966).

18. Inhabitants of Onondaga for a lock around Baldwin's dam on the

Seneca River, CBP, Box 1, "1831, Box 1, Folder 3"; John Stainton, CBP, Box 1, "1830, Box 1, Folder 1."

19. Petition of Inhabitants of Territory between Genesee River and Oak Orchard Creek, CBP.

20. William DeZeng, CBP, Box 1, "1829, Box 3, Folder 5."

21. White, *Marshall Court & Cultural Change*, 60. White cites J. Story, "Natural Law," in F. Lieber, ed., Encyclopedia Americana (1830), IX, 150, reprinted in J. McClellan, *Joseph Story and the American Constitution* (1971), 320.

22. For an analysis of New York's emergence as the preeminent port, see Robert G. Albion, *The Rise of New York Port* (1939); on the waterway's impact on upstate cities, see Whitford, *History of the Canal System*, 891–92.

23. J[oseph] and A[nn] Webb letter, October 26, 1833, Rochester Museum and Science Center.

24. William Wilcox, CBP, Box 4, "1837, Box 2, Folder 1"; Anson Cary, CBP, Box 6, "1841, Box 2, Folder 3."

25. Abraham Lansing, CBP, Box 5, "1840, Box 1, Folder 4." See also John Taylor, CBP, Box 5, "1840, Box 1, Folder 4"; David Diefendorff, Box 12, "1849, Box 1, Folder 1."

26. On the impact of the spread of credit relationships, see Edward J. Balleisen, "Navigating Failure: Bankruptcy in Antebellum America" (Ph.D. diss., Yale University, 1995).

27. While the number of people involved in manufacturing almost doubled during this period, they still represented a small portion of the population (7.1 percent). See Harvey H. Segal, "Canals and Economic Development," in *Canals and American Economic Development*, ed. Carter Goodrich, 236. Segal writes: "Our figures clearly indicate that the employment in commerce and manufacturing grew more rapidly in the Erie Canal group [of counties]" than in most of the rest of the state; 235. On manufacturing in the region, see also Richard Larry Ehrlich, "The Development of Manufacturing in Selected Counties in the Erie Canal Corridor, 1815–1860" (Ph.D. diss., State University of New York at Buffalo, 1972). No data exist on the number of farm laborers during this period. On strikes, see *Rochester Republican*, July 4, 1837; *Rochester Daily Advertiser*, February 8 and April 3, 1851; *Rochester Daily Democrat*, February 8 and April 2, 1851; New York Canal Commissioners, *Annual Report* (1851), 29–30; entry dated December 22, 1839,

Lyman Spalding Journal #2, Spalding Family Papers, Syracuse University. See also James Swinnich, "Strike and Rebellion Upon the Towpath" (student paper, State University of New York at Buffalo, 1981), Buffalo and Erie County Historical Society.

28. In 1847, the American Bethel Society estimated that 30,000 people worked on the Canal. *Eleventh Annual Report* (1847), 20.

29. See John Ashworth, *"Agrarians" & "Aristocrats": Party Political Ideology in the United States, 1837–1846* (1983, 1987); Lawrence Kohl, *The Politics of Individualism: Parties and the American Character in the Jacksonian Era* (1989).

30. On the American System, see Major L. Wilson, *Space, Time, and Freedom: The Quest for Nationality and the Irrepressible Conflict, 1815–1861* (1974), chapter 3.

31. Harry Scheiber has found a similar pattern in Ohio; Scheiber, *Ohio Canal Era*. For excellent overviews of the second party system and political rhetoric, see Ashworth, *"Agrarians" & "Aristocrats"*; Kohl, *Politics of Individualism*; Richard P. McCormick, *The Second American Party System: Party Formation in the Jacksonian Era* (1966); Meyers, *The Jacksonian Persuasion*; Edward Pessen, *Jacksonian America: Society, Personality, and Politics*, rev. ed. (1978); Harry L. Watson, *Liberty and Power: The Politics of Jacksonian America* (1990); Arthur Schlesinger, Jr., *The Age of Jackson* (1945); Bray Hammond, *Banks and Politics in America from the Revolution to the Civil War* (1957). On Democrats, see Jean Baker, *Affairs of Party: The Political Culture of Northern Democrats in the Mid-Nineteenth Century* (1983). On the Whigs, see Howe, *Political Culture of the American Whigs*. On Whigs in New York, see Elliot Robert Barkan, *Portrait of a Party: The Origins and Development of the Whig Persuasion in New York State* (1988). For an ethnocultural analysis of voting patterns in New York State, see Lee Benson, *The Concept of Jacksonian Democracy: New York as a Test Case* (1961). For overviews of party politics in New York, see Dixon Ryan Fox, *The Decline of Aristocracy in the Politics of New York, 1801–1840*, ed. Robert V. Remini (1965; orig. ed. 1919); Alvin Kass, *Politics in New York State, 1800–1830* (1965). Amy Bridges, *A City in the Republic: Antebellum New York and the Origins of Machine Politics* (1984), examines the birth of machine politics in New York City.

32. Joseph Hanford, CBP, Box 4, "1838, Box 1, Folder 2."

33. Anson Cary, CBP, Box 6, "1841, Box 2, Folder 3." Patrick Hen-

ry's speech at the Virginia Convention in Richmond on March 23, 1775, included the following phrases: "We are apt to shut our eyes against a painful truth—and listen to the song of that syren, till she transforms us into beasts," and "Gentlemen may cry, Peace, peace,—but there is no peace." William Hurt Henry, *Patrick Henry: Life, Correspondence and Speeches*, Vol. I (1891; repr. 1969), 262 and 266.

34. Anson Cary, CBP; Horwitz, *Transformation of American Law*, 101.
35. Stanley I. Kutler, *Privilege and Creative Destruction: The Charles River Bridge Case* (1971); Horwitz, *Transformation of American Law*, 130–39. Upstate farmers would not have meant that their property was literally sacrosanct, but rather that any "taking" required fair compensation.
36. Abraham Lansing and Levinus Lansing, CBP, Box 5, "1840, Box 1, Folder 4." Levinus Lansing filed for both.
37. Assembly Doc. 176, February 8, 1839; Assembly Doc. 296, March 12, 1839; Petition of Inhabitants of Dansville, CBP, Box 7, "1843, Box 2, Folder 4."
38. *Albany Evening Atlas*, May 20, 1844. I am very grateful to Reeve Huston for bringing this article to my attention.
39. Shaw, *Erie Water West* 250–51; 424.
40. On the evolution of nineteenth-century rhetoric, see Kenneth Cmiel, *Democratic Eloquence: The Fight over Popular Speech in Nineteenth-Century America* (1990). On vandalism, see New York Canal Commissioners, *Annual Report* (1820), 15; *Annual Report* (1851), 69; *Rochester Daily Union*, October 13, 1856.
41. Abraham Lansing and Levinus Lansing, CBP. W. J. Rorabaugh, *The Alcoholic Republic: An American Tradition* (1979). On temperance, see also Ian R. Tyrrell, *Sobering Up: From Temperance to Prohibition in Antebellum America, 1800–1860* (1979). For an excellent introduction to antebellum moral reform, see Ronald G. Waters, *American Reformers, 1815–1860* (1978).
42. John Taylor, CBP, Box 5, "1840, Box 1, Folder 4"; Levinus Lansing, CBP; Jacob Van Dorn, CBP, Box 3, "1835, Box 1, Folder 3"; Ephraim Beach, CBP, Box 10, "1846, Box 2, Folder 1."
43. Jacob Sanders and Robert Sanders, CBP, Box 7, "1842, Box 4, Folder 1." On eminent domain, see Harry N. Scheiber, "Property Law, Expropriation, and Resource Allocation by Government, 1789–1910," in Lawrence M. Friedman and Harry N. Scheiber,

eds., *American Law and the Constitutional Order: Historical Perspectives* (1978), 132–41; Horwitz, *Transformation of American Law*, chapter 3; Richard A. Epstein, *Takings: Private Property and the Power of Eminent Domain* (1985).

44. *Rochester Daily Democrat*, August 14, 1846. The "commonwealth studies" (particularly the works of the Handlins and Hartz cited in note 2 of this chapter) argue that Northern state legislatures adopted laissez-faire policies by the end of the antebellum period; in a complementary piece of scholarship, Morton Horwitz demonstrates that laissez-faire doctrines also increasingly characterized Northern judicial rulings; *Transformation of American Law*. My research suggests that many ordinary citizens in the upstate region would still have liked the government to intervene in economic development, but as Hartz has found for Pennsylvania and the Handlins for Massachusetts, experience with state-directed transportation schemes made upstate residents grow distrustful of the government's ability to intervene in a fair and equitable way.

45. Ronald Shaw writes: "In the villages and cities along the canal reactions to the stoppage of construction varied with party allegiance, but the stop and tax law enjoyed widespread support." He quotes favorable newspaper comments from Schenectady, Syracuse, Oswego, Batavia, Rochester, and Albany. Shaw, *Erie Water West*, 335–36. In the rest of the country, a rise in laissez-faire ideology accompanied an increase in state taxation levels in the 1840s; Horwitz, *Transformation of American Law*, 101.

46. Edwin Smith, CBP, Box 7, "1843, Box 2, Folder 3"; Fort Miller Dam Petition, CBP, Box 9, "1845, Box 2, Folder 2."

47. William Adams, CBP, Box 27, "1860, Box 6, Folder 2."

5: THE POLITICS OF BUSINESS

1. Women operated small businesses along the Canal, including taverns, grocery stores, and boardinghouses. But since only a few women addressed the Canal Board about issues related to business (as opposed to more general property claims), I will use the gender-specific term "businessmen." This discussion therefore reflects the biases of the available sources and does not seek to attribute to female merchants the same attitudes held by the men whose voices are recorded here.

2. Since party politics played such a central role in antebellum culture, men could be quite vocal about their affiliations and women about where their sympathies lay. They sometimes referred to political parties in their Canal Board claims as well as in the letters and diaries they kept. Democratic farmers in the western end of the state also identified their enemies—those "purse-proud monopolizers"—as being businessmen, suggesting that the businessmen they criticized were Whigs. See, for example, Handbill to Farmer regarding the Combination of Merchants and Forwarders, extra to the *Rochester Republican*, [1832], Box 9, No. 2305, O'Reilly Collection, Rochester Public Library. Throughout the 1830s, Democratic newspapers carried reports of farmers' meetings in which the resolutions passed denounced businessmen conspiring to keep down prices on produce. For discussions of Whig ideology and rhetoric, see John Ashworth, *"Agrarians" & "Aristocrats": Party Political Ideology in the United States, 1837–1846* (1983, 1988), 52–84; Daniel Walker Howe, *The Political Culture of the American Whigs* (1979), 23–42. Just as farmers saw it as their "vested right" to have convenient access to the parts of their land separated by a canal's running through their property, businessmen—as we will see—argued for the sanctity of their business investments based on their long-standing assumptions about the permanence of the location of the Canal and its infrastructure. These claimants to the Canal Board maintained that a combination of "settled expectations," practice, and custom had conferred property rights that the state had a duty to respect and, indeed, protect. If such rights were taken away, Canal Board petitioners argued, then the state owed its citizens financial compensation for their related losses.

3. *Plough Boy*, September 9 and October 7, 1820; *Geneva Gazette*, December 15, 1824; *Buffalo Emporium*, January 16 and 22, 1825; *People's Friend*, May 18 and July 13, 1825. Such battles would play themselves out in other parts of the country, particularly with the advent of the railroad. See, for example, William Cronon, *Nature's Metropolis: Chicago and the Great West* (1991), and Richard C. Wade, *The Urban Frontier: The Rise of Western Cities, 1790–1830* (1959).

4. Contemporaries and historians alike have characterized the celebration as demonstrating "universal jubilation." For the use of this term in particular, see John Seelye, " 'Rational Exultation': The

Erie Canal Celebration," *Proceedings of the American Antiquarian Society* 94:2 (1985), 247. William Leete Stone, *Narrative of the Festivities Observed in Honor of the Completion of the Grand Erie Canal* (1825), 295–316.

5. Pomroy Jones, *Annals and Recollections of Oneida County* (1851), 379. Although Jones does not mention the canal celebration or the funeral protest, he does note that the Canal passed half a mile away from the town's center. "No very satisfactory reasons," he continues, "have ever been adduced for such a location, and it was certainly very disastrous to the village, and for eighteen years [until the rerouting of the Canal] kept it behind the other villages upon the line of the canal." Moreover, had the Canal followed the lake route rather than the interior route, Rome would have been more centrally located. On funerals as forms of protest, see David Waldstreicher, "Rites of Rebellion, Rites of Assent: Celebrations, Print Culture, and the Origins of American Nationalism," *Journal of American History* (June 1995), 43. Ronald E. Shaw, *Erie Water West: A History of the Erie Canal, 1792–1854* (1966), 9; Austin A. Yates, ed., *Schenectady County, New York: Its History to the Close of the Nineteenth Century* (1902), 123; Henry O'Reilly, *Settlement in the West: Sketches of Rochester . . .* (1838), 332.

6. The residents of Rome and Schenectady also did not limit their protests to the symbolic realm; they actively petitioned state officials for changes to their situation—and with success. In 1836, the legislature passed a special act requiring that the Erie Canal be rerouted to flow through the town of Rome; Noble E. Whitford, *History of the Canal System of the State of New York, Together with Brief Histories of the Canals of the United States and Canada* (1906), 153; J. Smith to [Azariah Smith], November 24, 1825, in "Two Yankee Traders in New York: Letters on the Financing of Frontier Merchants, 1808–1830," ed. Albert V. House, *New England Quarterly* (September 1938), 630; *People's Friend*, December 7, 1825.

7. Horace Wheeler to Robert Rand, December 6, 1825, Horace Wheeler Letters, Rochester Historical Society.

8. Nathaniel Rochester to Henry Clay, June 16, 1823, Nathaniel Rochester Papers, University of Rochester; Henry Cole to Lyman Spalding, April 26, 1821, Lyman Spalding Papers, Cornell University; F. A. Fenn to Samuel Dakin, June 27, 1822, Samuel Dakin Papers, New York State Historical Association.

9. George S. Conover, ed., *History of Ontario County, New York* (1893), 198–204; David M. Ellis et al., *A History of New York State* (1967), 154; Clayton Mau, *The Development of Central and Western New York* . . . , 68–69; *Report on the Subject of a Communication between Canandaigua Lake and the Erie Canal* (1821), 10–11, Canal Collection, American Antiquarian Society.

10. Lyman Spalding to Jonathan J. Douglass, June 10, 1822, Lyman Spalding Papers, Cornell University; Lyman A. Spalding, *Recollections of the War of 1812 and Early Life in Western New York* (1949), 15–16; Holmes Hutchinson to Lyman Spalding, December 16, 1823, Lyman Spalding Papers, Cornell University.

11. *Niles' Weekly Register*, February 9, 1822. Although Niles refers to "Stockport," the context makes clear that the article is indeed about Lockport; Whitford, *History of the Canal System*, 918; William Lyon Mackenzie, *Sketches of Canada*, 144–45, in *Upstate Travels: British Views of Nineteenth Century New York*, ed. Robert Hayden (1982), 208–9. In 1850, Albany, Buffalo, Troy, Rochester, Syracuse, and Utica were bigger than Lockport, and Watervliet was just about the same size; Whitford, *History of the Canal System*, 914. A. W. Howe to Lyman Spalding, January 29, 1823, Lyman Spalding Papers, Cornell University.

12. Some commercial merchants bought produce outright from local merchants, but most operated as commission agents and worked for a share of the sale price of the commodities. In their advertisements, commercial merchants often stressed their commitment to keeping storage time to a minimum.

13. Mary Ann Archbald to Margaret [Wodrow], December 31, 1822, and December 31, 1824, Mary Ann (Wodrow) Archbald Papers, Smith College; A. W. Howe to Lyman Spalding, May 29, 1823, Lyman Spalding Papers, Cornell University.

14. H. B. Skinner, "Correspondence—Buffalo, NY," *Christian Herald*, October 26, 1843. Cathy Brekus provided me with this citation. Although as a missionary Skinner might have been unusually concerned about noting establishments selling alcohol, his description is consistent with others from the era.

15. Shaw, *Erie Water West*, 249; Frederick Backus, Canal Board Papers (hereafter CBP), Box 12, "1848, Box 1, Folder 2," New York State Archives.

16. DeWitt Clinton, Annual Message, 1828, in *Messages from the Governors [of New York]*, ed. Charles Z. Lincoln (1909), Vol. III, 200;

"Memorial of [those] . . . directly or indirectly interested, in navigation upon the Champlain Canal," CBP, Box 1, "1828, Box 2, Folder 1."

17. Petition of Canal Forwarders, CBP, Box 1, "1830, Box 2, Folder 3."

18. For examples of this exact choice of language, see Remonstrances of Inhabitants of Saratoga County, CBP, Box 4, "1836, Box 2, Folder 1," and Taxable Inhabitants of the Village of Waterford, CBP, Box 5, "1839, Box 4, Folder 3." Many other petitions made the same point in slightly different language.

19. *Niles' Weekly Register*, May 23, 1835; New York Canal Commissioners, *Annual Report* (1836), Assembly Doc. 73, January 25, 1837, 15–16.

20. Report of the Committee on Canals and Internal Improvements, on the Petitions of Inhabitants of the Counties of Schoharie and Greene, relative to a Canal from the Erie to Catskill, Assembly Doc. 212, March 2, 1838.

21. George Folts, CBP, Box 10, "1845, Box 3, Folder 1"; Re Albion Collector's Office, Box 12, "1848, Box 1, Folder 1."

22. S. P. Allen, *Digest of Claims, and the Action Thereon by the Legislature and the Canal Board, . . . , from 1818 to 1858* (1858), 251–52.

23. *A Remonstrance Adopted by the Inhabitants of the City of Schenectada [sic] at a Meeting Held on the 25th of February, 1836, Against the Change of the Route of the Erie Canal . . .* (1836), 6.

24. Proceedings of a Meeting at Frankfort, CBP, Box 4, "1836, Box 1, Folder 1"; Citizens of Little Falls, CBP, Box 11, "1847, Box 1, Folder 4." On good-faith statutes and common law, see Morton Horwitz, *The Transformation of American Law, 1780–1860* (1977), 60–62.

25. Persons engaged in the manufacture of salt, CBP, Box 11, "1847, Box 1, Folder 2"; memorial relative to toll on timber, CBP, Box 1, "1828, Box 2, Folder 1."

26. On the impact of business cycles on individuals, see Edward J. Balleisen, "Navigating Failure: Bankruptcy in Antebellum America" (Ph.D. diss., Yale University, 1995).

27. Lyman Spalding, CBP, Box 1, "1830, Box 1, Folder 1."

28. Spalding's manuscript diary indicates that a fire destroyed his mill, leading him to declare bankruptcy. Writing about Spalding, Ronald Shaw notes: "Charges of misappropriation of canal water led finally to a sheriff's sale of his property in 1846," Shaw, *Erie Water*

West, 237. The U.S. Supreme Court Recorder of the January Term, 1846, notes that Spalding spent from May 6 to September 29, 1842, in jail. *Lyman A. Spalding, Plaintiff in Error*, v. *The People of the State of New York* . . . , 22–23; Edward Balleisen and Jonathan Cedarbaum helped me find this case. Entry dated October 12, 1842, Lyman Spalding Journal #2, Spalding Family Papers, Syracuse University. Spalding's diaries for this period make repeated references to his campaigning for the Whigs and to his support for state-funded internal improvements and for protective tariffs.

29. Spalding, *Recollections of . . . Early Life in Western New York*, and scattered entries, Lyman Spalding Journals #2, 3, 4, and 5, Spalding Family Papers.

30. See, for example, Griffith J. Fish, CBP, Box 6, "1841, Box 2, Folder 3"; Inhabitants of Saratoga County, CBP, Box 4, "1836, Box 1, Folder 1"; Inhabitants of Kirkville, CBP, Box 4, "1837, Box 1, Folder 2"; Inhabitants and freeholders in City of Schenectady, CBP, Box 5, "1839, Box 2, Folder 3"; Taxable Inhabitants of the Village of Waterford, CBP, Box 5, "1839, Box 4, Folder 3"; *Remonstrance Adopted by the Inhabitants of . . . Schenectada*; Petition re Excavation at Little Falls, CBP, Box 5, "1839, Box 4, Folder 1"; Inhabitants of New Boston, CBP, Box 15, "1851, Box 3, Folder 2"; Citizens of Holley, CBP, Box 17, "1854, Box 2, Folder 4." Inhabitants of Lyons, CBP, Box 4, "1838, Box 1, Folder 1"; Inhabitants of Geddes, CBP, Box 4, "1838, Box 1, Folder 2."

31. Kirkville Petition, CBP, Box 4, "1837, Box 1, Folder 2."

32. Forwarders and Merchants of Albany, CBP, Box 9, "1845, Box 1, Folder 3"; O. N. Bush, CBP, Box 8, "1843, Box 5, Folder 3."

33. See, for example, Pierpont Dyer, CBP, Box 12, "1848, Box 1, Folder 2"; Petition re Albion collector's office, CBP, Box 12, "1848, Box 1, Folder 2"; *Remonstrance Adopted by the Inhabitants of . . . Schenectada*; Schenectady Petition, CBP, Box 5, "1839, Box 2, Folder 3"; Report of the Committee on Canals and Internal Improvements, on the Petition of the Proprietors of the Canal Basin at Rochester, known as "Child's Slip," Assembly Doc. 120, January 28, 1839, 5; Elias Pound, CBP, Box 12, "1848, Box 1, Folder 2."

34. *Proceedings of the Convention, Upon the Subject of an Immediate Enlargement of the Erie Canal; held at the Court-House in Rochester, on the 18th and 19th days of January, 1837* (1837), 9–10.

35. Although the Erie Canal was the first major connection between

the Great Lakes and Eastern markets, its success encouraged construction of several alternative routes, first canals and later railroads. The Welland Canal, completed in 1829, opened a passage between Lake Erie and Lake Ontario, from which goods could continue on their way via the St. Lawrence River. Ohio and Pennsylvania opened their canal systems in the early 1830s. On competing railroads, see the Epilogue. Rufus King, CBP, Box 22, "1860, Box 4, Folder 1"; Citizens of Orleans County, CBP, Box 22, "1860, Box 4, Folder 1."

36. See, for example, Petition re Palmyra collector's office, CBP, Box 4, "1837, Box 2, Folder 3," and Inhabitants of City of Schenectady, CBP, Box 6, "1842, Box 1, Folder 3." Most petitions assumed that phrases such as "community" and "public good" were self-explanatory.

37. Petition re Lyons collector's office, CBP, Box 9, "1844, Box 3, Folder 1."

38. Citizens of Rochester, CBP, Box 14, "1850, Box 1, Folder 4"; Petition for a Bridge in Utica, CBP, Box 3, "1834, Box 3, Folder 1"; and Inhabitants of Fort Edward, CBP, Box 7, "1843, Box 2, Folder 3."

39. H. Ely, CBP, Box 11, "1847, Box 1, Folder 3"; Petition from West Troy and Cohoes, CBP, Box 20, "1858, Box 1, Folder 3"; Citizens of Utica, CBP, Box 19, "1856, Box 3, Folder 2"; and H. Ely, CBP, Box 11, "1846, Box 1, Folder 2."

40. Inhabitants of Lenox and Sullivan, CBP, Box 15, "1852, Box 1, Folder 3"; Inhabitants of Schenectady, CBP, Box 6, "1842, Box 1, Folder 3"; J. D. Walbridge the younger, CBP, Box 10, "1846, Box 1, Folder 1"; Petitions re tolls on barley and malt, CBP, Box 21, "1859, Box 1, Folder 2"; Mayor and aldermen of Rochester, CBP, Box 6, "1842, Box 2, Folder 2."

6: THE PERILS OF PROGRESS

1. Reformers estimated that of the thirty thousand people working on the Canal in 1846, eight thousand were minors. American Bethel Society [hereafter ABS], *Eleventh Annual Report* (1847), 20. Carl F. Kaestle, *Pillars of the Republic: Common Schools and American Society, 1780–1860* (1983). Boatmen's Friend Society to the Forwarders, Merchants, and others . . . , *Rochester Daily Advertiser*, August 20, 1830.

2. ABS, *Eleventh Annual Report*, 20. Some freight boat crews included a cook as well, often the captain's wife. A passenger boat would have included two steersmen, a bowsman, a waiter, a cook, a cabin girl, and a steward.

3. Ronald E. Shaw, *Erie Water West: A History of the Erie Canal, 1792–1854* (1966), 87 and 242–43. Many types of cargo would have been unloaded directly into a warehouse, but it is unlikely that fresh oysters would have been stored.

4. The figure of 3,400 is for 1853, when 3,395 canal boats were registered with the state. Calculated from *A Certified Copy of the Register of Canal Boats Kept in the Canal Department . . . , as they stood on the 10th April, 1853*, New York State Library; Humphry Howland, August 4, 1827, in Giles Landon Claim, Canal Board Papers (hereafter CBP), Box 1, "1828, Box 2, Folder 1," New York State Archives.

5. When Frances Wilson escaped from a Cincinnati jail, a Syracuse newspaper reported that "the majority of this woman's life has been passed in driving stages and canal boat horses, dressed in male attire." *Syracuse Standard*, July 2, 1850, in "Tr[ansportation]—Canal—Erie—Boatmen, Cooks, Drivers, 1850–1853," Vertical Files, Onondaga Historical Association. Sarah Rosetta Wakeman worked briefly on the Chenango Canal before enlisting in the Union army; Lauren Cook Burgess, ed., *An Uncommon Soldier: The Civil War Letters of Sarah Rosetta Wakeman, alias Private Lyons Wakeman, 153rd Regiment, New York State Volunteers* (1994), 18.

6. For diaries of farmers who tended canal horses and boarded their drivers, see Cyrus Wilmarth Ledger, 1832–1837, Valentown Museum; David Hughes Diary, 1849–1852, New York State Historical Association. Hughes also sold large quantities of oats to the station barns that housed the horses during the Canal's open season. For an advertisement soliciting oats for canal horses, see *People's Friend*, February 9, 1825.

7. Daniel Wandell in relation to the use of steam on the Canal, CBP, Box 5, "1839, Box 4, Folder 3"; *Brockport Recorder*, October 8, 1828, and *Brockport Free Press and Monroe Democrat*, April 17, 1833; Jacob Abbot, *Marco Paul's Travels on the Erie Canal* (1987 [1843, 1852]), 138–39, vii.

8. Local newspapers throughout the state carried regular reports of crime. For a collection of crime reports in the vicinity of one

community, Syracuse, see the following vertical files at the Onondaga Historical Association: "Crime and Criminals," "Transportation—Canal—Erie—Boatmen, Cooks, Drivers," "Transportation—Canal—Erie—Accidents," "Crime—Canal Boat Rape at
Green Point." Police Watchbooks, 1836–1838, kept by Francis
Dana, Captain of the Night Watch in Rochester, Local History
Division, Rochester Public Library; City of Rochester, Police Department Watchbook, 1837, University of Rochester. The American Bethel Society reported in its *Second Annual Report* (1838) that
more than one-third of the inmates in the Auburn State Prison
had "followed the canals." The society cites the prison's 1838 annual report, which indicates that of 1,232 prisoners, 301 "had
followed the canals"; I have based my figure of one-fourth on this
report. ABS, *Second Annual Report* (1838), 19; Annual Report of
the Inspectors of the Auburn State Prison, Assembly Doc. 86,
January 16, 1838, 96–97; Pardon Thompson Claim, CBP, Box 1,
"1830, Box 1, Folder 1." Entries dated April 16, 1849, September
1, 1850, December 10, 1850, David Hughes Diary.

 9. Entry dated June 18, [1835,] Clarissa Burroughs Travel Diary,
Cornell University; Harriet Loring to George F. Gwinn, August
5, 1846, "Canals—Misc. Mss," Buffalo and Erie County Historical
Society Library.

10. *Laws of the State of New York, in relation to the Erie and Champlain
Canals, together with the Annual Reports of the Canal Commissioners,
and other Documents* . . . (1825), Vol. II, 577–78.

11. Herman Melville, *Moby-Dick; or, the Whale* (1930), 363. *Moby-Dick*
was originally published in 1851. Melville took a canal boat ride
on his honeymoon in 1847, and he may have worked on the Canal
during the summer of 1840. Gay Wilson Allen, *Melville and His
World* (1971), 90–92 and 43. On hurling obscenities at ladies, see
Niles' Weekly Register, October 7, 1826, cited in Shaw, *Erie Water
West*, 231.

12. Some missionaries seem to have recognized that drivers might have
an incentive to lie. The Bethel Society's *Fourth Annual Report*
estimated—as did many other Bethel publications—that one-half
of the drivers were orphans. The reformers went on to say: "We
have made somewhat extensive enquiries concerning this among
them, and four fifths of those of whom we enquired, we have found
to be orphans. We feel, therefore, safe in the remark, that probably

one half of the whole are *orphans.*" ABS, *Fourth Annual Report* (1840), 13. In the *Eleventh Annual Report*, the society estimated that three-fourths were orphans. ABS, *Eleventh Annual Report* (1847), 20. My use of the one-half estimate is therefore conservative. The New York State Legislature also referred to the large numbers of canal drivers who were orphans. Report of the majority of the Committee on Grievances, in relation to the closing of the locks of the canals on Sundays, Assembly Doc. 134, April 1, 1858, 3. ABS, *Eleventh Annual Report*, 27.

13. *Sailor's Magazine* [hereafter *SM*], February 1846, 168. Bethel reformers were not alone in recording captains' attempts to defraud their workers of their wages; see also *Syracuse Courier and Union*, December 21, 1858, in "Tr[ansportation]—Canal—Erie—Boatmen, Cooks, Drivers, 1857+," Vertical Files, Onondaga Historical Association. The *Onondaga Standard* reprinted an article from the *Syracuse Courier and Union* reporting that the body of an unknown boy was found drowned and that "the body was dressed in coarse striped cotton pants and shirt, and from appearances it was thought to have been a canal driver." *Onondaga Standard*, August 25, 1857. Ibid. Although the boy was drowned in the summertime, missionaries and newspapers reported that drivers often did not have winter clothing. For descriptions of the canallers' clothing, see M. Eaton, *Five Years on the Erie Canal: An Account of Some of the Most Startling Scenes and Incidents, during Five Years' Labor on the Erie Canal, and other Inland Waters* (1845), 34, 72, and 81. Freegift Wells, "Minutes of a Journey to Lyons, Wayne County and back to Watervliet," Microfilm roll 47/C/317, Western Reserve Historical Collection. This passage comes from a transcription prepared by Elizabeth Rice, located in "Canals—New York—Erie Canal—Eyewitness Accounts," Erie Canal Museum. Eaton, *Five Years*, 73–74.

14. Nathaniel Hawthorne, "The Canal Boat," *Mosses from an Old Manse* (1887), 493; the description of the driver's activities and rest is based on entry dated May 11 [no year] of Canal-drivers' Log, uncatalogued manuscript, Erie Canal Village. I chose Holden randomly from among approximately four thousand entries in this log. Freight boats changed their teams every ten to twelve miles, according to the *Albany Argus*, July 8, 1825. From 1853 to 1858, freight boats loaded with flour averaged 1.8 miles an hour; George

Rogers Taylor, *The Transportation Revolution, 1815–1860* (1951), 138. My estimate of six to seven hours includes a conservative estimate of time lost waiting at locks. Passenger boats changed horses every twenty miles, according to one traveler. *Notes on a Tour through the Western Part of the State of New York* (1829–1830 and 1916), 21, Item #79.48.11, Erie Canal Museum. Most passenger boats averaged three to four miles an hour; Taylor, *Transportation Revolution*, 142. So the number of hours worked by a driver pulling a passenger boat would be about the same as one pulling a freight boat. Common wisdom has it that drivers worked "six hours on, six hours off." *SM*, April 1847, 252.

15. *SM*, November 1835, 138, and January 1836, 188. In the January issue, the magazine printed a chart showing the number of canalside grog shops, totaling 1,515, broken down by town and category ("taverns which sell ardent spirits," "groceries which sell ardent spirits," "groceries wh. sell fer'd. liq'rs"). *Buffalo Spectator* in *SM*, May 1838, 386. On accidents in general, see, for example, clippings in the vertical files on accidents at the Onondaga Historical Association. Newspapers throughout the region regularly reported canal-related accidents, and travelers frequently recorded accidents in their letters and journals. ABS, *Second Annual Report* (1838), 19.

16. *Onondaga Standard*, December 14, 1853, in "Tr[ansportation]—Canal—Erie—Boatmen, Cooks, Drivers, 1850–1853," Vertical Files, Onondaga Historical Association. *Onondaga Standard*, March 18, 1857, in "Tr[ansportation]—Canal—Erie—Boatmen, Cooks, Drivers, 1857+," Vertical Files, Onondaga Historical Association. The boys referred to in the quotation in the text were also lodged in jail, though not charged with any crime. See also *Onondaga Standard*, March 17, 1857.

17. ABS, *Third Annual Report* (1839), [6], Institutions Collection, American Antiquarian Society; *SM*, November 1854, 72; *SM*, February 1846, 168; on middle-class boys creating "social space," see E. Anthony Rotundo, "Boy Culture: Middle-Class Boyhood in Nineteenth-Century America," in Mark C. Carnes and Clyde Griffen, eds., *Meanings for Manhood: Constructions of Masculinity in Victorian America* (1990), 15, 25.

18. On the dress of working-class youth in New York City, see Christine Stansell, *City of Women: Sex and Class in New York, 1789–1860* (1986), 90.

19. Whitney R. Cross, *The Burned-Over District: The Social and Intellectual History of Enthusiastic Religion in Western New York, 1800–1850* (1950), 3; Paul E. Johnson, *A Shopkeeper's Millennium: Society and Revivals in Rochester, New York, 1815–1837* (1978), 12. Curtis D. Johnson, *Islands of Holiness: Rural Religion in Upstate New York, 1790–1860* (1989) and *Redeeming America: Evangelicals and the Road to Civil War* (1993).

20. For background on Bissell and his role in bringing Finney to Rochester, see Johnson, *Shopkeeper's Millennium,* 16; Josiah Bissell to CG Finney, September 15, 1829, Charles Finney Papers, Oberlin College Archives. Paul Johnson most generously brought this letter to my attention and provided me with his transcription of it. A copy of the letter is also in Blake McKelvey, ed., "Letters Postmarked Rochester: 1817–1879," in *Rochester Historical Society Publications* (1943).

21. American Seamen's Friend Society, *Second Annual Report* (1830), 11, Institutions Collection, American Antiquarian Society; *Rochester Daily Advertiser,* August 20, 1830.

22. The *Third Annual Report* of the American Bethel Society noted: "We have now engaged on the Erie Canal, in Bethel operations, Baptists, Methodists, Presbyterian, Congregationalists and Dutch Reformed Churches . . ." *Third Annual Report* (1839), 10. For a different interpretation of the role of evangelical reformers on the Canal, see Roger E. Carp, "The Limits of Reform: Labor and Discipline on the Erie Canal," *Journal of the Early Republic* (Summer 1990), 191–219. Carp writes: "After 1831 . . . popular concern for canal workers, whether young or adult, all but disappeared," 212. I will suggest that support for the American Bethel Society, founded in 1836, reflected popular concern for canal workers throughout the antebellum period. Johnson notes that the Bethel Presbyterian Church in Rochester was founded by wealthy Finney converts; Johnson, *Shopkeeper's Millennium,* 116–17 and 154; ABS, *Fourth Annual Report* (1840), 12.

23. In 1847, the Western Seamen's Friend Society became an auxiliary of the American Bethel Society. It specialized in reforming boatmen in Cleveland and points farther west. ABS, *Twelfth Annual Report* (1848), 6.

24. ABS, *Twenty-fourth Annual Report* (1860), 68, in American Seamen's Friend Society, *Thirty-second Annual Report* (1860); *SM,* September 1847, 20. The number of full-time, paid missionaries

peaked at twelve in 1847. Given the rate of travel, this meant that boat workers were likely to come in contact with one of these missionaries either every day or, at least, every two days.

25. ABS, *Second Annual Report* (1838), 20. As Charles E. Rosenberg has shown, nineteenth-century Americans often drew a literal connection between physical and moral disease. Rosenberg, *The Cholera Years: The United States in 1832, 1849, and 1866* (1962 and 1987).

26. Eaton, *Five Years*, 32–33.

27. ABS, *Seventh Annual Report* (1843), 11, and ABS, *Eleventh Annual Report* (1847), 12; Abigail Marks to Silas Curtis family, January 15, 1844, Curtis Family Papers, University of Rochester.

28. *SM*, November 1854, 71.

29. ABS, *Twenty-seventh Annual Report* (1863), 62; Eaton, *Five Years*, 43; ABS, *Fourth Annual Report* (1840), 12.

30. Johnson, *Shopkeeper's Millennium*, 121.

31. As late as the 1830s, English pounds were sometimes used in financial transactions in the upstate region. A shortage of American currency and the proximity to the British territory of Canada probably encouraged this practice.

32. Eleazor Conkey Diary (typescript), Erie Canal Museum.

33. Eleazor Conkey Log, Erie Canal Museum; Eugene F. Moran, Sr., "The Erie Canal as I have Known It," *Bottoming Out: Useful and Interesting Notes Collected for Members of the Canal Society of New York State*, III:2 (1959), 5–7; Horatio Alger, Jr., *From Canal Boy to President, or the Boyhood and Manhood of James A. Garfield* (1881); *Brockport Free Press and Monroe Democrat*, April 17, 1833.

34. *SM*, September 1846, 30; ABS, *Seventh Annual Report* (1843), 11; *SM*, April 1850, 239; *SM*, April 1847, 254.

35. ABS, *Second Annual Report* (1838), 14–15; *Sheet Anchor* in *SM*, November 1845, 78; William F. Liddle and John C. Homan, CBP, Box 15, "1851, Box 2, Folder 3."

36. *SM*, September 1847, 30. For mention of a strike among boat captains, see *Syracuse Daily Journal*, June 14, 1856, in "Tr[ansportation]—Canal—Erie—Boatmen, Cooks, Drivers, 1854–1856," Vertical Files, Onondaga Historical Association. On drivers, see *Onondaga Standard*, May 12, 1858, in "Tr[ansportation]—Canal—Erie—Boatmen, Cooks, Drivers, 1857+," Vertical Files, Onondaga Historical Association. These newspaper

accounts offer virtually no details about the strikes. ABS, *Twelfth Annual Report* (1848), 18.

37. ABS, [*First*] *Annual Report* (1837), 12, Institutions Collection, American Antiquarian Society.

38. *Ibid.*, 12–13. See the following Legislative documents: Senate Doc. 122, April 18, 1843; Senate Doc. 66, February 20, 1844; Senate Doc. 119, April 10, 1844; Assembly Doc. 148, March 5, 1845; Senate Doc. 77, March 11, 1858; Senate Doc. 91, March 20, 1858; Assembly Doc. 134, April 1, 1858; Assembly Doc. 137, April 1, 1858. For a discussion of how elites in Rochester divided over Sabbatarianism, see Johnson, *Shopkeeper's Millennium*, 83–88. *SM*, November 1854, 70; January 1838, 183.

39. See printed petition from the Forwarders, Merchants, and Business Men, Upon the Canals to the Canal Commissioners, CBP, Box 9, "1844, Box 3, Folder 2." Although the Canal Board Papers contain only one copy of this petition, most printed petitions (as opposed to handwritten ones) were distributed in multiple copies. A New York State Senate Committee noted in 1844 that "the petitioners [for Sabbath closing of the locks] are very numerous, and from the most respectable portion of our citizens; the names of boatmen [i.e., captains], forwarders, and merchants are in great numbers on the memorials." Report on the Committee on Canals in relation to the observance of the Sabbath on the Canals, Senate Doc. 119, April 10, 1844, 2. The collection of petitions to the legislature was damaged in the fire at the New York State Library and are not available to the public. In 1843, Timothy Stillman, the Bethel Society's corresponding secretary, wrote a letter to Canal Commissioner William Bouck in which he alluded to including four petitions in support of the Sabbath closing of the locks and suggests that others were still being circulated. The petitions were signed by boat captains and the "forwarders and agents by whom they are employed." Timothy Stillman to William C. Bouck, Bouck Family Papers, #2206, Cornell University Library. *Rochester Daily Democrat*, January 4, 1845; ABS, *Third Annual Report* (1839), 14; ABS, *Second Annual Report* (1838), 15. While it is not possible to verify this claim about profits, it nonetheless provides evidence of the sorts of concerns the missionaries addressed.

40. ABS, *Second Annual Report* (1838), 13; *SM*, April 1850, 239. Several annual reports point out the generous financial assistance of

women's auxiliaries. Lists of contributors, usually by the name of their association, are appended to each of the society's annual reports. See also *SM*, September 1836, 27. Although Mary Ryan, in her discussion of Young Men's Associations in Utica, shows that most young men involved in the associations were predominantly lawyers or clerks, Utica was a manufacturing town rather than a commercial center and thus may not be representative of all upstate communities. Ryan, *Cradle of the Middle Class: The Family in Oneida County, New York, 1790–1865* (1981). In his study of young men's voluntary associations, Glenn Wallach has found that benevolent societies were more likely to draw their leaders from mercantile backgrounds than were the groups promoting self-help. Wallach, "Obedient Sons: Youth and Generational Consciousness in American Culture, 1630–1850s" (Ph.D. diss., Yale University, 1991), chapter 3.

41. Silas Marks to Nancy and Abigail Curtis, August 29, 1837, Curtis Family Papers. "Pioneering" probably refers to the support of Sabbath observance on the Canal. The most visible Sabbath-observing boat line was the Pioneer Line. Historians have also argued that the middle classes defined themselves, in large part, in terms of piety. See, for example, Johnson, *Shopkeeper's Millennium*, and " 'Art' and the Language of Progress in Early-Industrial Paterson: Sam Patch at Clinton Bridge," *American Quarterly* (1988), 433–49; Stansell, *City of Women*; Anthony F. C. Wallace, *Rockdale: The Growth of an American Village in the Early Industrial Revolution* (1978); Ryan, *Cradle of the Middle Class*; Stuart Blumin, *The Emergence of the Middle Class: Social Experience in the American City, 1760–1900* (1989); Karen Halttunen, *Confidence Men and Painted Women: A Study of Middle-Class Culture in America, 1830–1870* (1982); John S. Gilkeson, Jr., *Middle-Class Providence, 1820–1940* (1986). For another important look at middle-class efforts to regain social control through reform, see David J. Rothman, *The Discovery of the Asylum: Social Order and Disorder in the New Republic* (1971 and 1990).

42. Cross, *The Burned-Over District*; Ryan, *Cradle of the Middle Class*; Nancy A. Hewitt, *Women's Activism and Social Change: Rochester, New York, 1822–1872* (1984); Alice Felt Tyler: *Freedom's Ferment: Phases of American Social History from the Colonial Period to the Outbreak of the Civil War* (1944). Bethel missionaries commented on

the mistreatment of canal animals. See, for example, *SM*, November 1845, 78, and December 1849, 123. According to the Bethel Society, the number of captains accompanied by their families increased over time. Bethel missionaries supported this change primarily because women were seen as reintroducing morality to the Canal and because a family-based economy was preferable to a wage economy, which the reformers saw as morally corrupt. A related reason that reformers saw this arrangement as an improvement was that it discouraged men from visiting prostitutes and from hiring cabin girls who sold sexual services on the side.

43. ABS, *[First] Annual Report*, 13; *SM*, September 1851, 404–5.
44. For employers' views of alcohol in other industries, see Johnson, *Shopkeeper's Millennium*; Wallace, *Rockdale*; Sean Wilentz, *Chants Democratic: New York City and the Rise of the American Working Class, 1788–1850* (1984). We know that Joy was a proprietor and agent of a boat company from a petition that he filed with the Canal Board regarding laws giving preference to packet boats at locks. *Rochester Daily Advertiser and Telegraph*, February 25, 1830; *SM*, August 1833, 383.
45. *SM*, April 1848, 254.
46. Reprinted in ABS, *Third Annual Report* (1839), 22; ibid., 5.
47. Forwarders, Merchants, and Business Men, Upon the Canals, CBP, Box 9, "1844, Box 3, Folder 2."

EPILOGUE:
BECOMING SECOND NATURE

1. Report of the Minority of the Committee on Grievances on the Petitions for and Remonstrances against the Closing of the Canal Locks on Sunday, Assembly Doc. 137, April 1, 1858, 2.
2. George Rogers Taylor, *The Transportation Revolution, 1815–1860* (1951), 167; Roberta Balstad Miller, *City and Hinterland: A Case Study of Urban Growth and Regional Development* (1979), 85; Ronald W. Filante, "A Note on the Economic Viability of the Erie Canal, 1825–1860," *Business History Review* (Spring 1974), 95–102. David M. Ellis et al., *A History of New York State* (1957, 1967), 250. For a thorough treatment of the political wrangling surrounding railroad policy in New York, see Lee Bensen, *Merchants, Farmers & Railroads: Railroad Regulation and New York Politics, 1850–1887*

(1955). More general studies of the influence of railroads on economic development include Albert Fishlow, *American Railroads and the Transformation of Ante-bellum Economy* (1966); Robert Fogel, *Railroads and American Economic Growth: Essays in Econometric History* (1964); Carter Goodrich, *Government Promotion of American Canals and Railroads, 1800–1890* (1960); Julius Rubin, "Canal or Railroad?: Imitation or Innovation in the Response to the Erie Canal in Philadelphia, Baltimore, and Boston," *Transactions of the American Philosophical Society* (November 1961), 5–106.

3. William Seward, Annual Message, 1839, in *Messages from the Governors [of New York]*, ed. Charles Z. Lincoln (1909), Vol. III, 732–33.

4. Quoted in David Walker Howe, *The Political Culture of the American Whigs* (1979), 202. For the most comprehensive treatments of free-labor ideology, see Eric Foner, *Free Soil, Free Labor, Free Men: The Ideology of the Republican Party before the Civil War* (1970), and Jonathan Glickstein, *Concepts of Free Labor in Antebellum America* (1991).

5. "The Irrepressible Conflict," speech delivered in Rochester, October 15, 1858, in *The Works of William H. Seward*, Vol. IV, rev. ed., ed. George E. Baker (1884), 292.

6. Ibid., 291.

SOURCES

Because *The Artificial River* does not fit neatly into a single established body of historical literature, I will not attempt to offer a comprehensive treatment of the secondary works that have influenced my own; I hope instead that readers will consult the endnotes for relevant citations and for brief discussions of pertinent scholarly debates. My intentions here are to offer general suggestions for additional secondary reading on the Erie Canal, and then to direct future researchers to some of the rich primary sources on antebellum New York State.

The term "the transportation revolution" was coined by George Rogers Taylor, whose *The Transportation Revolution, 1815–1860* (1951) remains the standard source on the nation's internal improvements. Caroline E. MacGill's *History of Transportation in the United States before 1860* (1917) similarly offers a wealth of information on the ways in which technological innovations influenced the speed and cost of transportation. The best scholarly overview of the history of the Erie Canal—one that provided essential background for my own study— is Ronald E. Shaw, *Erie Water West: A History of the Erie Canal, 1792– 1854* (1966); Shaw's *Canals for a Nation: The Canal Era in the United States, 1790–1860* (1990) offers an excellent introduction to American artificial waterways generally. Based on extensive research, Shaw's books offer comprehensive treatments of the political, technological, and economic histories of canal-building. In 1984, Shaw also published a useful review essay of the scholarly literature on canals: "Canals in the Early Republic: A Review of the Recent Literature," *Journal of the Early Republic* (Summer 1984), 117–42. The classic work on the waterways of New York is Noble E. Whitford's two-volume *History of the Canal System of the State of New York, Together with Brief Histories of the*

Canals of the United States and Canada, which was published as a supplement to the *Annual Report of the State Engineer and Surveyor . . . for the Fiscal Year 1905* (1906). In addition to offering a great deal of background material, Whitford's study provides an inventory of published official documents relating to New York's internal improvements.

Other important works focus on particular aspects of canal history. For the Erie's economic influence, see Nathan Miller, *The Enterprise of a Free People: Aspects of Economic Development in New York State during the Canal Period, 1792–1838* (1962); Carter Goodrich, ed., *Canals and American Economic Development* (1961); Goodrich, *Government Promotion of American Canals and Railroads, 1800–1890* (1960). L. Ray Gunn, *The Decline of Authority: Public Economic Policy and Political Development in New York State, 1800–1860* (1988), provides crucial background on the politics of economic development. Harry N. Scheiber's *Ohio Canal Era: A Case Study of Government and the Economy, 1820–1861* (1969) is a sophisticated account whose relevance extends beyond the bounds of Ohio. While all of the vast work of Blake McKelvey illustrates the Canal's influence on urban development, see, in particular, "The Erie Canal, Mother of Cities," *The New York Historical Quarterly* (January 1951), 55–71, and "Rochester and the Erie Canal," *Rochester History* (July 1949), 1–24. For an astute analysis of the local impact of transportation on Syracuse, see Roberta Balstad Miller, *City and Hinterland: A Case Study of Urban Growth and Regional Development* (1979).

Peter Way's *Common Labour: Workers and the Digging of North American Canals, 1780–1860* (1993) focuses on the construction of canals generally and makes important contributions to the field of labor history. Patricia Anderson's *The Course of Empire: The Erie Canal and the New York Landscape, 1825–1875* (1984) provides a perceptive analysis of paintings featuring the Erie Canal; the book also reproduces artwork from museums across the country. Although at times overwhelming in its detail, an excellent unpublished dissertation on the political ideologies of the canal era is Roger Evan Carp, "The Erie Canal and the Liberal Challenge to Classical Republicanism, 1785–1850" (Ph.D. diss., University of North Carolina at Chapel Hill, 1986).

Readers interested in additional secondary sources on the Erie Canal should begin by consulting Lionel D. Wyld's *The Erie Canal: A Bibliography*, rev. ed. (1990). This 19-page annotated pamphlet covers scholarly works, popular histories, fiction, and some basic primary documents. A popular history published since the appearance of Wyld's bibliography is Russell Bourne, *Floating West: The Erie and Other American Canals* (1992).

Few of these earlier studies were able to take advantage of new historical methodologies emphasizing the social and cultural experiences of ordinary men and women. A notable exception to this generalization is Whitney Cross's ground-breaking *The Burned-Over District: The Social and Intellectual History of Enthusiastic Religion in Western New York, 1800–1850* (1950); chapter 4 looks at the impact of the Erie Canal on evangelical revivalism. Although they do not focus primarily on the transportation revolution, some of the finest social histories of the past two decades are case studies of upstate towns that should be consulted by anyone interested in learning more about the region. See, for example, Paul E. Johnson, *A Shopkeeper's Millennium: Society and Revivals in Rochester, New York, 1815–1837* (1978); Mary Ryan, *Cradle of the Middle-Class: The Family in Oneida County, New York, 1790–1865* (1981); Nancy Hewitt, *Women's Activism and Social Change: Rochester, New York, 1822–1872* (1984). Two other useful recent works about nineteenth-century New York State are Nancy Grey Osterud, *Bonds of Community: The Lives of Farm Women in Nineteenth-Century New York* (1991), and Curtis D. Johnson, *Islands of Holiness: Rural Religion in Upstate New York, 1790–1860* (1989). Without the work of these scholars, and many others, my own work would not have been possible.

For all that has been written about the transportation revolution, much remains to be done. By offering details about the primary sources I used in writing *The Artificial River*, I hope to save future researchers from some of the frustrations that I faced in tracking down what turned out, in the end, to be abundant source material. Much of my narrative is pieced together from scattered letters, diaries, account books, petitions, claims, newspaper articles, tracts, and broadsides. While I stumbled upon many of these sources by sheer luck or under the skillful guidance of archivists and librarians, there are systematic ways to begin searching for relevant sources before arriving in upstate New York. An indispensable starting place is the 46-volume *Guide to Historical Resources . . .* (1980–). Organized by county, these volumes offer information about the manuscript holdings of institutions varying in size from university libraries to local historical societies. Many of these institutions have also made information about their collections available on the on-line database RLIN.

Perhaps one of the most ironically gratifying compliments I have ever received came from an archivist who confided in a mutual friend that the bulk of my manuscript sources are intrinsically "dull beyond belief." While it is true that the official documents pertaining to the New York canals are in many ways tedious, they nonetheless have buried within them—sometimes in quite unexpected places—invaluable information about daily life in the Canal corridor. One of my favorite examples, cited in the main text of the book, is a letter from a citizen encouraging the state to use steam-powered boats on the Erie Canal. While on the surface this document seems to tell us little about what life was actually like for people living along the waterway's banks, a closer look suggests otherwise: the author of the letter reminds state officials that if they adopt steam power, they will be less dependent on the "profain" boys who drive the horses who pull the boats. When other citizens filed claims enumerating, for page after dense page, the contents of their flooded cellars, they unwittingly left detailed records of their consumption patterns. The Canal Board Papers cover the period from 1828 to 1926 and fill more than fifty cubic feet of storage space. Several dozen other sizable archival series make up the canal collection at the New York State Archives; the complete holdings are listed in "The Mighty Chain: A Guide to Canal Records in the New York State Archives," a 117-page finding aid available free of charge from the Office of Cultural Education, State Archives and Records Administration, Albany, NY 12230. The archives' holdings are also listed on the Internet at gopher://unix6.nysed.gov.

Because so many New Yorkers were interested in internal improvements—if for no other reason than that they were helping to pay for them—the state regularly published documents related to canal policy. Many of these are indexed in Adelaide R. Hasse, *Index of Economic Materials in Documents of the United States, New York, 1789–1904* (1907); Hasse interpreted "economic" in the broadest possible sense, so this finding aid covers a much wider range of material than its title suggests. It provides the most reliable way to locate material in the government documents collection at the New York State Library in Albany.

In an era when persuasion played such a vital role in politics, tracts were a popular way for citizens to try to sway one another about canal policy. Copies of such publications are now found in rare-book collections throughout the country. While they cannot be systematically located, many of them are at the New York State Library. A large number have also been gathered together by the American Antiquarian Society in Worcester, Massachusetts, in its Canal Collection. More easily available to researchers are travel diaries kept by tourists, many of which were written with an eye toward publication. The rage for keeping diaries also inspired a number of farces along the lines of the Dunlap play featured in chapter 3. For particular titles of tracts and diaries, farcical and not, readers should consult the following list of Primary Sources as well as the bibiliographies in other secondary works mentioned above.

Historians of all stripes find newspapers to be invaluable sources, but anyone who has done such research knows just how laborious it can be. In New York, a few finding aids can ease this process. During the Great Depression, the National Youth Administration sponsored a project to index Rochester's nineteenth-century newspapers; the legacy is the *Index to Newspapers Published in Rochester, New York, 1818–1897*, which resides in the local history division of the Rochester Public Library. Although the Rochester index is apparently unique, the Onondaga Historical Association in Syracuse has kept extensive vertical files of nineteenth-century newspaper clippings from that city arranged by topic. Local histories—of villages, towns, counties, or land purchases—often contain reprints of newspaper articles from the antebellum period. For the more intrepid, the New York State Library and Cornell University Library have enormous microfilm collections of unindexed newspapers from around the state, and local libraries generally house collections of regional papers. The American Antiquarian Society also has an impressive collection of newspapers, including many not available on microfilm elsewhere. National newspapers, particularly *Niles' Weekly Register* and *Hunt's Merchant Magazine*, contain a wealth of material on antebellum New York and are widely available at research libraries.

New York's historical sources offer fruitful opportunities for researchers whose interests lead them to track the lives of particular individuals. New York took its own census in years ending in 5, which nicely complements the federal censuses done in years ending with 0. The forms that census takers filled out as they went door to door are available on microfilm. For the federal census from 1800 to 1850, the New York State Library has a printed index of names. Many upstate towns also published city directories, most of which are available in

American Directories through 1860: A Collection on Microfiche . . . (1969); Dorothea Spear's *Bibliography of American Directories through 1860* (1961) provides a handy reference to available directories.

The Erie Canal quickly assumed a cherished place in American folklore, offering yet another approach to upstate history. Folktales have been collected by Lionel D. Wyld in *Boaters and Broomsticks: Tales and Historical Lore of the Erie Canal* (1986) and in *Low Bridge! Folklore and the Erie Canal* (1962). Another useful source is Marvin Rapp's *Canal Water and Whisky: Tall Tales from the Erie Canal Country* (1965). William Hullfish has put together a collection of ballads in *The Canaller's Songbook* (1984). The fictionalized works of Walter D. Edmonds and Samuel Hopkins Adams offer vivid detail about canal life based on a combination of historical research and folklore.

Popular interest in the canals of New York has remained strong to the present day, as witnessed by the success of the Erie Canal Museum in Syracuse and the Erie Canal Village in Rome. These two living museums offer researchers numerous physical artifacts as well as manuscript collections. The museum's holdings are particularly extensive. A still-vibrant Canal Society of New York State has since 1956 periodically published a newsletter called *Bottoming Out,* which is filled with excerpts from newspapers, letters, and other primary documents still in private hands. The New York State Library has a complete run of that publication.

The Artificial River has profited from all these sources, and many more. Appended to this bibliographic note is a list of specific primary sources that may be of interest to other researchers.

PRIMARY SOURCES

A. Manuscript Collections

American Antiquarian Society, Worcester, Mass.

Broadsides Collection
Canal Collection
Engravings
Institutions Collection
Lithographs
Morse Collection of American Historical Pottery

Buffalo and Erie County Historical Society Library, Buffalo, N.Y.

Ira A. Blossom Papers
Canals—Miscellaneous Manuscripts
Cary Family Papers
Hawley Family Papers
Vertical File

Cornell University Library, Ithaca, N.Y.

Botsford Family Papers
William C. Bouck Papers
Clarissa Burroughs Travel Diary
Chapman Papers
William B. Harris Farm Journal
Henry Morgan Papers
Elijah Smith Papers
Lyman Spalding Papers
State Agricultural Society Papers

Erie Canal Museum, Syracuse, N.Y.

M. A. Anderson Letter
Ephraim Arnold Letter
Bethel Missionary Letter
Canal-Related Material Collection
Eleazor Conkey Diary
Eleazor Conkey Log
Eyewitness Accounts
Davis Hurd Collection
Paul C. Livingston Collection
Morgan Collection
Wood Collection

Erie Canal Village, Rome, N.Y.

Canal-drivers' Log

New York State Archives, Albany, N.Y.

Contracts and Accounts for Construction and Repair
Minutes of the Canal Commission and Superintendent of Public
Works

Petitions and Appeals to the Canal Board ("Canal Board Papers")
Scrapbooks of Newspaper Articles Relating to the Canals, 1817–
   1826

New York State Historical Association, Cooperstown, N.Y.

Charles Camp Diary
Samuel Dakin Papers
David Hughes Diary
Mary Ann Johnson Diary
Sibyl Tatum Diary

New York State Library, Albany, N.Y.

Broadsides Collection
Aaron Burr to William Bell
Aaron Burr to Samuel Reid
Check Roll of Labor Performed, 1829
Alexander Coventry Diary
Erie Canal Transportation Company Account Book
Clarissa Mann Letter
New York State Canals Papers
New York State Manuscript Census Schedules
Passenger Lists
Hezekiah B. Pierpont to William Bell
Peter B. Porter to William C. Bouck Letters
Petition of Sundry Inhabitants of the Counties of Herkimer and
   Montgomery
Stewart Scott Diary
Stephen Van Rensselaer to Henry Dearborn
Elkanah Watson Papers
John G. Wheelock Deposition

Oneida County Historical Society, Utica, N.Y.

Broadhead Family Papers
John S. Coleman Papers
Erie Canal Collection
Joshua Hathaway Papers
Seymour Family Papers

Onondaga Historical Association, Syracuse, N.Y.

John F. Clark Diary
Lincoln Family Papers
Vertical Files

Rochester Historical Society, Rochester, N.Y.

Horace Wheeler Letters
P[ierson] A. Reading Letter

Rochester Museum and Science Center, Rochester, N.Y.

Donald McKenzie Papers
William C. Prindle Letterbook
J[oseph] and A[nn] Webb Letter

Rochester Public Library, Rochester, N.Y.

Myron Adams Diary
Gould Diary
Monroe County Agricultural Society Record Book
O'Reilly Collection
Police Docket, 1836–1839
Police Watchbooks, 1836–1838
Rochester Village Records
Hamlet Scrantom Diary

University of Rochester, Rush Rhees Library, Rochester, N.Y.

N. Bronson to Theren Bronson
Chandler Family Papers
Hemin Chapin Family Papers
Curtis Family Papers
Gale-Sisson Letters
Garbutt Family Papers
Michael Hutchinson Jenks Journal
Journal of a Trip to Niagara Falls in 1822
King Family Papers
Leicester-Bromley Family Papers
Police Watchbook, 1837
Porter Family Papers
Kendrah Robson Diary

Nathaniel Rochester Papers
Rochester Family Papers
Joseph Buell Ward Papers

Smith College, Sophia Smith Collection, Northampton, Mass.

Mary Ann (Wodrow) Archbald Papers (microfilm)

Syracuse University, George Arents Library, Syracuse, N.Y.

Asa Eastwood Papers
Spalding Family Papers

Tonawanda-Kenmore Historical Society, Tonawanda, N.Y.

Churchill Letters

Valentown Museum, Valentown, N.Y.

Webb Harwood Letter
Cyrus Wilmarth Ledger

B. Periodicals

Albany Argus, 1813–1850
American Farmer (Owego), 1803–1814
Anti-Masonic Enquirer (Rochester), 1828–1834
Bellows Falls Intelligencer (Vermont), 1822–1826
Brockport Free Press, 1830–1833
Brockport Recorder, 1828–1830
Buffalo Emporium, 1824–1827
Cabinet (Schenectady), 1818
Cherry-Valley Gazette, 1820–1829
Columbian (New York), 1809–1817
Dublin Journal (Ireland), 1817–1825
The Elucidator (Utica), 1826–1834
The Exile (New York), 1817–1818
Genesee Farmer (Rochester), 1831–1834
Geneva Gazette, 1817–1833
Hampden Journal (Springfield, Mass.), 1824–1825
Hunt's Merchant Magazine, 1839–1865
Lockport Observatory, 1823–1827

Monroe Chronicle (Brockport), 1833–1834

Monroe Republican (Rochester), 1821–1827

New York Commercial Advertiser, 1815–1820

New York Tribune, 1841–1865

Niles' Weekly Register, 1811–1849

Onondaga Standard (Syracuse), 1829–1862

Ontario Freeman (Canandaigua), 1823–1825

Orange Farmer (Goshen and Montgomery), 1820–1823

People's Friend (Little Falls), 1824–1829

Plough Boy (Albany), 1819–1823

Republican Advocate (Batavia), 1824–1825

Republican Monitor (Cazenovia), 1823–1841

Rochester Daily Advertiser, 1826–1856

Rochester Daily Advertiser and Telegraph, 1829–1830

Rochester Daily American, 1844–1857

Rochester Daily Democrat, 1834–1853

Rochester Daily Union, 1852–1856

Rochester Observer, 1827–1832

Rochester Republican, 1816–1865

Rochester Telegraph, 1818–1829

Rochester Union and Advertiser, 1856–1865

Roman Citizen, 1840–1856

Rome Sentinel, 1852–1855

Sailor's Magazine, and Naval Journal, 1828–1837

Sailor's Magazine and Seamen's Friend, 1837–1860

Schoharie Observer, 1820–1823

Utica Intelligencer, 1826–1831

Western Argus (Lyons), 1830–1836

C. Government Documents and City Directories

Albany City Directory, 1815–1817, 1823, 1825, 1844–1845, 1855. In *American Directories through 1860: A Collection on Microfiche* . . . New Haven: Research Publications, 1969.

Buffalo City Directory, 1828, 1832, 1835, 1847–1848, 1855. In *American Directories through 1860: A Collection on Microfiche* . . .

Certified Copy of the Register of Canal Boats kept in the Canal Department, . . . , A. 1853.

Certified Copy of the Register of Canal Boats kept in the Canal Department, . . . , A. 1854.

Digest of Claims, and the Action Thereon by the Legislature and the Canal Board, together with the Awards Made by the Board of Canal Appraisers, from 1818 to 1858. S. P. Allen, Clerk of the Senate. Rochester: A. Strong and Co., 1858.

Laws of the State of New York, in relation to the Erie and Champlain Canals, together with the Annual Reports of the Canal Commissioners, and other Documents . . . Albany: Published by the Authority of the State, E. and E. Hosford, Printers, 1825.

Laws, Regulations, Rates of Toll, and Names of the Principal Places, with their Distances from each other, of the New-York State Canals . . . Albany, Weed, Parson & Co., 1850.

New York Canal Commissioners. *Annual Report,* 1811–1862.

New York Legislature: Assembly. *Assembly Documents,* 1830–1860.

New York Legislature: Senate. *Senate Documents,* 1830–1860.

New York Secretary of State. *Census of the State of New York,* 1825. Albany, 1826.

New York Secretary of State. *Census of the State of New York for 1835* . . . Albany: Printed by Croswell, Van Benthuysen & Burt, 1836.

New York Secretary of State. *Census of the State of New York for 1845* . . . Albany: Carrol & Cook.

New York Secretary of State. *Census of the State of New York for 1855* . . . Albany: Printed by C. Van Benthuysen, 1857.

New York Secretary of State. *Census of the State of New York for 1865* . . . Albany: Printed by C. Van Benthuysen & Sons, 1867.

Official Report of the Canal Commissioners of the State of New-York, and the Acts of the Legislature respecting Navigable Communications between the Great Western and Northern Lakes and the Atlantic Ocean, The. New York: T. & W. Mercein, 1817.

Report of the Committee on Canals, on so much of the Governor's Message as relates to the Completion of the State Canals. Albany: Charles Van Benthuysen, 1851.

Report of the Committee on Canals, on the Petition of David E. Evans, and others. Albany: Croswell and Van Benthuysen, 1827.

Report of the Joint Committee of the Legislature of New-York, on the Subject of the Canals . . . Albany: Websters and Skinners, 1817.

Report of the Joint Committee of the Senate and Assembly, Relative to the Internal Improvements of the State . . . Albany: J. Buel, 1819.

Revised Statute. Chapter IX., Title IX., Relating to the Canals; passed at the Extra Session of the Legislature of New-York, December 3, 1827. Albany: E. Croswell, 1827.

Rochester City Directory, 1827, 1834, 1838, 1841, 1845–1846, 1859. In *American Directories through 1860: A Collection on Microfiche* . . .

U.S. Census, 1810. Washington, 1811.

U.S. Census, 1820. Washington: Printed by Gales and Seaton, 1821.

U.S. Census, 1830. Washington: Printed by Duff Green, 1832.

U.S. Census, 1840. Washington: Printed by Blair and Rives, 1841.

U.S. Census, 1850. J.D.B. DeBow. Washington: Robert Armstrong, Public Printer, 1853.

U.S. Census, 1860. Joseph C. G. Kennedy. Washington: Government Printing Office, 1864.

United States National Youth Administration. *Index to Newspapers Published in Rochester, New York, 1818–1897.* Rochester: Rochester Public Library, n.d.

Utica City Directory, 1817, 1828, 1832, 1837 1838, 1840–1841, 1844–1845, 1860–1861. In *American Directories through 1860: A Collection on Microfiche* . . .

D. Books, Pamphlets and Articles

Abdy, E. S. *Journal of a Residence and Tour in the United States of North America, from April, 1833 to October, 1834.* Vol. I. London: John Murray, 1835.

Addington, Henry Unwin. *Youthful America: Selections from Henry Unwin Addington's Residence in the United States of America, 1822, 23, 24, 25.* Ed. Bradford Perkins. University of California Publications in History, Vol. 65. Berkeley and Los Angeles: University of California Press, 1960.

Albany Basin, and Erie Canal. Albany: Printed by T. G. Wait, 1836.

American Bethel Society. *Annual Report.* Buffalo: 1837–1843, 1847–1848, 1860, 1863.

American Seamen's Friend Society. *Annual Report.* New York: 1829–1860.

Barrett, Richard. *Richard Barrett's Journal, New York and Canada, 1816: Critique of the Young Nation by an Englishman Abroad.* Ed. Thomas Brott and Philip Kelley. Winfield, Kans.: Wedgestone Press, 1983.

Brown, William. *America: A Four Years' Residence in the United States and Canada* . . . Leeds: William Brown, 1849.

Campbell, Allan. Report on a Direct Route for the Eastern Termination of the Erie Canal. Albany: Packard and Van Benthuysen, 1836.

Campbell, William W. *The Life and Writings of DeWitt Clinton.* New York: Baker and Scribner, 1849.

Chapman, George W. *Manual of Canal Laws Relating to the New York State Canals*; . . . Albany: Weed, Parsons and Company, 1873.

Colden, Cadwallader D. *Memoir, Prepared at the Request of a Committee of the Common Council of the City of New York, and Presented to the Mayor of the City, at the Celebration of the Completion of the New York Canals.* New York: Printed by Order of the Corporation of New York, by W.A. Davis, 1825.

Conway, Alan, ed. *The Welsh in America: Letters from the Immigrants.* Minneapolis: University of Minnesota Press, 1961.

Copy of the Register of Canal Boats, as appears from the book of Registry, of those boats in the Comptroller's office . . . 1833.

Cuming, F. H. *An Address, Delivered at the Laying of the Cap-Stone, of the Ten Combined Locks at Lockport, on the Anniversary of St. John the Baptist, June 24, 1825.* Lockport: Orsamus Tuner, 1825.

Darby, William. *A Tour from the City of New York, to Detroit* . . . , *1818* . . . Reprint ed. Chicago: Quadrangle Books, 1962.

Dunlap, William. *A Trip to Niagara; or, Travellers in America. A Farce, in Three Acts.* New York: E. B. Clayton, 1830.

[Dwight, Theodore, Jr.] *Things as They Are: or, Notes of a Traveller* . . . New York: Harper & Brothers, 1834.

Eaton, M. *Five Years on the Erie Canal: An Account of Some of the Most Startling Scenes and Incidents, during Five Years' Labor on the Erie Canal, and other Inland Waters.* Utica: Bennett, Backus, & Hawley, 1845.

Emerson, Ralph Waldo. *The Collected Works of Ralph Waldo Emerson.* Notes and introduction by Robert E. Spiller; text established by Alfred R. Ferguson. Cambridge, Mass.: The Belknap Press of Harvard University Press, 1971.

"Equal Rights." *Review of the Pamphlet of Oswego, Against the Intended Enlargement of the Erie Canal.* Buffalo: Day, Stagg, and Cadwallader, 1826.

Eyton, T. C. *A History of the Oyster and the Oyster Fisheries.* London: John Van Voorst, 1858.

Facts and Observations in Relation to the Origin and Completion of the Erie Canal. New York: N. B. Holmes, 1825.

Facts and Observations in Relation to the Origin and Completion of the Erie Canal. 2nd ed. Providence: F. Y. Carlile and H. H. Brown, 1827.

Giles, Charles. *The Convention of Drunkards: A Satirical Essay on Intemperance . . . and an Ode on the Completion of the Erie Canal.* New York, 1839.

Gilman, Caroline. *The Poetry of Travelling in the United States.* New York: S. Colman, 1838.

Hall, Basil. *Forty Etchings from Sketches Made with the Camera Lucida, in North America, in 1827 and 1828.* Edinburgh: Cadell & Co., and London: Simpkin & Marshall, and Moon, Boys, & Graves, 1829.

———. *Travels in North America in the Years 1827 and 1828.* Vol. I. Philadelphia: Carey, Lea & Carey, 1829.

Hall, Margaret. *The Aristocratic Journey, Being the Outspoken Letters of Mrs. Basil Hall Written during a Fourteen Months' Sojourn in America, 1827–1828.* Ed. Una Pope-Hennesscy. New York: G. P. Putnam's Sons, 1931.

Hawley, Jesse. *An Essay on the Enlargement of the Erie Canal.* Lockport: Printed at the Courier Office, 1840.

Hawley, Merwin. *The Erie Canal: Its Origin, Its Success, and Its Necessity.* Buffalo: Joseph Warren and Co., 1868.

———. *The Erie Canal. The Question of the Origin of the Erie Canal.* 1872.

Hawthorne, Nathaniel. "The Canal Boat." *Mosses from an Old Manse.* Boston and New York: Houghton, Mifflin and Company, 1887.

Hopkins, John Henry. " 'Journal of My Tour in Fall of 1825,' Accompanied by Sketches in Watercolor and India Ink." *American Magazine and Historical Chronicle* 4:1 (1988), 23–29.

Hopson, W. B. *An Essay on the Oyster Industry of the United States.* New York: The McWilliams Printing House, 1885.

Hosack, David. *Memoir of De Witt Clinton; with an appendix containing numerous documents illustrative of the principal events of his life.* New York: J. Seymour, 1829.

House, Albert V., ed. "Two Yankee Traders in New York: Letters on the Financing of Frontier Merchants, 1808–1830." *New England Quarterly* 11:3 (September 1938), 607–31.

Improvement of the Internal Navigation of the State . . . , The. Albany: S. Southwick, 1812.

Internal Improvement. *Proceedings of Meetings of the Citizens of Rochester, Buffalo, Lockport and Palmyra* . . . Rochester: Shepard, Strong, and Dawson, 1839.

[Johnson, Edwin Ferry.] *An Appeal to the Representatives of the People of the State of New-York in Relation to the Proposed Enlargement of the Erie Canal.* 1836.

Jones, Pomroy. *Annals and Recollections of Oneida County.* Rome: By the Author, 1851.

Kapp, Samuel L. *A Discourse on the Life and Character of DeWitt Clinton* . . . Washington: printed by William Greer, 1828.

Lanman, Charles. *Recollections of Curious Characters and Pleasant Places.* Edinburgh: David Douglas, 1881.

Levasseur, A. *Lafayette in America in 1824 and 1825; or, Journal of a Voyage to the United States.* 2 vols. Philadelphia: Carey and Lea, 1829.

Lieber, Francis, ed. Encyclopedia Americana. S.v. "Oyster." Philadelphia: Carey & Lea, 1832.

Lincoln, Charles Z., ed. *Messages from the Governors.* Vols. II and III. Albany: J. B. Lyon Company, 1909.

Loomis, Elisha. "Diary of Trip Rochester to Mackinac Island." Ed. Philip P. Mason. *Michigan History* 38 (1853), 27–41.

[Lumsden, James.] *American Memoranda, by A Mercantile Man, during a Short Tour in the Summer of 1843.* Glasgow: Bell & Bain, 1844.

Mackay, Alex. *The Western World; or Travels in the United States in 1846–47* . . . Vol. II. Philadelphia: Lea & Blanchard, 1849.

McKelvey, Blake, ed. "Letters Postmarked Rochester: 1817–1879." In *Rochester Historical Society Publications* 21. Rochester: Published by the Society, 1943.

Maxmilian, Prince of Wied. *Travels in the Interior of North America.* Trans. H. Evans Lloyd. London: Ackerman and Co., 1843.

Melville, Herman. *Moby-Dick; or, the Whale.* New York: Random House, 1930.

"Niagara Falls Tourist of the Year 1817: Being the Journal of Captain Richard Langslow of the Honorable East India Service, A." *Publications of the Buffalo Historical Society* 5 (1902), 111–33.

Notes on a Tour through the Western Part of the State of New York. Philadelphia, 1829–1830.

O'Callaghan, E. B. *The Documentary History of the State of New York.* Vol. II. Albany: Weed, Parsons, & Co., 1849.

O'Reilly, Henry. *Settlement in the West: Sketches of Rochester* . . . Rochester: William Alling, 1838.

Oyster: Where, How, and When to Find, Breed, Cook and Eat It, The. London: Trubner & Co., 1861.

[Paulding, J. K.] *The New Mirror for Travellers; and Guide to the Springs.* New York: G. & C. Carvill, 1828.

Pickering, Joseph. *Inquiries of an Emigrant: and Being the Narrative of an English Farmer from the Year 1824 to 1830.* London: Effingham Wilson, 1832.

Power, Tyrone. *Impressions of America, During the Years 1833, 1834, and 1835.* Vol I. London: Richard Bentley, 1836.

Proceedings of the Convention upon the subject of an Immediate Enlargement of the Erie Canal . . . Buffalo: Charles Faxon, 1837.

Public Documents, relating to the New-York Canals, which are to Connect the Western and Northern Lakes, with the Atlantic Ocean . . . *Printed under the direction of the New-York Corresponding Association, for the Promotion of Internal Improvements.* New York: William A. Mercein, 1821.

Randel, John, Jr. *Description of a Direct Route for the Erie Canal, at its Eastern Termination* . . . Albany: G. J. Loomis, 1822.

Remonstrance Adopted by the Inhabitants of the City of Schenectada [sic] at a Meeting Held on the 25th of February, 1836, Against the Change of the Route of the Erie Canal . . . , A. Schenectady: Printed at the Reflector Office, 1836.

Report of the Commissioners appointed by Joint Resolutions of the Honorable the Senate and Assembly of the State of New-York . . . *to Explore the Route of an Inland Navigation from Hudson's River to Lake Ontario and Lake Erie.* Albany: S. Southwick, 1811.

Report, on the Subject of a Communication between Canandaigua Lake and the Erie Canal. Canandaigua: J. D. Bemis and Co., 1821.

Reports and Speeches in Favor of the . . . *Enlargement of the Erie Canal* . . . Albany: Printed by Weed, Parsons and Co., 1851.

Scott, Kenneth, and Rosanne Conway, comps. *New York Alien Residents, 1825–1848.* Baltimore: Genealogical Publishing Co., Inc., 1978.

Seward, William H. *The Works of William H. Seward.* Ed. George E. Baker. Vols. II–IV. Boston: Houghton, Mifflin and Company, 1884.

Shirreff, Patrick. *A Tour through North America* . . . Edinburgh: Oliver and Boyd, 1835.

Spalding, Lyman A. *Recollections of the War of 1812 and Early Life in Western New York.* Occasional Contributions of the Niagara County Historical Society, No. 2. Lockport, N.Y.: Niagara County Historical Society, 1949.

Stone, William L[eete]. "A Night of Peril." *The Atlantic Souvenir for 1832.* Philadelphia: Carey and Lea, 1832.

————. *Narrative of the Festivities Observed in Honor of the Completion of the Grand Erie Canal.* New York, 1825.

Sweet, S. H. *Documentary Sketch of New York State Canals.* Albany: Van Benthuysen, 1863.

Tacitus [DeWitt Clinton]. *Canal Policy of the State of New-York* . . . Albany: E. and E. Hosford, 1821.

Traveller's Pocket Directory and Stranger's Guide; Exhibiting Distances on the Erie Canal and Stage Routes in the State of New York, The. Schenectady: S. Wilson, 1831; reprint, Schenectady: John P. Papp, 1978.

Tocqueville, Alexis de. *Democracy in America.* Trans. George Lawrence; ed. J. P. Mayer. New York: Harper and Row, 1969.

Tucker, Louis Leonard, ed. *A Knickerbocker Tour of New York State, 1822: "Our Travels, Statistical, Geographical, Mineorological, Geological, Historical, Political, and Quizzical."* Albany: New York State Library, 1968.

Tudor, Henry. *Narrative of a Tour in North America* . . . London: James Duncan, 1834.

Turner, O[rsamus]. *History of the Pioneer Settlement of Phelp's and Gorham Purchase, and Morris' Reserve* . . . Rochester: William Alling, 1851.

————. *Pioneer History of the Holland Land Purchase of Western New York* . . . Buffalo: George H. Derby and Co., 1850.

Twenty-Four Letters from Labourers in America to their Friends in England. London: Edward Rainford, 1829; reprint, California State Library, n.d.

Tyron, Warren S., comp. and ed. *A Mirror for Americans: Life and Manners in the United States, 1790–1870, as Recorded by American Travelers,* Vol. I. Chicago: University of Chicago Press, 1952.

Upstate Literature. Ed. Frank Bergmann. Syracuse: Syracuse University Press, 1985.

View of the Grand Canal, from Lake Erie to the Hudson River . . . , A. New York: John Low, 1825.

"Visit of Gerard T. Hopkins: A Quaker Ambassador to the Indians who Visited Buffalo in 1804." *Publications of the Buffalo Historical Society* 6 (1903), 217–22.

Wager, Daniel E., ed. *Our County and Its People: A Descriptive Work on Oneida County, New York.* N.p.: Boston History Company, 1896.

"Water Ways of New York, The." *Harper's* 48 (December 1873), 1–17.

Western Seaman's Friend Society. *Report.* Cleveland: 1849–1850, 1850–1851, 1859–1860, 1862–1863.

White, Philip L., ed. "An Irish Immigrant Housewife on the New York Frontier." *New York History* 68:2 (April 1967), 182–88.

Williams, Edwin. *The New-York Annual Register* . . . New York, 1830–1845.

INDEX